Contents

Maps

Foreword

We would like to express our gratitude to the German National Tourist Board, German Information Center, Berlin Tourist Office, GermanRail, Inc., Lufthansa German Airlines, LTU International Airways, and KD German Rhine Line for their help and support. Special thanks go to Hedy Wuerz, Helga Brenner-Khan, Birgit Fickert, Jan Friedrich, Lucille Hoshabjian, Jan Myers, Rudolf Masata, Michael Brodersen, Gisela Höppner, and Hubert Wegmann.

While every care has been taken to assure the accuracy of the information in this guide, the passage of time will always bring change and, consequently, the publisher cannot accept responsibility for errors that may occur.

All prices and opening times quoted here are based on information supplied to us at press time. Hours and admission fees may change, however, and the prudent traveler will avoid inconvenience by calling ahead.

Fodor's wants to hear about your travel experiences, both pleasant and unpleasant. When a hotel or restaurant fails to live up to its billing, let us know and we will investigate the complaint and revise our entries where the facts warrant it.

Send your letters to the editors of Fodor's Travel Publications, 201 East 50th Street, New York, NY 10022.

Highlights'93 and Fodor's Choice

Highlights '93

For visitors from abroad on their first arrival in Berlin, crossing over into the East at **Checkpoint Charlie** used to be an unnerving experience. You were not allowed to cross unless your papers were in order. The tension would quickly mount as stern-looking border guards examined documents, checked identities, then motioned visitors through a security tract with automatic doors that opened with a buzz. Now, with the Cold War divide gone and the East German flag furled, the first thing those same visitors want to do is see where all this used to happen. Vestiges of Checkpoint Charlie remain—the original signboard marking the border and some barbed wire to protect token sections of the Berlin Wall from being chipped down. Russian and Polish emigrés sell papier-maché Gorby dolls and jars of cheap dried caviar, all under cigarette billboards stating this is "now Marlboro country" and it is time to "Test the West."

The remaining pieces of the **Berlin Wall,** in central Mühlenstrasse between the Jannowitzbrücke and Oberbaumbrücke bridges, and at Bernauerstrasse in Wedding (where a "wall museum" has been proposed), have been left standing as a historic reminder of what once divided Berlin. The scar left by the Wall and the border fortifications is still visible, but for much of its length the strip of land beside it resembles a huge building site as developers set about putting it to new uses. Construction is likely to take place in the ugly wilderness between Pariser Platz and Vosstrasse, the site of Hitler's former Chancellery and the bunker where he spent his final hours with Eva Braun. The bunker, much to the dismay of the local Jewish community, is being turned into a memorial.

Changes are taking place in Berlin as quickly as reunification of the two Germanys in October 1990. Week after week and month after month, city planners, investors, and bulldozers appear anew. The pace of change is faster than even the most cynical Berliner imagined. West Berliners always boasted about their fashionable shopping street the Kurfürstendamm—the locals call it the Ku'damm—with its 2 miles of conspicuous consumption and often seedy nightlife. But now there's the **Unter den Linden** in the East, steeped in history and being restored to its former glory. The huge **Meissen** porcelain showroom is still there, as is, for the time being, the ex–Soviet embassy, fronted by a bust of Lenin. New investment is pouring into the area. The tail end of Unter den Linden, where the Brandenburg Gate stands, has now been opened to buses and taxis, and fashionable western boutiques already line the avenue's lower stretch. **Galeries Lafayette,** one of Paris's premier department stores, is erecting a huge store on Friedrichstrasse, just off Unter den Linden, but it could be four years before it's complete.

East Berlin's beautiful **Platz der Akademie** can once again claim a place among Europe's loveliest squares. The transformation has given the square back its historic name, **Platz der Gendarmenmarkt,** after the city police station that once stood there. This process of renaming streets, squares, buildings, bridges, and monuments to eradicate the vestiges of the communist past, now under way throughout the former German Democratic Republic, will radically change the map of the city and could lead to some confusion for visitors. The names of Marx, Lenin, and Engels are being replaced in eastern Berlin, although, ironically, they still adorn street signs in the western part of Berlin and in cities throughout western Germany, where acquaintance with the founders of communism hasn't been so close.

The barren **"death strip"**—the stretch of dry sand and a few blades of grass along the eastern side of the Wall that was known as no-man's land—is slowly being transformed into a pleasant enviromental area. With Berlin's bid to host the Olympic games in the year 2000, the marketing organization that has been set up to promote the city's candidacy is getting companies to sponsor the planting of trees, shrubs, and grass. In the meantime the American, British, and French embassies are busy reclaiming the land they owned surrounding the Brandenburg Gate so that plans can be drawn up for their new premises once the government moves from Bonn to Berlin.

The fusion of most public services of the two previously autonomous halves of Berlin is not yet complete, and this could cause additional inconvenience for visitors. Although the amalgamation of the two separate transport systems was achieved with surprising speed and smoothness, some new bus routes are still being mapped out, moribund U-bahn and S-bahn stations reopened, and lines extended and renumbered. Both halves of Berlin were recently united under a single city telephone code, 030—formerly the code of only West Berlin. The telephone service in eastern Berlin won't be up to western standards until at least 1995, but the system is being improved all the time.

The hotel and restaurant scene in eastern Berlin is in upheaval as the official government trustees—the Treuhand—struggle with the enormous task of returning state-confiscated and -run properties to their former owners or selling them off to private entrepreneurs and corporate-operated chains. We've tried to keep up with the changes as much as possible, but it's always a good idea to call in advance before heading for that highly touted eastern Berlin hotel or restaurant; it may have changed ownership or name, or it may have closed down completely.

At the Kulturforum, the celebrated **Philharmonie concert hall** reopened in spring 1992 after a major overhaul, and a new building housing the print and drawing collection formerly shown at Dahlem is scheduled to open in summer 1993. This is the first step in a 20-year program to reunite the state art and ethnographic collections that were split during the war. The plan at the moment is to move as much as possible from the west to the Museumsinsel (Museum Island) in the east. To help pay for this momumental project admission is now being charged for those public museums in western Berlin that used to be free, and admission prices for their East Berlin counterparts have been raised.

For the most part, Berlin still carries scars from the Second World War; with the era of communism in the East and the island mentality of the West, it will take time and patience before the two halves are one again. It is almost as though two people are being joined together with a new heart.

Fodor's Choice

No two people will agree on what makes a perfect vacation, but it's fun and helpful to know what others think. We hope you'll have a chance to experience some of Fodor's Choices during your visit to Berlin and eastern Germany. For detailed information about each entry, refer to the appropriate chapters of the book.

Castles and Palaces

Albrechtberg, Meissen

Schloss Charlottenburg, Berlin

Schloss Sanssouci, Potsdam

Spandauer Zitadelle, Berlin

Wartburg castle, Eisenach

Zwinger Palace, Dresden

Churches

Berliner Dom, Berlin

Deutscher Dom and Französischer Dom, Berlin

Dom, Magdeburg

Marienkirche, Berlin

Nikolaikirche, Berlin

Nikolaikirche, Leipzig

Thomaskirche, Leipzig

Memorable Sights

Looking down on the stage of the Semperoper, Dresden

Berlin from the top of the Funkturm, Alexanderplatz

Climbing the terraces at the base of Schloss Sanssouci, Potsdam

Facing the Schauspielhaus on Gendarmenmarkt, Berlin

The modern Kaiser Wilhelm Gedächtniskirche, Berlin, at night

Strolling down Unter den Linden, Berlin

Watching the sun set from the Brühlsche Terrasse, Dresden

Monuments and Memorials

Berlin Wall remains

Brandenburger Tor, Berlin

Buchenwald concentration camp, outside Weimar

Frauenkirche, Dresden

Kaiser Wilhelm Gedächtniskirche, Berlin

Neue Wache, Berlin

Pergamon Altar, Pergamonmuseum, Berlin

Statue of Goethe and Schiller, Theaterplatz, Weimar

Völkerschlachtdenkmal, Leipzig

Museums

Ägyptisches Museum, Berlin

Gemäldegalerie, Dahlem, Berlin

Museum der Bildenden Künste, Leipzig

Grüne Gewölbe, Dresden

Neue Nationalgalerie, Berlin

Pergamonmuseum, Berlin

Porzellansammlung, Dresden

Sempergalerie Collection, Dresden

Parks, Gardens, Forests

Botanischer Garten, Leipzig

Englischer Garten, Berlin

Glienicke Park, Berlin

Grunewald, Berlin

Park an der Ilm, Weimar

Pfaueninsel, Berlin

Sanssouci Park, Potsdam

Schlossgarten Charlottenburg, Berlin

Schloss Wörlitz Park, Wörlitz

Tiergarten, Berlin

Restaurants

Bamberger Reiter, Berlin (*Very Expensive*)

Frühsammer's restaurant an der Rehwiese, Berlin (*Very Expensive*)

Ermeler-Haus, Berlin (*Expensive*)

Hohe Lilie, Erfurt (*Expensive*)

Sekundogenitur, Dresden (*Moderate*)

Trio, Berlin (*Moderate*)

Weisser Schwan, Weimar (*Moderate*)

Wirtshaus Moorlake, Berlin (*Moderate*)

Auerbachs Keller, Leipzig (*Inexpensive*)

Blockhaus Nikolskoe, Berlin (*Inexpensive*)

Zur Letzten Instanz, Berlin (*Inexpensive*)

Hotels

Bristol Hotel Kempinski, Berlin (*Very Expensive*)

Dresdner Hof, Dresden (*Very Expensive*)

Grand Hotel, Berlin (*Very Expensive*)

Hilton Hotel, Berlin (*Very Expensive*)

Hotel Bellvue, Dresden (*Very Expensive*)

Hotel Berlin, Berlin (*Very Expensive*)

Elephant, Weimar (*Expensive*)

Schweizerhof Berlin, Berlin (*Expensive*)

Auf der Wartburg, Eisenach (*Moderate*)

Charlottenhof, Berlin (*Moderate*)

Germany

North Sea

Baltic Sea

DENMARK

POLAND

HOLLAND

Rügen

Fehmarn

Elbe

Oder

Elbe

Oder

Neisse

Ems

0 — 100 miles
0 — 150 km

N

Flensburg

Husum

Kiel

Neustadt

Wismar

Lübeck

Hamburg

Barth Stralsund

Greifswald

Anklam

Rostock

Güstrow

Teterow

Neubrandenburg

Neustrelitz

Waren

Schwerin

Neustadt-Gleve

Pritzwalk

Neuruppin

Oranienburg

Ludwigslust

Perleberg

Wittenberge

Salzwedel

Stendal

Brandenburg

Potsdam

Berlin

Frankfurt an der Oder

Lübben

Cottbus

Wittenberg

Magdeburg

Dessau

Bernburg

Bitterfeld

Halle

Leipzig

Meissen

Dresden

Görlitz

Nordhausen

Mühlhausen

Kassel

Göttingen

Halberstadt

Wolfsburg

Braunschweig

Hannover

Hildesheim

Minden

Bielefeld

Osnabrück

Rheine

Münster

Dortmund

Hagen

Essen

Duisburg

Düsseldorf

Meppen

Oldenburg

Emden

Wilhelmshaven

Caroliensiel

Norden

Cuxhaven

Bremerhaven

Bremen

FORMER BORDER BETWEEN EAST AND WEST GERMANY

Berlin

Spree

River

Dovestr.

Lev etzowstr.

Paulstr.

Lüneburgerstr.

Altonaerstr.

John-Foster-Dulles

Bachstr.

Spreeweg

Str. des 17 Juni

Marchstr.

Grosser
Stern

Str. des 17 Juni

Tiergarten

Ernst-
Reuter-
Pl.

Hofjäger-Allee
Klingelhöferstr.

Harden bergstr.

Tiergarten str.

Budapesterstr.

Kurfürstenstr.

Lützowstr.

Kurfürstendamm

Tauenzienstr.

Lietzenburgerstr.

Nürnbgrstr.

Kleiststr.

Bülowstr.

Spichern

Nachodstr.

Motzstr.

Hohenstaufenstr.

Hohenzollern-Damm

Martin-Luher-Str.

Potsdamerstr.

Uhlandstr.

Bundesallee

Grunewaldstr.

Hauptstr.

Berlinerstr.

Badenschestr.

Volkspark

Bundesallee

Hauptstr.

Ebersstr.

West angente

Allee

Moltkestr.

Entlastungsstr.

Unter den Linden

Otto Grotewohlstr.

Friedrichstr.

Gendarmen-
markt

Karl-Liebknecht-Str.

Marx-
Engels
Pl.

Rathausstr.

Wallstr.

Leipzigerstr.

Potsdamerpl.

FORMER LOCATION OF BERLIN WALL

Oranienstr.

Ritterstr.

Potsdamerstr.

Wilhelmstr.

Friedrichstr.

Lindenstr.

Schönebergerstr.

Möckernstr.

Prinzenstr.

Gitschinerstr.

Urban - str.

Yorckstr.

Möckernstr.

Yorckstr.

Gneisenaustr.

Baerwaldstr.

Monumentenstr.

Kreuzbergstr.

Mehringdamm

Victoria
Park

Volkspark
Hasenheide

N

Kolonnenstr.

Dudenstr.

Columbiadamm

0   750 yards

0   750 meters

World Time Zones

MONDAY
SUNDAY

International Date Line

+12 +13 -9

-4

-3

25

-10

-7

3

7

-5 -4

4 14 15

8 9 13

-11 5 -8 -6 17 16

6 10 18

-10 11

2 12 19 22

-5 20

-4 -3

23

+11

+12 21 24

-3

+11 +12 - -11 -10 -9 -8 -7 -6 -5 -4 -3 -2

Numbers below vertical bands relate each zone to Greenwich Mean Time (0 hrs.).
Local times frequently differ from these general indications,
as indicated by light-face numbers on map.

Prime Meridian

+7 +8 +9 +10 +11

Prime Meridian

+1 +2

+4 +5 +6

+8

33

32 45

26 27 34 36 +3

54

59 +9

30 31 35 37

28 38 39

40

60

29 41

+8

55

42 46 +3:30 +4:30

48

+5

56

57

47 +1 +2 +3 +5:30 +6:30 49 +8

50 51

52 +8

43 +3

53 +8 +9

44 +2

+8 +9:30 +10

58 61

-1 0 +1 +2 +3 +4 +5 +6 +7 +8 +9 +10
Greenwich
Mean Time

Mecca, **47**	Ottawa, **14**	San Francisco, **5**	Toronto, **13**
Mexico City, **12**	Paris, **30**	Santiago, **21**	Vancouver, **4**
Miami, **18**	Perth, **58**	Seoul, **59**	Vienna, **35**
Montréal, **15**	Reykjavík, **25**	Shanghai, **55**	Warsaw, **36**
Moscow, **45**	Rio de Janeiro, **23**	Singapore, **52**	Washington, D.C., **17**
Nairobi, **43**	Rome, **39**	Stockholm, **32**	Yangon, **49**
New Orleans, **11**	Saigon (Ho Chi Minh	Sydney, **61**	Zürich, **31**
New York City, **16**	City), **51**	Tokyo, **60**	

Introduction

By Robert Tilley

British-born Robert Tilley lives in Germany and is a broadcast and print journalist whose work has appeared in German and British publications.

Berlin isn't a city at all, really—it's more like a country. It's certainly a way of life, a state of mind. Take Heine's word for it. The German poet wrote: "[Berlin] . . . just provides the gathering place for a lot of people, among them many of intellect, for whom it's quite immaterial where they are." In more prosaic terms, Germany's new capital, restored to its old status, is an amorphous, sprawling conurbation. The size of a small European state (and bigger than Andorra, Liechtenstein, or San Marino), it's a patchwork quilt of eight towns, 59 villages, and 27 farms and estates, fused together in 1920 to form Greater Berlin, nearly 900 square kilometers and with a city border 234 kilometers (138 miles) in length, longer than the railway line connecting it with the nearest western German city, Hanover.

Berlin's way of life? The history of Berlin has molded its lifestyle in a way that no other European city can match: imperial capital; meeting point of European culture and all forms of artistic expression; refuge for oppressed minorities; 1920s pleasureground; home of German fascism; military citadel flattened by war, occupied by victorious armies, and then rent asunder by a 28-mile-long wall that divided it into two halves that symbolized the Cold War confrontation between Western democracy and communist totalitarianism. And in no other European city can you see historical influences so evidently at work in the way it functions. The Berliners really do live from day to day, with a phlegmatic, unconventional but at the same time practical approach to life that's the despair of other Germans. Goethe thought them to be an "audacious lot."

The Berliners are born survivors, an attribute that makes them excellent business people: sharp, quick-witted, inquisitive, outgoing, and—as you'll undoubtedly find as a visitor—warmhearted hosts. Their humor is naturally sardonic and self-deprecatory, a dry form of wit with instant appeal to Americans and British. When did you ever hear reference to German humor? Yet the Berliner *Schnauze*, or Berlin wit, is renowned beyond German borders and respected even by those who feel its sometimes cruel lash. Its acerbic tone was to be savored in the graffiti that decorated the hated Wall, and wonderfully captured by the most famous spray-painted and prophetic line: "Will the last one over please switch out the lights."

You can find examples of Berlin wit all over the city, and not all of them are contemporary. Several historical monuments are deliberately humorous in style, most notably the equestrian statue of Frederick the Great on Unter den Linden, in which the figures of his two outspoken critics Lessing and Kant are positioned under the horse's tail. Frederick was a typical Berliner, so hospitable a host that guest rooms at his Potsdam palace, Sanssouci, outnumbered his own chambers.

Berlin flourished under Frederick's enlightened rule, but the city was already a great German capital when he ascended the throne in 1740. It's a young city by European standards, beginning life in the early Middle Ages as two trading communities on and around the Spree River island where eastern Berlin's great museums now stand, the so-called Museumsinsel. The island was called Cölln and a nearby riverbank settlement, Berlin. The Margrave Heinrich the Tall combined them into one administrative town in 1307, and it is from that date that the city's history really begins. Paradoxically, several other areas of what is now Greater Berlin are older—Spandau and Köpenick, for instance. Until 1920 they nurtured their own, independent, histories, and even today they zealously guard their ancient traditions. You'll hear their denizens say that they are "off to Berlin" when talking about a shopping trip or an outing to the theater in the city center. Several Berlin parish churches are far older than the city of which they are now a part.

Berlin is a city of churches, most of them Protestant. Ironically, Berliners fiercely resisted the Reformation, and in 1524 the Prince-Elector Joachim Nestor banned Luther's New Testament. His successor, Joachim II, opened the gates of Berlin to the Reformation. A century later, the city was again caught up in religious strife, suffering heavily in the Thirty Years' War, which swept a destructive course through much of Germany. It was at the height of the war that Berlin's first great ruler, the Prince Elector Friedrich Wilhelm, took power, laying the foundation of the Prussian-Brandenburg state. It was Friedrich Wilhelm who first welcomed to Berlin the foreign refugees who were to play such a major role in creating the vibrant city we know today. He encouraged the Huguenots to settle there, and they brought badly needed skills that helped the city increase the volume of its trade sixfold within 10 years.

In those days Berlin's rulers lived in what is now the eastern part of the city, in a palace badly damaged in World War II and later blown up by East Berlin's then communist masters. An enduring, grand reminder of that chapter of Berlin history is the famous avenue, Unter den Linden, once a tree-lined riding path connecting the palace with the royal hunting grounds of the present Tiergarten park.

It was Friedrich Wilhelm's successor, the Prince Elector Friedrich III, who began the construction of Berlin's most famous palace, the Charlottenburg, intending it to serve as a summer residence in the sylvan peace of the western reaches of the expanding city. Friedrich was the first of the

highly cultured rulers to whom Berlin will be ever in-
debted, and he is the true father of the Prussian state. Under his enlightened rule arose academies of arts and
sciences, and the theater and music flourished. Small wonder that he won the favor of the German Emperor Leopold,
who bestowed on him the title of King of Prussia.

Friedrich was crowned in 1701 in Königsberg, but he chose
Berlin as his royal residence. He dipped deep into the city
and state coffers to finance the kind of court he thought
worthy of the new kingdom of Prussia—too deep for the
likes of his ascetic son Friedrich Wilhelm I. When his father
died, the funeral was the last display of Prussian pomp for
27 years. Friedrich Wilhelm initiated a severe austerity
program, diverting money into the equivalent of a modern
defense budget, which he regarded as essential for the security of the new Prussian state. The people dubbed him
their "Soldier King."

Friedrich Wilhelm's death swung the pendulum back
again. His son Friedrich II—Frederick the Great—
possessed his grandfather's aesthetic sensibilities,
and under his 46-year rule Berlin flourished as never before. The monumental grandeur of Berlin (and of nearby
Potsdam) began to take shape under such architects as
Georg von Knobelsdorff, and Frederick's court attracted
the cream of European artistic talent; Voltaire came for a
visit and stayed three years.

Frederick's successor, his nephew Friedrich Wilhelm II,
continued the work of building Berlin into a leading European cultural and political capital. The architects Carl
Langhans and Karl Friedrich Schinkel gave Berlin its Neoclassical stamp, with Langhans building its most famous
structure, the Brandenburger Tor. But 15 years after the
completion in 1791 of the massive victory arch, Napoléon
and his troops marched through it, heralding two years of
occupation of the city by the French. Napoléon robbed the
arch of its crowning sculpture, the Quadriga, but Berlin
won it back again in 1814.

The industrial age brought further problems for Berlin. A
simmering cauldron of discontent, its source being workers, students, and intellectuals, boiled over in 1848 into
open rebellion, pressuring the Prussian court into unparal-
leled concessions. There was a reactionary backlash, however, and the freedoms won by the Berlin proletariat were
lost again in an undemocratic constitution that was to last
until 1918. In the latter half of the 19th century, industrialization brought Berlin remarkable prosperity but also enormous poverty. By the turn of the century more than 1,000
factories had been established in Berlin and railways and
canals had been built, but alongside them sprung up over-
crowded tenements in which nearly two million people eked
out miserable existences.

Meanwhile, Prussia's military victories over Austria and France paved the way for German unification (1871) and Prussian dominance over the new nation. Piloted by Bismark, the country was largely conservative and militaristic, but Berlin, steadily becoming a modern capital, remained resolutely liberal. Thus revolution was never far away, and in November 1918, after Germany's defeat in World War I, it broke out again, forcing the abdication of Kaiser Wilhelm II.

Berlin flourished anew during the Weimar Republic that followed. During that brief, heady burst of democracy, Berlin became a cultural and entertainment capital as well. The joyous 1920s brought to prominence the likes of Bertholt Brecht, Kurt Weill, Erich Kastner, George Grosz, Fritz Lang, Marlene Dietrich, and a thousand other names that made this period a golden age for Berlin.

But it was an ephemeral time, an incandescence that ended in dark years of recession, runaway inflation, social unrest, and the rise of fascism. We all know what followed. Berlin was destined for damnation: Hitler's militaristic capital, bombed to ruins and then occupied by the Red Army, cut in four ways like a cake by the victorious Allies, then split into two zones and finally divided for nearly three decades by a hideous wall.

The fall of the Wall in November 1989, and the demise of the communist regime that built it, opened the way for Berlin's rebirth as the premier city of Germany and the restoration of its status as capital of the nation. The debate over the merits of Bonn and Berlin was long and often passionate, but there was never really any doubt about the outcome. The selection of Berlin by the German Bundestag in June 1991, was more of an emotional vote than a political or economic one, and an impassioned speech by interior Minister Wolfgang Schäuble is given the credit by grateful Berliners for swinging the vote their way. Historic Berlin—the city of the first Prussian king and of Frederick the Great—has returned to claim its birthright.

Lawmakers have given the government 12 years to make the move from Bonn. It won't be an easy time, for even three years after the fall of the Wall Berlin is still a divided city, cleft no longer by a physical barrier but by the differences created by the parallel development of the capitalist West and the communist East. In the long run, however, the unifying forces must inevitably succeed and Berlin will emerge as an even more extraordinary metropolis, growing by the early 21st century into the largest and most powerful industrial city between the Atlantic and the Urals. The infrastructures that took shape in the two halves of Berlin give the city a sound foundation, not only economically but culturally. After inheriting three opera houses and more than a dozen world-class museums, newly united Berlin is set to become Germany's cultural capital and an important

European center of the arts. The Reichstag, historic seat of the German imperial parliament, will return to its old function, and around the century-old building, on the now-open banks of the Spree River, will arise a new suburb of administrative buildings. Part of the land that once served as the mined border between East and West Germany will be developed, with office blocks, parks, and gardens springing up where armed guards and dogs once patrolled.

As champions of Bonn have pointed out, every long-term advantage of shifting the capital to Berlin will be more than matched by immediate drawbacks. "Enormous economic and social challenges face the city as it wrestles with the problems thrown up by unification and the task of resuming its premier position within Germany," said a leading German economist. "Berlin . . . will inevitably attract great amounts of investment capital, entrepreneurship, labor, and know-how, but the attendant complications are likely to be awesome." At press time (spring 1992), unemployment was high as eastern Berlin's creaking economic base was jacked up to western levels, and as western Berlin lost the special tax status it enjoyed as a divided and isolated city. However, with construction booming in eastern Berlin, many are finding work rebuilding part of the city, which is in desperate need of restoration.

Adding to the strains—but also contributing greatly to Berlin's fascination—is its great ethnic diversity, a modern manifestation of the open society that the city has always encouraged. More than a quarter of a million foreigners from 156 countries have made their home in Berlin, half of them Turks (Berlin, wags say, is Turkey's second-largest city). The Turks, who have made the district of Kreuzberg virtually their own, were lured to Berlin by the availability of relatively high-paying jobs on automobile assembly lines, in factories, and under conditions the Germans disdained. They contributed greatly to the German economic boom of the 1960s and 1970s, and it's a measure of Berlin's openness that their integration is almost complete. Less assimilated but nonetheless integral to everyday Berlin are the Third World refugees, the dropouts (West Berliners were exempted from the draft) and junkies, the punks and skinheads, the has-beens and ne'er-do-wells who find in this big-hearted metropolis a tolerance missing in most other German cities.

Yes, Berlin has its problems, and they're going to multiply. But it has the human and humane resources to solve them and make Berlin a great German—indeed, a great European—capital once again.

1 Essential Information

Before You Go

Government Tourist Offices

Contact the German National Tourist Office at 122 E. 42nd St., 52nd Floor, New York, NY 10168, tel. 212/661–7200; or 11766 Wilshire Blvd., Suite 750, Los Angeles, CA 90071, tel. 310/575–9799.

In Canada 175 Bloor Street E, North Tower, Suite 604, Toronto, Ont. M4W 3R8, tel. 416/968–1570.

In the U.K. Nightingale House, 65 Curzon Street, London W1Y 7PE, England, tel. 0371/495–0081.

Tour Groups

Most escorted group tours team Berlin with a number of other European countries and German cities, giving you an economical, efficient overview of the most famous sights and attractions. Keep in mind, however, that when choosing a group tour you must step to the beat of the tour guide's drum. If freedom and flexibility are more important to you, or if you're interested strictly in Berlin, consider an independent package. Tour operators' offerings include multi-day accommodation packages, fly/drive plans, and preferred nightly hotel rates.

When evaluating any tour, be sure to find out exactly what expenses are included (particularly tips, taxes and service charges, side trips, additional meals, and entertainment); ratings of all hotels on the itinerary and the facilities they offer; cancellation policies for both you and the tour operator; and, if you are traveling alone, the cost of a single supplement.

Listed below is a sampling of operators and packages to give you an idea of what is available. For additional resources, contact your travel agent or the German National Tourist Office. Most tour operators request that bookings be made through a travel agent—there is no additional charge for doing so.

General-Interest Tours **TWA Getaway Vacations** (tel. 800/GETAWAY) lets you explore Berlin, Prague, and Vienna, or Berlin, Moscow, and St. Petersburg at a leisurely 10-day pace. **Maupintour** (Box 807, Lawrence, KS 66044, tel. 800/255–4266 or 913/843–1211) offers a two-week united Germany tour. **Olson-Travelworld** (Box 10066, Manhattan Beach, CA 90226, tel. 800/421–2255, 800/421–5785 in California, or 310/546–8400) offers comprehensive, 17-day tours of Germany. **Caravan Tours** (401 N. Michigan Ave., Suite 3325, Chicago, IL 60611, tel. 312/321–9800 or 800/CARAVAN) covers the country in a brisk 13 days. Both **Trafalgar Tours** (21 E. 26th St., New York, NY 10010, tel. 800/854–0103 or 212/689–8977) and **American Airlines Fly AAway Vacations** (tel. 800/321–2121 or 817/355–1234) hit the highlights of Germany and Austria in 15 days, including a stop in Berlin. **American Express Vacations** (300 Pinnacle Way, Norcross, GA 30093, tel. 800/241–1700 or 800/421–5785 in Georgia) combines a stop in Berlin with such other German cities as Hamburg, Dresden, Heidelberg, and Frankfurt.

U.K.-based Operators **Cresta Holidays** (Cresta House, Victoria St., Altrincham, Cheshire WA14 1ET, tel. 0361/927–7000) has flight/hotel packages and special offers. **DER Travel Service** (18 Conduit St.,

London W1R 9TD, tel. 0371/408–0111) offers package holidays by air, car, or rail with 3–10 nights in Berlin, Christmas and New Year's packages, and shopping weekends to Berlin's Christmas markets. **GTF Tours** (182–186 Kensington Church St., London W8 4DP, tel. 0371/229–2474) has flight/accommodation packages to Berlin for one or more nights. **Hamilton Travel Ltd** (6 Heddon St., London W1R 7LH, tel. 0371/439–3199) offers economical scheduled fares to Berlin. **Scandinavian Seaways** (Scandinavia House, Parkeston Quay, Harwich, Essex CO12 4QG, tel. 0255/241234) offers a 5-day package to Berlin, with sightseeing tours and a New Year's festive holiday. **Sovereign Cities** (Groundstar House, London Rd., Crawley, West Sussex RH10 2TB, tel. 0293/547700) offers flight/hotel packages to Berlin from two to seven nights, with optional excursions.

Special-Interest Tours
Art/Architecture

Esplanade Tours (581 Boylston St., Boston, MA 02116, tel. 617/266–7465) offers several in-depth art and architecture tours led by noted lecturers.

Barge Cruising

Drift in leisure and luxury down the Rhine, Lahn, and Mosel rivers (crossing into France) with **Floating Through Europe** (271 Madison Ave., New York, NY 10016, tel. 212/685–5600).

Health/Fitness

DER Tours offers spa packages at five classic spas in the Black Forest and Bavaria.

Music

Dailey-Thorp Travel (315 W. 57th St., New York, NY 10019, tel. 212/307–1555) offers deluxe opera and music tours, including "Musical Heartland of Europe." The tour features operas in Berlin, Dresden, and Prague. Itineraries vary according to available performances.

Wine/Cuisine

Travel Concepts (373 Commonwealth Ave., Suite 601, Boston, MA 02115–1815, tel. 617/266–8450) offers the "German Wine Academy." Usually based at Kloster Eberbach, a 12th-century monastery, the program includes tastings and visits to vineyards and wine cellars in 7 of Germany's 11 wine-producing regions. **DER Tours** (11933 Wilshire Blvd., Los Angeles, CA 90025, tel. 213/479–4140 or 800/421–4343) offers a tour called "Romantic Rhine and Wine." **KD German Rhine Line** (170 Hamilton Ave., White Plains, NY 10601, tel. 914/948–3600; 323 Geary St., San Francisco, CA 94102, tel. 415/392–8817) holds a 7-day "floating wine seminar" on the Rhine and Mosel rivers at the height of the autumn grape harvest, with lectures and wine tastings aboard and ashore.

Package Deals for Independent Travelers

Lufthansa (tel. 800/645–3880) has fly/drive and fly/rail packages, as well as preferred nightly rates at a wide range of hotels throughout Germany.

The fly/drive program from **United Vacations** (tel. 800/328–6877) combines special rental car and hotel rates in Berlin. Sightseeing tours and one-way airport transfers are also available.

Travel Bound (599 Broadway, Penthouse, New York, NY 10012, tel. 800/456–8656 or 212/334–1350) offers special rates at Berlin hotels as well as half-day sightseeing tours.

TWA Getaway Vacations (*see* General-Interest Tours, above) has two-night packages in first-class as well as budget hotels; extra nights are available.

Globetrotters (139 Main St., Cambridge, MA 02142, tel. 800/999–9696 or 617/621–9911) also gives you preferred hotel rates; stay for just one night or as many as you choose.

When to Go

It's always high season in Berlin. Even in its most dismal month, cold, wet February, the city entices thousands of visitors from all over the world to its glittering annual film festival. Nonetheless, the spring and summer months from April through September are the best times for a visit. In December and January, you might find yourself trudging around the city's sights through ankle-deep snow, while the weather in March and October is unpredictable. Since Berlin does not have an off-season, the only way to enjoy reduced rates in the city's higher-priced hotels is to cram your visit into a weekend. Most leading hotels offer weekend rates, often with sightseeing tours and theater/concert tickets thrown in. A weekend is, of course, much too short for Berlin, but one way of spinning out your stay for a minimal cost is to make sure it encompasses a Saturday and Sunday.

Climate The climate of Berlin and environs is temperate, although winter temperatures can often plunge to Siberian lows and some summer days can be swelteringly hot. Snowfalls are often heavy, and the eastern part of both the city and the country are rarely prepared for them. So, if you're traveling in the east during a heavy winter, prepare for delays on the roads, railways, and at airports.

The following are the average daily maximum and minimum temperatures for Berlin.

Jan.	36F	2C	May	67F	19C	Sept.	68F	20C
	27	– 3		47	8		50	10
Feb.	38F	3C	June	72F	22C	Oct.	56F	13C
	27	– 3		54	12		43	6
Mar.	47F	8C	July	76F	24C	Nov.	45F	7C
	32	0		58	14		36	2
Apr.	56F	13C	Aug.	74F	23C	Dec.	38F	3C
	40	4		56	13		31	– 1

Current weather information for foreign and domestic cities may be obtained by calling **The Weather Channel Connection** at 900/WEATHER from a touch-tone phone. In addition to the weather report, The Weather Channel Connection offers local time and travel tips as well as hurricane, foliage, and ski reports. The call costs 95¢ per minute.

Festivals and Seasonal Events

Berlin is a premier—some would say *the* premier—German festival city. Scarcely a week passes without at least one major event getting under way. What follows are the city's most notable festivals:

January–February The museums are open throughout the year, of course, but during the **Berliner Museumstage** special exhibitions and concerts are held.

Internationale Grüne Woche, Berlin's annual agricultural and produce fair, is held at the Messegelände, the fairgrounds at the radio and television tower, the Funkturm.

Internationale Filmfestspiele is the world-famous Berlin Film Festival.

March **Internationale Tourismus-Börse** is Europe's biggest travel and tourism fair. Berliners say farewell to winter at the **Frühlingsfest,** a popular spring fair on the central Lützowplatz.

April–May Berlin galleries join in presenting a giant fine arts fair during the **Berliner Kunsttage.**

Freie Berliner Kunstaustellung is another major fine arts festival open to all Berlin artists.

Whitsun: During **Frühkonzerte im Freien,** music is in the air everywhere, with bands, pop groups, and small ensembles touring Berlin's parks, open-air cafés, pubs, and restaurants.

May–June All Berlin becomes a stage for **Theatertreffen** when scores of theater groups perform anywhere they can find an audience—in tents, tavern taprooms, parks, marketplaces, and even on the pavements of downtown Berlin.

The garden setting for **Jazz in the Garden,** held Friday in June, is the sculpture-strewn grounds of the Neue Nationalgalerie.

Held in Spandau's old town center, **Kiezfest** is one of Berlin's most popular summer festivals.

Horizonte, Festival der Weltkulturen is an international culture exchange presented in the Kongresshalle, Tiergarten, and other venues.

June–July **Bläser-Serenaden** is a series of brass ensemble concerts performed in the courtyard of the Grunewald Jagdschloss, a Renaissance hunting lodge.

Barrel-organ enthusiasts of the world turn their handles in one of Berlin's most unusual musical get-togethers, the **Internationales Drehorgelfest,** held outside the Gedächtniskirche.

Berliner Bachtage is a week-long festival celebrating the great German composer.

Jugglers do their thing on Los-Angeles-Platz in the **Gauklerfest.**

Insiders say that **Jazz in July** at the Quasimodo Club is Berlin's leading international jazz festival.

July–August **Deutsch-Amerikanisches Volksfest** in Dahlem celebrates German-American friendship.

Glienicker Schlosskonzerte are chamber-music concerts presented in the enchanting open-air courtyard setting of the Remisenhof of the Glienicker Schloss.

Sommerkonzerte are organ recitals in the Eosander chapel of Schloss Charlottenburg.

August–September Kreuzberg's summer festival, **Kreuzberger Festliche Tage,** celebrated on and around the Kreuzberg hill in Victoria Park, is a huge party.

Turmstrassenfest is the Moabit district's attempt to outdo Kreuzberg.

September–October **Berliner Festwochen** is Berlin's major music and theater festival.

Allgemeine Auto-Ausstellung Berlin, the annual motor show, is held at the fairgrounds.

Dozens of Berlin groups blow the dust off the Music Instrument Museum exhibition in a three-day jazz festival, the **Jazztreffen im Musikinstrumenten-Museum.**

Berlin's 20th annual **International Marathon** is set for September 26, 1993.

November The German national contest of young songwriters, the **Treffen Junger Liedermacher,** takes place in various venues.

December **Weihnachtsmärkte,** the Christmas markets, spring up all over Berlin, the best of them around the Gedächtniskirche and in Spandau's old town.

What to Pack

Pack light—luggage restrictions on international flights are tight. Airlines generally allow two pieces of check-in luggage and one carry-on piece per passenger. No piece of check-in luggage can exceed 62 inches (length + width + height) or weigh more than 70 pounds. The carry-on luggage cannot exceed 45 inches (length + width + height) and must fit under the seat or in the overhead luggage compartment. Passengers in first and business classes are also allowed to carry on one garment bag. It is always best, however, to check with your airline ahead of time to find out about its luggage restrictions.

What you pack depends more on the time of year than on any particular dress code. Winters can be bitterly cold; summers are warm but with days that suddenly turn cool and rainy.

For Berlin, pack as you would for an American city: dressy outfits for formal restaurants and nightclubs, casual clothes elsewhere. Jeans are as popular in Germany as anywhere else, and are perfectly acceptable for sightseeing and informal dining. In the evening, men will probably feel more comfortable wearing a jacket and tie in more expensive restaurants. Many German women are extremely fashion-conscious and wear stylish outfits to restaurants and the theater, especially in the larger cities.

If you plan to swim in a pool, take a bathing cap. They're obligatory in Germany, for both men and women. For stays in budget hotels, take your own soap. Many do not provide soap or provide only one small bar. You will need an electrical adapter for your hair dryer or other small appliances. The current is 220 volts, 50 cycles.

Taking Money Abroad

Before going, you may want to chart the U.S. dollar for a couple of weeks against the German Deutschemark. This can be risky, but the savings may warrant the trouble: if the dollar is weakening, consider buying traveler's checks in Deutschemarks and paying in advance for such costly items as hotel rooms and train or plane tickets. If the dollar is improving, buy traveler's checks in U.S. currency, and use a credit card (American Express, in particular, is widely accepted in Berlin and excursion destinations) to pay for costly items after you've arrived at your destination. Overseas credit charges often don't appear on your bill for two or three months, and you pay the exchange rate of the day the vendor posted the charge. Always carry some cash with you, however, especially in smaller cities and rural areas where credit cards and traveler's checks are not widely accepted. Some shops offer a cash discount in place of credit-card payment—don't be shy to ask. Regardless of how the dollar is faring abroad, it's wise to exchange a small amount of money into German Deutschemarks before you go to avoid lines at airport currency-exchange booths. Most U.S. banks will exchange your money for Deutschemarks. If your local bank can't provide this service, you can exchange money through **Thomas Cook Currency Service.** To find the office nearest you, contact them at 630 Fifth Ave., New York, NY 10111, tel. 212/757–6915.

The most recognized traveler's checks are **American Express, Barclay's, Thomas Cook,** and those issued through such major commercial banks as **Citibank** and **Bank of America.** American Express now issues **Travelers Cheques for Two**—a system that allows both you and your traveling companion to sign and use the same checks. Some banks will issue the checks free to established customers, but most charge a 1% commission fee. Buy part of the traveler's checks in small denominations to cash toward the end of your trip. This will save you from having to cash a large check and ending up with more foreign money than you need. Remember to take the addresses of offices where you can get refunds for lost or stolen traveler's checks.

The best places to change money are banks and bank-operated currency-exchange booths in airports and railway stations. Hotels and privately run exchange firms will give you a significantly lower rate.

Getting Money from Home

Cash Machines Where possible, use automated-teller machines (ATMs) to withdraw money from your checking account with a bank card, or, though it's more expensive, advance cash with your credit card. Before leaving home ask your local bank for a Personal Identification Number (PIN) for your bank and credit cards. Also request a list of affiliated cash-machine networks (i.e., **Cirrus** and **Plus**), their ATM locations, the fees for withdrawals or cash advances made overseas, and limits on these transactions within given time periods. Not all German ATMs have prompts in English, so learn the German equivalent for key words such as *withdraw, amount, cancel,* etc.). Cash advances can also be made through bank tellers. Either way, you pay interest from the day of posting, and some banks tack on an extra service charge.

Bank Transfers Just have your bank send money to another bank in Germany. It's easiest to transfer money between like branches; otherwise, the process takes a couple days longer and costs more.

American Express
Cardholder
Services The company's **Express Cash** system links your U.S. checking account to your Amex card. Overseas you can withdraw up to $1,000 in a 21-day period (more if your card is Gold or Platinum). For each transaction there's a 2% fee (minimum $2, maximum $6). Call 800/227–4669 for information. Cardholders can also cash personal or counter checks at any American Express office for up to $1,000, of which $500 may be claimed in cash and the balance in traveler's checks carrying a 1% commission.

Wiring Money   You don't have to be a cardholder to have an **American Express MoneyGram** sent to you overseas. Just have a friend at home fill out a MoneyGram for up to $10,000 at an American Express MoneyGram agency (call 800/543–4080) for locations). Payment of up to $1,000 may be made with a credit card (AE, D, MC, V); the balance must be in cash. Your friend then telephones you with a reference number and the MoneyGram agent authorizes a funds transfer to the participating office nearest you. Present proper I.D. and the reference number for payment. Fees are roughly 5%–10%, depending upon the amount and method of payment.

If there are no American Express offices nearby, you can use **Western Union** (tel. 800/325–6000). A friend at home can bring cash or a check to the nearest Western Union office or pay over the phone with a credit card. Delivery usually takes two business days, and fees are roughly 5% to 10%.

German Currency

The unit of currency in Germany is the Deutschemark (DM), divided into 100 pfennings (pf). Bills are DM 1,000, 500, 200, 100, 50, 20, and 10. Coins are DM 5, 2, and 1, and 50, 10, 5, 2, and 1 pf. At press time the exchange rate was about DM 1.46 to the U.S. dollar, DM 1.30 to the Canadian dollar, and DM 2.86 to the pound sterling.

The Deutschemark became the official currency of united Germany in July 1990. However, great discrepancies still exist in the standard of living between western and eastern Germany.

What It Will Cost

Germany has an admirably high standard of living—perhaps the highest in Europe—which inevitably makes it an expensive country to visit, particularly if you spend time in the cities. Many items—gas, food, hotels, and trains, to name but a few— are often more expensive than in the United States.

Although Germany's largest city, Berlin is not its most expensive. Restaurant bills are generally lower (particularly in the eastern half of the city), hotel package-deals are more numerous, and theater/concert ticket prices tend to be lower than in, say, Hamburg or Munich. Until unification, East Berlin and eastern German excursion cities such as Potsdam and Magdeburg were a budget-traveler's dream. Currency reform and political union rapidly changed that, and today the former communist-ruled areas that attract tourists are at a rough price parity with western German areas.

Passports and Visas

Americans   Only a valid passport is required to enter Germany for a stay of up to 90 days. To obtain a new passport, apply in person; renewals can be obtained in person or by mail. First-time applicants should apply to one of the 13 U.S. Passport Agency offices at least five weeks before departure. In addition, local county courthouses, many state and probate courts, and some post offices accept passport applications. Necessary documents include: (1) a completed passport application (Form DSP-11); (2) proof of citizenship (certified birth certificate issued by the

Hall of Records of your state of birth, or naturalization papers); (3) proof of identity (valid driver's license or state, military, or student ID card with your photograph and signature); (4) two recent, identical, 2-inch-square photographs (black-and-white or color head shots with white or off-white background); and (5) a $65 application fee for a 10-year passport ($40 for a five-year passport available to those under 18). You may pay with a check, money order, or exact cash amount; no change is given. Passports are mailed to you in 10 to 15 working days. To renew your passport by mail, send a completed Form DSP-82 with two recent, identical passport photographs, your current passport (provided it is less than 12 years old and was issued after your 16th birthday), and a check or money order for $55.

A tourist/business visa is not required for U.S. citizens staying up to three months in Germany, but longer stays generally require a visa. Check with the German Embassy, 4645 Reservoir Rd. NW, Washington, DC 20007, tel. 202/298–4000.

Canadians Only a valid passport is required to enter Germany for a stay of up to 90 days. Send your completed application (available at any post office or passport office) to the **Bureau of Passports,** Suite 215, West Tower, Guy Favreau Complex, 200 René Lévesque Blvd. W, Montreal, Quebec H2Z 1X4. Include $25, two photographs, a guarantor, and proof of Canadian citizenship. Applications can also be made in person at the regional passport offices in Edmonton, Halifax, Montreal, Toronto, Vancouver, or Winnipeg. Passports are valid for five years and are nonrenewable.

Visas are not required for Canadian citizens to enter Germany for stays of up to three months.

Britons All British citizens require a passport to enter Germany. Application forms are available from travel agencies and main post offices, or from the **Passport Office** (Clive House, 70 Petty France, London SW1H 9BR, tel. 0371/279–3434 for recorded information, or 0371/279–4000). Send the completed form to a regional passport office or apply in person at a main post office. The application must be countersigned by your bank manager, or by a solicitor, barrister, doctor, clergyman, or justice of the peace who knows you personally. In addition, you'll need two photographs and a £15 fee for a standard 32-page passport, £30 for a 94-page passport. The occasional tourist might opt for a British Visitors' passport. It is valid for one year, costs £7.50 and is nonrenewable. You'll need two passport photographs and identification. Apply at your local post office.

Visas are not required for British citizens to enter Germany.

Customs and Duties

On Arrival There are two levels of duty-free allowance for visitors to Germany.

For goods obtained anywhere outside the EC or for goods purchased in a duty-free shop within an EC country, the allowances are (1) 400 cigarettes or 200 cigars or 100 cigars or 500 grams of tobacco (these allowances are halved if you live in Europe), plus (2) 2 liters of still table wine, plus (3) 1 liter of spirits over 22% volume or 2 liters of spirits under 22% volume (fortified and sparkling wines) or 2 more liters of table wine, plus (4)

60 milliliters of perfume and 250 milliliters of toilet water, plus (5) other goods to the value of DM 115.

For goods obtained (duty and tax paid) within another EC country, the allowances are (1) 300 cigarettes or 150 cigarillos or 75 cigars or 400 grams of tobacco, plus (2) 5 liters of still table wine, plus (3) 1.5 liters of spirits over 22% volume or 3 liters of spirits under 22% volume (fortified or sparkling wines) or 3 more liters of table wine, plus (4) 90 milliliters of perfume and 375 milliliters of toilet water, plus (5) other goods to the value of DM 780.

Tobacco and alcohol allowances are for visitors aged 17 and over. Other items intended for personal use can be imported and exported freely. There are no restrictions on the import and export of German currency.

On Departure   **U.S. Customs:** Before your trip, it's a good idea to obtain *Know Before You Go,* a free, invaluable customs brochure that outlines what returning residents may and may not bring back to this country, and at what cost. Contact the U.S. Customs Service (1301 Constitution Ave., Washington, DC 20229).

If you are bringing any foreign-made equipment from home, such as cameras, it's wise to carry the original receipt with you or register it with U.S. customs before you leave (Form 4457). Otherwise you may end up paying duty on your return. U.S. residents may bring home duty-free up to $400 worth of foreign goods, as long as they have been out of the country for at least 48 hours and haven't made an international trip in 30 days. Each member of the family is entitled to the same exemption, regardless of age, and exemptions can be pooled. For the next $1,000 worth of goods, a flat 10% rate is assessed; above $1,400, duties vary with the merchandise. Included for travelers 21 or older are 1 liter of alcohol, 100 cigars (non-Cuban), and 200 cigarettes. Only one bottle of perfume trademarked in the U.S. may be imported. However, there is no duty on antiques or art over 100 years old. Anything exceeding these limits will be taxed at the port of entry, and may be taxed additionally in the traveler's home state. Gifts valued at under $50 may be mailed to friends or relatives at home duty-free, but not more than one package per day to any one addressee may be sent, and packages may not include perfumes costing more than $5, tobacco, or liquor.

Canadian Customs: Canadian residents have an exemption ranging from $20 to $300, depending on the length of stay out of the country. For the $300 exemption, you must have been out of the country for one week. For any given year, you are allowed one $300 exemption. You may also bring in duty-free up to 50 cigars, 200 cigarettes, 2.2 pounds of tobacco, and 40 ounces of liquor, provided these are declared in writing to customs on arrival and accompany the traveler in hand or in checked-through baggage. Personal gifts should be mailed as "Unsolicited Gift—Value under $40." Request the Canadian customs brochure "I Declare" for further details.

British Customs: Returning to the United Kingdom, there are two levels of duty-free allowances; tobacco and alcohol allowances are for travelers aged 17 and over.

For goods obtained anywhere outside the EC or for goods purchased in a duty-free shop within Germany, the allowances are

(1) 200 cigarettes or 100 cigarillos or 50 cigars or 250 grams of tobacco (these allowances are doubled if you live outside of Europe); (2) two liters of still table wine and, in addition, (a) one liter of alcoholic drink over 22% volume (most spirits) or (b) two liters of alcoholic drink under 22% by volume (fortified or sparkling wines) or (c) two more liters of table wine; (3) 60 milliliters of perfume and 250 milliliters of toilet water; (4) other goods to a value or £32.

For goods obtained (duty and tax paid) within Germany, the allowances are (1) 300 cigarettes or 150 cigarillos or 75 cigars or 400 grams of tobacco; (2) 5 liters of still table wine and, in addition, (a) 1.5 liters of spirits over 22% volume or (b) 3 liters of spirits under 22% volume (fortified or sparkling wines) or (c) 3 more liters of table wine; (3) 90 milliliters of perfume and 375 milliliters of toilet water; (4) other goods to the value of £420.

In addition, no animals or pets of any kind may be brought into the United Kingdom. The penalties for doing so are severe and are strictly enforced.

Traveling with Film

If your camera is new, shoot and develop a few rolls of film before leaving home. Pack some lens tissue and an extra battery for your built-in light meter.

Film doesn't like hot weather. If you're driving in summer, don't store film in the glove compartment or on the shelf under the rear window. Put it behind the front seat on the floor, on the side opposite the exhaust pipe.

On a plane trip, never pack unprocessed film in check-in luggage; if your bags get X-rayed, you can say goodbye to your pictures. Always carry undeveloped film with you through security and ask to have it inspected by hand. (It helps to isolate your film in a plastic bag, ready for quick inspection.) Inspectors at American airports are required by law to honor requests for hand inspection; abroad, you'll have to depend on the kindness of strangers.

The old airport scanning machines—still in use in some Third World countries—use heavy doses of radiation that can turn a family portrait into an early morning fog. The newer models—used in all U.S. and most German airports (those in the eastern part have less modern equipment)—are safe for anything from five to 500 scans, depending on the speed of your film. The effects are cumulative; you can put the same roll of film through several scans without worry. After five scans, however, you're asking for trouble.

Language

The Germans are great linguists and you'll find that English is spoken in virtually all hotels, restaurants, airports and stations, museums, and other places of interest. Berliners are particularly cosmopolitan and enjoy the opportunity to show off their ability to speak English.

Staying Healthy

Sanitation and health standards in Germany are as high as those anywhere in the world, and there are no serious health risks associated with travel there. If you have a health problem that might require purchasing prescription drugs while in Germany, have your doctor write a prescription using the drug's generic name. Brand names vary widely from one country to another.

In Washington, DC, the Department of State **Citizens Emergency Center** (tel. 202/647–5225) provides information about health conditions in other nations; what U.S. citizens can do in the event of an emergency overseas; whether any notices, cautions, or warnings exist in the area to which you're traveling; and how to obtain passports and visas.

The **International Association for Medical Assistance to Travelers** (IAMAT) is a worldwide association that offers a list of approved physicians and clinics whose training meets British and American standards. For a list of German physicians and clinics that are part of this network, contact IAMAT (417 Center St., Lewiston, NY 14092, tel. 716/754–4883; in **Canada,** 40 Regal Rd., Guelph, Ontario N1K 1B5; in **Europe,** 57 Voirets, 1212 Grand-Lancy, Geneva, Switzerland). Membership is free.

Inoculations are not required for entry to Germany.

Insurance

Travelers may seek insurance coverage in four areas: health and accident, loss of luggage, flight, and trip cancellation. Your first step is to review your existing health and homeowner policies; some health-insurance plans cover health expenses incurred while traveling, some major-medical plans cover emergency transportation, and some homeowner policies cover the theft of luggage.

Health and Accident Several companies offer coverage designed to supplement existing health insurance for travelers:

Carefree Travel Insurance (Box 310, 120 Mineola Blvd., Mineola, NY 11501, tel. 516/294–0220 or 800/323–3149) provides coverage for emergency medical evacuation and accidental death and dismemberment. It also offers 24-hour medical phone advice.

International SOS Assistance (Box 11568, Philadelphia, PA 19116, tel. 215/244–1500 or 800/523–8930), a medical assistance company, provides emergency evacuation services, worldwide medical referrals, and optional medical insurance.

Travel Assistance International (1133 15th St. NW, Suite 400, Washington, DC 20005, tel. 202/331–1609 or 800/821–2828) provides emergency evacuation services, 24-hour medical referrals, and medical insurance.

Travel Guard International, underwritten by Transamerica Occidental Life Companies (1145 Clark St., Stevens Point, WI 54481, tel. 715/345–0505 or 800/782–5151), offers reimbursement for medical expenses with no deductibles or daily limits, as well as emergency-evacuation services.

Wallach and Company, Inc. (Box 480, Middleburg, VA 22117-0480, tel. 703/687–3166 or 800/237–6615), offers comprehensive medical coverage, including emergency evacuation services worldwide.

Lost Luggage On international flights, airlines are responsible for lost or damaged property of up to $9.07 per pound (or $20 per kilo) for checked baggage, and up to $400 per passenger for unchecked baggage. If you're carrying valuables, either take them with you on the plane or purchase additional insurance for lost luggage. Some airlines will issue extra luggage insurance when you check in, but many do not. Insurance for lost, damaged, or stolen luggage is available through travel agents or directly through various insurance companies. Luggage loss coverage is usually part of a comprehensive travel insurance package that includes personal accident, trip cancellation, and sometimes default and bankruptcy. Two companies that issue luggage insurance are **Tele-Trip** (Box 31685, 3201 Farnam St., Omaha, NE 68131-0618, tel. 800/228–9792), a subsidiary of Mutual of Omaha, and **The Traveler** (Ticket and Travel Dept., 1 Tower Sq., Hartford, CT 06183-5040, tel. 203/277–0111 or 800/243–3174). Tele-Trip operates sales booths at airports, and also issues insurance through travel agents. Rates vary according to the length of the trip. The Traveler will insure checked or hand luggage at $500–$2,000 valuation per person, for a maximum of 180 days. Rates for 1–5 days for $500 valuation are $10; for 180 days, $85. Other companies with comprehensive policies include **Access America, Inc.,** a subsidiary of Blue Cross-Blue Shield (Box 11188, Richmond, VA 23230, tel. 800/334–7525 or 800/284–8300); **Near Services** (450 Prairie Ave., Suite 101, Calumet City, IL 60409, tel. 708/868–6700 or 800/654–6700); **Travel Guard International;** and **Carefree Travel Insurance** (*see* Health and Accident Insurance, above).

Before you go, itemize the contents of each bag in case you need to file an insurance claim. Be certain to put your home or business address on each piece of luggage, including carry-on bags. If your luggage is lost or stolen and later recovered, the airline will deliver the luggage to your home free of charge.

Flight Flight insurance, which covers passengers in the case of death or dismemberment, is often included in the price of a ticket when paid for with American Express, MasterCard, or other major credit cards.

Trip-Cancellation Consider purchasing trip-cancellation insurance if you are traveling on a promotional or discounted ticket that does not allow changes or cancellations. You are then covered if an emergency causes you to cancel or postpone your trip. Trip-cancellation insurance is usually included in combination travel-insurance packages available from most tour operators, travel agents, and insurance agents.

Renting, Leasing, and Purchasing Cars

Renting If you're flying into Berlin you can save money by arranging to pick up and return your car at the airport. You'll have to weigh the added expense of renting a car from a major company with an airport office against the savings on a car from a budget company with offices in town. You could waste precious hours trying to locate the budget company in return for only a small financial savings. If you're arriving and departing from different airports, look for a one-way car rental with no return fees. If you're traveling to more than one country, make sure your rental contract permits you to take the car across borders and that the insurance policy covers you in every country you visit. Be prepared to pay more for a car with an automatic transmission. Since these cars aren't as readily available as those with manual transmission, you should reserve them in advance.

Rental rates vary widely, depending on size and model, number of days you use the car, insurance coverage, and whether special drop-off fees are imposed. In most cases, rates quoted include unlimited free mileage and standard liability protection. Not included are collision damage waiver (CDW), which eliminates your deductible payment should you have an accident; personal accident insurance; gasoline; and European value added taxes (VAT). In 1993, the VAT is expected to be raised from 14% to 15% throughout Germany.

Driver's licenses issued in the United States, Canada, and Britain are valid in Germany. You might also take out an international driving permit before you leave, to smooth out difficulties if you have an accident or as an additional identification. Permits are available for a small fee through local offices of the American Automobile Association (AAA) and the Canadian Automobile Association (CAA), or from their main offices (**AAA,** 1000 AAA Dr., Heathrow, FL 32746, tel. 800/336–4357; **CAA,** 2 Carlton St., Toronto, Ontario M5B 1K4, tel. 416/964–3002).

It's best to arrange a car rental before you leave. You won't save money by waiting until you arrive in Germany, and you may find that the type of car you want is not available at the last minute. Rental companies usually charge according to the exchange rate of the dollar at the time the car is returned or when the credit-card payment is processed. Two companies with special programs to help you hedge against the falling dollar, by guaranteeing advertised rates if you pay in advance, are **Budget Rent-a-Car** (3350 Boyington St., Carrollton, TX 75006, tel. 800/527–0700) and **Connex Travel International** (23 N. Division St., Peekskill, NY 10566, tel. 800/333–3949).

Other budget rental companies serving Germany include **Europe by Car** (1 Rockefeller Plaza, New York, NY 10020, tel. 800/223–1516 or 800/252–9401 in CA), **Auto Europe** (Box 1097 Sharps Wharf, Camden, ME 04843, tel. 800/223–5555), **Foremost EuroCar** (5430 Van Nuys Blvd., Suite 306, Van Nuys, CA 91401, tel. 800/272–3299), and **Kemwel** (106 Calvert St., Harrison, NY 10528, tel. 800/678–0678).

Other companies include **Avis** (tel. 800/331–1212), **Hertz** (tel. 800/654–3131), and **National** or **Europcar** (tel. 800/CAR–RENT).

Leasing For trips of 21 days or more, you may save money by leasing a car. Under a leasing arrangement, you are technically buying a car and then selling it back to the manufacturer after you've used it. You receive a factory-new car, tax-free, and with international registration and extensive insurance coverage. Rates vary with the make and model of car and length of time used. Car leasing programs are offered by Renault, Citroën, and Peugeot in France, and by Volkswagen, Ford, Audi, and Opel, among others, in Belgium. Delivery to Germany can be arranged for an additional fee. Before you go, compare long-term rental rates with leasing rates. Remember to add taxes and insurance costs to the car rentals, something you don't have to worry about with leasing. Companies that offer leasing arrangements include **Kemwel, Europe by Car,** and **Auto Europe,** all listed above.

GermanRail offers Rail and Drive packages, which combine a train Flexipass (*see* Rail Passes, below) with three days of unlimited-mileage car rental. Packages start at $185 (for a five-day Flexipass and three-day car rental over a month-long period).

Purchasing Given the weakness of the dollar, purchasing a car in Germany is less appealing today than it was a decade ago. The advantage is that you'll get what amounts to a free car rental during your stay in Europe. If you plan to purchase a car in Germany, be certain the prices quoted are for cars built to meet specifications set down by the U.S. Department of Transportation. You will also be subject to a U.S. customs duty. For more information, contact **Kemwel** or **Europe by Car,** both listed above, or ask your local car dealer to put you in touch with an importer.

Rail Passes

The **EurailPass,** valid for unlimited first-class train travel through 20 countries, including Germany, is an excellent value if you plan to travel around the Continent. The ticket is available for periods of 15 days ($430), 21 days ($550), one month ($680), two months ($920), and three months ($1,150). Three people traveling together can purchase the 15-day pass for $340 each. During the off-season (Oct.–Mar.) two people can enjoy the cut-price deal. For those under 26 (on the first day of travel), there is the **Eurail Youthpass,** for one or two months' unlimited second-class train travel at $470 and $640.

For travelers who like to spread out their train journeys, there is the **Eurail Flexipass.** With the 15-day pass ($280), travelers get five days of unlimited first-class train travel spread out over a 15-day period; a 21-day pass gives you nine days of travel ($450), and a one-month pass gives you 14 days ($610).

The EurailPass is available only if you live outside Europe or North Africa. The pass must be bought from an authorized agent before you leave for Europe. Apply through your travel agent, or contact **GermanRail** (747 Third Ave., New York, NY 10017, tel. 212/308–3100).

The new **GermanRail (DB) Flexipass,** now valid for the entire German rail network, is available to non-Europeans and must be purchased outside of Europe. The "flexible" nature of the pass allows you to spread your days of train travel over a month-long period. A first-class pass costs $240 for five days, $360 for 10 days, and $450 for 15 days. A second-class pass costs $160 for five days, $240 for 10 days, and $300 for 15 days. A Youthpass (second-class only) for people aged 12–25 ranges from $110 to $180. GermanRail passes can be used on buses operated by the DB, as well as on tour routes along the Romantic and Castle Roads served by Deutsche Touring (*see* Getting Around, below). Cruises on the Rhine, Main, and Mosel rivers operated by the Köln-Düsseldorfer (KD) Line are also included with the pass.

Student and Youth Travel

The **International Student Identity Card** (ISIC) entitles students to youth rail passes, special fares on local transportation, Intra-European student charter flights, and discounts at museums, theaters, sports events, and many other attractions. If purchased in the United States, the $14 cost of the ISIC also includes $3,000 in emergency medical insurance, $100 a day for up to 60 days of hospital coverage, and a collect phone number to call in case of emergencies. Apply to the **Council on International Student Exchange** (CIEE, 205 E. 42nd St., New York, NY 10017, tel. 212/661–1414). In Canada, the ISIC is available for CN$13 from **Travel Cuts** (187 College St., Toronto, Ont. M5T 1P7, tel. 416/979–2406).

The **Youth International Educational Exchange Card** (YIEE), issued by the **Federation of International Youth Travel Organizations** (FIYTO, 81 Islands Brugge, DK-2300 Copenhagen S, Denmark), provides similar services to nonstudents under the age of 26. In the United States, the card is available from CIEE (address above). In Canada, the YIEE is available from the **Canadian Hostelling Association** (CHA, 1600 James Naismith Drive, Suite 608, Gloucester, Ont. K1B 5N4, tel. 613/748–5638).

An **International Youth Hostel Federation** (IYHF) membership card is the key to inexpensive dormitory-style accommodations at more than 5,000 youth hostels in 70 countries around the world. Hostels provide separate sleeping quarters for men and women at rates ranging from $7 to $20 a night per person and are situated in a variety of facilities, including converted farmhouses, villas, and restored castles, as well as specially constructed modern buildings. IYHF membership is available in the United States through American Youth Hostels (AYH, Box 37613, Washington, DC 20013, tel. 202/783–6161) and in Canada through the **Canadian Hostelling Association** (address above). The cost for a first-year membership is $25 for adults 18–54. Renewal thereafter is $20 a year. For youths (17 and under), the rate is $10 a year, and for senior citizens (55 and older) the rate is $15 a year. Family membership is available for $35 a year.

Council Travel, a CIEE subsidiary, is the foremost U.S. student travel agency, specializing in low-cost charters and serving as the exclusive U.S. agent for many student airfare bargains and student tours. CIEE's 72-page *Student Travel Catalog* and "Council Charter" brochure are available free from any Council Travel office in the United States (enclose $1 postage if ordering by mail). Contact the CIEE headquarters (205 E. 42nd St., New York, NY 10017) for the branch office nearest you.

Students who would like to work abroad should contact CIEE's **Work Abroad Department** (205 E. 42nd St., New York, NY 10017, tel. 212/661–1414, ext. 1130). The council arranges various types of paid and voluntary work experiences overseas for up to six months. CIEE also sponsors study programs in Europe, Latin America, and Asia, and publishes many books of interest to the student traveler. These include *Work, Study, Travel Abroad: The Whole World Handbook* ($12 plus $1.50 book-rate postage or $3 first-class postage); and *Volunteer! The Comprehensive Guide to Voluntary Service in the U.S.*

and Abroad ($8.95 plus $1.50 book-rate postage or $3 first-class postage).

The Information Center at the **Institute of International Education** (IIE) has reference books, foreign university catalogs, study-abroad brochures, and other materials, which may be consulted by students and nonstudents alike, free of charge.

The Information Center (809 UN Plaza, New York, NY 10017, tel. 212/883–8200) is open Monday–Friday 10–4. *It is not open on holidays.*

IIE administers a variety of grant and study programs offered by U.S. and foreign organizations, and publishes a well-known annual series of study-abroad guides, including *Academic Year Abroad, Vacation Study Abroad,* and *Study in the United Kingdom and Ireland.* The institute also publishes *Teaching Abroad,* a book of employment and study opportunities overseas for U.S. teachers. For a current list of IIE publications with prices and ordering information, write to Publications Service, Institute of International Education, 809 UN Plaza, New York, NY 10017. Books must be purchased by mail or in person; telephone orders are not accepted.

General information on IIE programs and services is available from its regional offices in Atlanta, Chicago, Denver, Houston, San Francisco, and Washington, DC.

Traveling with Children

Publications Ask the German National Tourist Board for the booklet **"Berlin Loves Children,"** filled with information about family restaurants and accommodations, children's museums, puppet theaters, and other child-friendly activities in Berlin. Although it is written in German, it offers an excellent starting point.

Family Travel Times is a newsletter published 10 times a year by **TWYCH** (Travel with Your Children, 45 W. 18th St., 7th Floor Tower, New York, NY 10011, tel. 212/206–0688). Subscription costs $35 and includes access to back issues and twice-weekly opportunities to call in for specific advice.

Great Vacations with Your Kids, by Dorothy Jordan and Marjorie Cohen, offers complete advice on planning your trip with children, from toddlers to teens ($12.95 paperback, E.P. Dutton, 375 Hudson St., New York, NY 10014, tel. 212/366–2000).

Innocents Abroad: Traveling with Kids in Europe, by Valerie Wolf Deutsch and Laura Sutherland, is a new guide to child- and teen-friendly activities, food, and transportation in Britain and on the Continent, with individual sections on each country ($14.95 paperback, New American Library, Penguin USA, 375 Hudson St., New York, NY 10014, tel. 212/366–2000).

Kids and Teens in Flight, a useful brochure about children flying alone, is available from the U.S. Department of Transportation. To order a free copy, call 202/366–2220.

Hotels Although few hotels in Berlin have extensive facilities or programs for children, **Hotel Berlin,** part of the **Dial Berlin Consortium** (tel. 800/237–5469 for reservations) has several L-shaped rooms with dividing curtains for family use. They also offer children's menus. At both the **Intercontinental Berlin** and

Intercontinental's Schweizerhoss hotels (tel. 800/327–0200), one child under 14 can stay free in his or her parents' room.

Home Exchange Exchanging homes is a surprisingly low-cost way to enjoy a vacation abroad, especially a long one. The largest home-exchange service, **Intervac U.S./International Home Exchange** (Box 590504, San Francisco, CA 94159, tel. 415/435–3497 or 800/756–4663) publishes three directories a year. Membership, which costs $45, entitles you to one listing and all three directories. **Loan-a-Home** (2 Park La., 6E, Mount Vernon, NY 10552, tel. 914/664–7640) is popular with academics on sabbatical and businesspeople on temporary assignment. There's no annual membership fee or charge for listing your home, however one directory and a supplement costs $35. Loan-a-Home publishes two directories (in December and June) and two supplements (in March and September) each year. The set of four books costs $45 per year.

Getting There On international flights, children under two years not occupying a seat pay 10% of adult fare. Various discounts apply to children from ages two to 12. Reserve a seat behind the bulkhead of the plane, which offers more legroom and can usually accommodate a bassinet (which some airlines will supply). At the same time, inquire about special children's meals or snacks, offered by most airlines. (See "TWYCH's Airline Guide," in the February 1990 and 1992 issues of *Family Travel Times*, for a rundown on children's services offered by 46 airlines.)

Regulations about infant travel on airplanes are in the process of changing. Until they do, however, if you want to be sure your infant is secure, you should buy a separate ticket and bring your own infant car seat (but check with the airline in advance—some don't allow them). Some airlines allow babies to travel in their own car seats at no charge if there's a spare seat available; otherwise, safety seats will be stored and the child will have to be held by a parent. For the booklet *Child/Infant Safety Seats Acceptable for Use in Aircraft*, write to the **Federal Aviation Administration** (800 Independence Ave. SW, Washington, DC 20591, tel. 202/267–3479). If you opt to hold your baby on your lap, do so with the infant outside the seat belt so he or she won't be crushed in case of a sudden stop.

Baby-sitting Services First check with the hotel desk for recommended child-care arrangements. Also, most local tourist offices in Germany maintain updated lists of baby-sitters. The baby-sitters have all been screened. Expect to pay approximately DM 25 per hour.

Hints for Disabled Travelers

The recent changes in eastern Germany and Berlin mean that many organizations are combining, changing names, or disappearing. For the time being, you should contact the Berlin Tourist Office for all information concerning accessibility and special services. GermanRail (747 Third Ave., New York, NY, tel. 212/308–3103) publishes a 50-page booklet, **"Travel Guide for Our Handicapped Passengers,"** outlining services for the disabled in more than 400 train stations throughout Germany, including Berlin. Most stations are equipped with narrow wheelchairs that are used to transport handicapped passengers to their seats.

The **Information Center for Individuals with Disabilities** (Fort Point Pl., 1st floor, 27–43 Wormwood St., Boston, MA 02210, tel. 617/727–5540) offers useful problem-solving assistance, including lists of travel agents that specialize in tours for the disabled.

Moss Rehabilitation Hospital Travel Information Service (1200 West Tabor Rd., Philadelphia, PA 19141–3099, tel. 215/456–9603) provides (for a small fee) information on tourist sights, transportation, and accommodations in destinations around the world.

Mobility International USA (Box 3551, Eugene, OR 97403, tel. 503/343–1284), an internationally affiliated organization, coordinates exchange programs for disabled people around the world and offers information on accommodations and organized study programs. The annual fee is $20.

The **Society for the Advancement of Travel for the Handicapped** (347 Fifth Ave., Suite 610, New York, NY 10016, tel. 212/447–7284) offers access information. Annual membership costs $45, or $25 for senior travelers and students. Send a stamped, self-addressed envelope.

Travel Industry and Disabled Exchange (TIDE, 5435 Donna Ave., Tarzana, CA 91356, tel. 818/368–5648) provides (for a $15 per-person annual membership fee) a quarterly newsletter and a directory of travel agencies and tours to Europe, Canada, New Zealand, and Australia, all specializing in travel for the disabled.

Hotels Most Berlin hotels offer some wheelchair-accessible rooms. The totally accessible **Hotel Mondial** (Kurfürstendamm 47, D-1000, Berlin 15, tel. 030/884–110), sponsored by an association of injured war veterans, is a must for all disabled visitors planning an extended stay. Situated in the heart of western Berlin, the Hotel Mondial has no steps or revolving doors and offers specially designed rooms and bathrooms and a physical therapy center. As there are only 75 rooms, reservations are advised. Other hotels with wheelchair-accessible facilities include the **Berlin Penta** (tel. 800/223–8585), **Hotel Berlin** (tel. 800/237–5469), and **Novotel Berlin** (tel. 800/221–4542).

Publications *The Itinerary* (Box 2012, Bayonne, NJ 07002, tel. 201/858–3400) is a bimonthly travel magazine for the disabled. Subscriptions cost $10 for one year, $20 for two. *Access to the World: A Travel Guide for the Handicapped,* by Louise Weiss, offers tips on travel and accessibility around the world. It is available from Henry Holt & Co. for $12.95 (tel. 800/247–3912; the order number is 0805001417).

Twin Peaks Press (Box 129, Vancouver, WA 98666, tel. 206/694–2462 or 800/637–2256 for orders only) specializes in books for the disabled. *Travel for the Disabled* offers helpful hints as well as a comprehensive list of guidebooks and facilities geared to the disabled. *The Directory of Travel Agencies for the Disabled* lists more than 350 agencies throughout the world. Twin Peaks also offers a "Traveling Nurse's Network," which provides registered nurses to accompany and assist disabled travelers.

Hints for Older Travelers

Visitors holding senior citizen passes issued by German Federal Railways receive a 50% discount on all rail routes in the country (*see* Getting Around in Staying in Germany, below).

The **American Association of Retired Persons** (AARP, 601 E St. NW, Washington, DC 20049, tel. 202/434–2277) has two programs for independent travelers: (1) the "Purchase Privilege Program," which offers discounts on hotels, airfare, car rentals, and sightseeing; and (2) the "AARP Motoring Plan," provided by Amoco, which offers emergency aid and trip-routing information for an annual fee of $39.95 per couple. The AARP also arranges group tours, including apartment living in Europe, through **American Express Vacations** (400 Pinnacle Way, Suite 450, Norcross, GA 30071, tel. 800/927–0111). AARP members must be 50 or older. Annual dues are $5 per person or per couple.

When using an AARP or other identification card, ask for a reduced hotel rate at the time you make your reservation, not when you check out. At participating restaurants, show your card to the maitre d' before you're seated, since discounts may be limited to certain set menus, days, or hours. When renting a car, be sure to ask about special promotional rates which may offer greater savings than the available discount.

Elderhostel (75 Federal St., 3rd Floor, Boston, MA 02110–1941, tel. 617/426–7788) is an innovative, low-cost educational program for people 60 and older. Participants live in dorms on some 1,600 campuses around the world. Mornings are devoted to lectures and seminars; afternoons, to sightseeing and field trips. The all-inclusive fee for two- to three-week international trips, including room, board, tuition, and round-trip transportation, ranges from $1,800 to $4,500.

National Council of Senior Citizens (1331 F St. NW, Washington, DC 20004, tel. 202/347–8800) is a nonprofit advocacy group with some 5,000 local clubs across the country. Annual membership is $12 per person or per couple. Members receive a monthly newspaper with travel information and an ID card for reduced-rate hotels and car rentals.

Mature Outlook (6001 N. Clark St., Chicago, IL 60660, tel. 800/336–6330), a subsidiary of Sears Roebuck & Co., is a travel club for people over 50, with hotel and motel discounts and a bimonthly newsletter. Annual membership is $9.95 per couple. Instant membership is available at participating Holiday Inns.

Further Reading

Berlin is the setting for many good spy novels, including Len Deighton's *Funeral in Berlin* and *Berlin Game*, John Le Carré's *The Spy Who Came in from the Cold*, Ken Follett's *Key to Rebecca*, Adam Hall's *Berlin Memorandum*, Fredrick Knebel's *Crossing in Berlin*, and Ian McEwan's *The Innocent*.

For fiction about Berlin in the days of the Weimar Republic, pick up Vicki Baum's *Grand Hotel*, Alfred Döblin's *Berlin-Alexanderplatz*, and Christopher Isherwood's *Goodbye to Berlin*. Leon Uris's *Armageddon: A Novel of Berlin* is set at the end of World War II. Contemporary novels about Berlin include

Peter Schneider's *The Wall Jumper* and Philip Kerr's *March Violets*.

Notable memoirs include *Zoo Station*, by Ian Walker, a British journalist who lived in the city in the mid-1980s, *Berlin Diaries*, the secret journals of a Russian emigré living in Nazi Berlin, and Lillian Hellman's *Pentimento*, about the author's friend who was active in the Nazi resistance.

Walter Hubatsch's *Frederick the Great: Absolutism and Administration* and Christopher Duffy's *Frederick the Great: A Military Life* examine the life of the man who was largely responsible for transforming Berlin and Prussia into dominant forces in Germany and Europe. Histories of the Weimar era include John Willett's *Weimar Years* and Alex de Jonge's *The Weimar Chronicle*. For excellent accounts of the war years, read William Shirer's *The Rise and Fall of the Third Reich*, George Clare's *Berlin Days 1946–1947*, and Hugh Trevor-Roper's *The Last Days of Hitler*.

For a look at life in the city after the fall of the Wall, try *After the Wall: East Meets West in New Berlin*, by John Borneman. *Portrait of a City* features photographs by Stéphane Duroy that chronicle the divided city over the last decade and includes images of the smashing of the Wall. The most recent studies of the Germans available in English include *Germany and the Germans* by John Ardagh, *Germany, the Empire Within* by Amity Shlaes, and *The New Germany* by David Marsh.

Arriving and Departing

From North America by Plane

Since the air routes between North America and Germany are heavily traveled, the passenger has a choice of many airlines and fares. But fares change with stunning rapidity, so consult your travel agent on what bargains are currently available.

Be certain to distinguish among (1) nonstop flights—no changes, no stops; (2) direct flights—no changes but one or more stops; and (3) connecting flights—two or more planes, one or more stops.

Airlines The U.S. airline that serves Berlin is **Delta** (tel. 800/241–4141), with direct flights from Atlanta and New York. **Lufthansa** (tel. 800/645–3880), the German national carrier, has no direct flights between the United States and Berlin, requiring changes in Frankfurt, Düsseldorf, or other German cities.

Flying Time The flying time to Berlin from New York is 8.25 hours.

Enjoying the Flight Since the air on a plane is dry, it helps to drink a lot of nonalcoholic liquids; drinking alcohol contributes to jet lag. Feet swell at high altitudes, so it's a good idea to remove your shoes while in flight. Sleepers usually prefer window seats to curl up against; those who like to move about the cabin should ask for aisle seats. Bulkhead seats (located in the front row of each cabin) have more legroom, but seat trays are attached to the arms of your seat rather than to the back of the seat in front of you. Bulkhead seats are generally reserved for the disabled, the elderly, and parents traveling with infants.

Discount Flights The major airlines offer a range of tickets that can increase the price of any given seat by more than 300%, depending on the day of purchase. As a rule, the further in advance you buy the ticket, the less expensive it is and the greater the penalty (up to 100%) for canceling. Check with airlines for details.

The best buy is not necessarily an APEX (advance purchase) ticket on one of the major airlines. APEX tickets carry certain restrictions: They must be bought in advance (usually 21 days); they restrict your travel, usually with a minimum stay of seven days and a maximum of 90; and they also penalize you for changes—voluntary or not—in your travel plans. But if you can work around these drawbacks, they are among the best-value fares available.

Travelers willing to put up with some restrictions and inconveniences in exchange for a substantially reduced air fare may be interested in flying as an air courier. A person who agrees to be a courier must accompany shipments between designated points. A telephone directory listing courier companies by the cities to which they fly is available for $5 (sent with a self-addressed, stamped, business-size envelope) from Pacific Data Sales Publishing, 2554 Lincoln Blvd., Suite 275-I, Marina Del Rey, CA 90291. "A Simple Guide to Courier Travel" may be purchased for $15.95 (includes postage and handling); send a check to Box 2394, Lake Oswego, OR 97035. For more information, call 800/344–9375.

Charter flights offer the lowest fares but often depart only on certain days, and seldom on time. Though you may be able to arrive at one city and return from another, you may lose all or most of your money if you cancel your ticket. Don't sign up for a charter flight unless you've checked with a travel agency about the reputation of the packager. It's particularly important to know the packager's policy concerning refunds should a flight be canceled. One of the most popular charter operators to Europe is **Council Charter** (205 E. 42nd St., New York, NY 10017, tel. 800/800–8222 or 212/661–0311), a division of CIEE (Council on International Educational Exchange). Other companies advertise in the Sunday travel section of newspapers.

Somewhat more expensive—but up to 50% below the cost of APEX fares—are tickets purchased through companies known as consolidators, which buy blocks of tickets on scheduled airlines and sell them at wholesale prices. Here again, you may lose all or most of your money if you change plans, but at least you will be on a regularly scheduled flight with less risk of cancellation than on a charter. Once you've made your reservation, call the airline to make sure you're confirmed. Among the best known consolidators are **UniTravel** (Box 12485, St. Louis, MO 63132, tel. 800/325–2222 or 314/569–2501) and **Access International** (101 W. 31st St., Suite 1104, New York, NY 10001, tel. 212/465–0707 or 800/825–3633). Others advertise in the Sunday travel section of the newspapers as well.

Yet another option is to join a travel club that offers special discounts to its members. Three such organizations are **Moment's Notice** (425 Madison Ave., New York, NY 10017, tel. 212/486–0500); **Discount Travel International** (114 Forrest Ave., Narberth, PA 19072, tel. 215/668–7184 or 800/334–9294); and **Worldwide Discount Travel Club** (1674 Meridian Ave., Suite 300, Miami Beach, FL 33139, tel. 305/534–2082). These cut-rate tickets should be compared with APEX tickets on the major airlines.

Smoking Regulations If cigarette smoke bothers you, it is best to request a nonsmoking seat at the time that you book your ticket. If a U.S. airline representative tells you there are no seats available in the nonsmoking section, insist on one: Department of Transportation regulations require U.S. flag carriers to find seats for all nonsmokers on the day of the flight, provided they meet check-in time restrictions. On foreign carriers, ask for a seat far from the smoking section.

From the U.K. by Plane

British Airways and **Lufthansa** are the main airlines flying from London to Berlin. **British Airways** (tel. 081/897–4000) flies four times a day from Heathrow to Berlin's Tegel airport. **Lufthansa** (tel. 0371/408–0442) flies three times daily from Gatwick to Tegel. Less expensive flights are offered by the charter company **Danair**/GTF (tel. 0371/229–2474), which flies several times weekly to Tegel.

From the U.K. by Train

British Rail operates up to 10 services a day to Germany under its Rail Europe banner. Eight of the departures are from Victoria (via the Dover–Ostend ferry or jetfoil) with the other two from Liverpool Street (via Harwich–Hook of Holland).

Berlin is reached via Hannover in about 20 hours, with up to four departures a day—two from Victoria, two from Liverpool Street.

A one-way fare to Berlin is £80; the round-trip fare is £160. Book through British Rail travel centers (tel. 0371/834–2345).

From the U.K. by Bus

Europabus service runs three times weekly from London to Berlin. The buses leave London's Victoria Coach Station Wednesday, Thursday, and Friday at 7 PM and arrive in Berlin the next evening at 7:30. Buses leave Berlin's central bus station (at the Funkturm in West Berlin) Wednesday, Saturday, and Sunday at 10 AM and arrive in London at 10 AM. The one-way fare is DM 165 (roundtrip DM 300). Reservations can be made through **Eurolines London,** 52 Grosvenor Garden, Victoria, London, tel. 0371/730–8235.

From the U.K. by Car

Berlin is 476 miles from the closest Channel port, the Hook of Holland (Ostend, in Belgium, is 45 miles farther along the coast).

For the Hook of Holland, ferries depart from Harwich—the east coast port reached from London via A12 (about 2½ hours drive). **Sealink** operates one ferry daily and one overnight; both sail year-round. It is an eight-hour crossing, and passengers' fares start at £27 (£9 supplement for first-class travel), car rates range from £32 to £63, and a two-berth cabin costs from £6 to £14.

Like Sealink, **Olau Line** operates newer, high-quality ships on its Netherlands route. There is one daily and one overnight departure from the north Kent port of Sheerness (two hours from London via A2/M2) to Vlissingen. The fare is £22; car rates start at £25.

From the Hook, take the A12 to Apeldoorn and then the A1 to Oshnabrueck and Hannover. There you can pick up E30 to Berlin. From Vlissingen, take the A67 to Venlo and then the A2 to Dortmund. Just east of Dortmund, take E37 north, then E30 to Berlin.

P&O European Ferries operates services from Dover to both Zeebrugge (up to six a day) and Ostend, 19 miles southwest down the coast. Crossing time to Ostend is four hours, half an hour longer to Zeebrugge. Passengers' fares to both Belgian ports are £13, with car rates from £24 to £78.

P&O also operates a ferry service into Zeebrugge from Felixstowe (another English east coast port just north of Harwich); while **North Sea Ferries** operates from much farther north at Hull to Zeebrugge and Rotterdam Europoort, two miles south of the Hook.

There is a **Motorail** service from Paris to Munich. A distance of 575 miles, the journey takes 10 hours and there is one departure a day.

For ferry reservations: **Sealink**, tel. 01/834–8122; **P&O**, tel. 01/734–4431; **Olau**, tel. 0795/666666; **North Sea Ferries**, tel. 0482/795141; **French Motorail**, tel. 0371/409–3518 (information only).

It is recommended that motorists acquire a green card from their insurance companies. This gives comprehensive insurance coverage for driving in Germany. The most comprehensive breakdown insurance and vehicle and personal security coverage is sold by the **Automobile Association** (AA) in its Five Star scheme.

Staying in Germany

Getting Around

By Plane Germany's internal air network is excellent, with frequent flights linking all major cities. Services are operated by **Lufthansa** and by Germany's other leading airline, **LTU**. Some internal flights are also offered by **Air Europe, British Airways,** and **Delta.** In addition, three small airlines operate services between a limited number of northern cities and the East and North Frisian islands, though many of these flights operate only in the summer. Details of all internal services are available from travel agents; otherwise, contact Lufthansa (tel. 069/690–71222; 069/690–3050–9) and LTU (tel. 0211/421–6325 or 089/921–1879–7).

LTU ticket holders get free travel to and from the Düsseldorf airport on VRR/VRS buses and commuter trains within a 25-mile radius of Düsseldorf, Köln, and Essen, plus discounts on Deutsche Bundesbahn and Reichsbahn rail travel through Germany.

Lufthansa runs an excellent train, the "Lufthansa Express," linking Düsseldorf, Köln, Bonn, and Frankfurt airports and acting as a supplement to existing air services. Only passengers holding air tickets may use the train, but there is no extra charge for it. Service is first-class. Luggage is automatically transferred to your plane on arrival at the airport. German Railways operates a similar service called "Rail and Fly" (*see* below), and trains on the Köln-Munich line stop at Frankfurt airport instead of at Wiesbaden for connections with flights to and from Frankfurt.

By Train German Federal Railways—or **DB,** meaning Deutsche Bundesbahn, as it is usually referred to—operates one of the most comprehensive and fastest rail systems in Europe. DB runs trains in what was formerly West Germany, while train service in eastern Germany is still operated by the Reichsbahn. The two systems are expected to merge in the near future, but in the meantime are increasingly integrating their networks. For instance, there are many more trains now linking the eastern cities of Leipzig, Dresden, Halle, Magdeburg, Potsdam, Rostock, and Schwerin—as well as Berlin—with western cities. DB offers a range of discounted fares and inclusive tickets, from family rovers to a Senior Citizen Card, but probably the best deal for the foreign visitor is the new Flexipass, which is valid for trains in east, as well as west (*see* Before You Go, above).

All major cities in western Germany are linked by fast Intercity (IC) hourly service. A DM 6 (DM 10 first class) surcharge is made regardless of distance on all Intercity journeys, and there is also a small charge for seat reservations. (Holders of GermanRail Flexipasses pay no supplements.) IC provides excellent connections at the main nodal points—Hannover, Dortmund, Köln, Mannheim, Würzburg, Munich, and Frankfurt—and changing trains couldn't be easier. You only have to cross to the other side of the platform. Special train maps on platform notice boards give details of the layout of each IC train arriving on that line, showing where first- and second-class cars and the restaurant car are situated, as well as where they will stop along the length of the platform. If you have a reservation, it will give the number of the car with your seats; locate this car on the map so that you can stand on the platform exactly where your car will stop when the train pulls in. It is possible to check your baggage for Frankfurt Airport from any of 52 stations throughout Germany. Except on weekends, there is guaranteed overnight delivery.

Super high-speed Intercity Express (ICE) trains, capable of speeds up to 165 mph, were introduced last year on the Hamburg–Munich line. Travel times have been cut by as much as 30% on these comfortable trains, allowing passengers to cross Germany from the north coast to Bavaria in under six hours.

Although the eastern German Reichsbahn has train classifications similar to the DB, their trains remain much slower because of the poor condition of tracks and bridges. Many trains have first- and second-class cars, and longer distance routes provide dining cars or buffet facilities. Since fewer people have cars in the east, trains are more heavily used and seat reservations are strongly advised for long journeys.

Rail passengers in possession of a valid round-trip air ticket can buy a heavily discounted "Rail and Fly" ticket for DB trains connecting with German airports: Hamburg, Bremen, Hannover, Düsseldorf, Köln/Bonn, Saarbrücken, Stuttgart, and Munich.

The IC network is complemented by "FD" trains (*Fernexpresszüge*), which are long-distance express trains, and by "D" trains (*Schnellzüge*), which are the ordinary fast trains. On both, a small supplement—currently DM 6—must be paid if you are traveling under 50 kilometers (30 miles). No supplements are necessary for traveling on the semi-fast "E" trains (*Eilzuge*) or local services. The moral of the tale is simple: Don't use fast trains for short hops.

Note that in high season you will frequently encounter lines at ticket offices for seat reservations. Unless you are prepared to board the train without a reserved seat, taking the chance of a seat being available, the only way to avoid these lines is to make an advance reservation by phone. Call the ticket office (*Fahrkarten Schalter*) of the rail station from which you plan to depart. Here again, you will probably have to make several attempts before you get through to the reservations section (*Reservierungen-Platzkarten*), but you will then be able to collect your seat ticket from a special counter without having to wait in line.

Tourist Rail Cards Holders of British Rail Senior Citizens' Rail Cards can buy an "add-on" **European Senior Citizens' Rail Card** that permits half-price train travel in most European countries, including Germany. Senior citizens from other countries who intend to stay in Germany for some time should consider buying the DB **Senioren Pass.** This is available in two forms: the Senioren Pass "A" (which costs DM 75) allows half-price travel Monday–Thursday and Saturday while Senioren B (DM 110) permits half-price travel any day of the week. Both are valid for a year and can be bought before going to Germany.

Travelers under 26 who have not invested in a **Eurail Youthpass,** or in any of the other rail passes, should inquire about discount travel fares under a Billet International Jeune (BIJ) scheme. The special one-trip tariff is offered by EuroTrain International, with offices in London, Dublin, Paris, Madrid, Lisbon, Rome, Zurich, Athens, Brussels, Budapest, Hanover, Leiden, Vienna, and Tangier. You can purchase a Eurotrain ticket at one of these offices or at travel-agent networks, mainline rail stations and specialist youth-travel operators.

DB Regional Rail Rovers (**Tourenkarten**) cover some 73 areas, including all the main tourist regions. They are excellent value for the money. Valid for any 10 days within a 21-day vacation period, they cost around DM 50 for one person, DM 68 for two people traveling together, and DM 83 for a family (one or two parents, plus any number of unmarried children under 18 and grandparents). Unless you are going to Germany on a vacation run by the railways themselves, the Tourenkarte has to be bought when you arrive in Germany. However, there is one catch: To be eligible you must travel at least 250 kilometers (155 miles) on a German train to reach your vacation area and the same distance when you leave. So check distances carefully on your map—it may be worth making a slight detour to qualify.

For further information, contact **GermanRail** (747 Third Ave., New York, NY 10017, tel. 212/308–3100).

By Bus   Germany has a good bus network. A large proportion of services are operated by the railways (**Bahnbus**) and are closely integrated with train services, while on less busy rail lines, services are run by buses in off-peak periods—normally midday and weekends. Rail tickets are valid on these services. The railways, in the guise of **Deutsche Touring**, also operate the German sections of the Europabus network. Contact them at Am Römerhof 17,6000-Frankfurt/Main 90, for details about a range of 2–7 day package tours.

One of the best services is provided by the Romantic Road bus between Würzburg (with connections to and from Frankfurt and Wiesbaden) and Füssen (with connections to and from Munich, Augsburg, and Garmisch-Partenkirchen). This is an all-reserved-seats bus with a stewardess, offering one- or two-day tours in each direction in summer, leaving in the morning and arriving in the evening. Details and reservations are available from Deutsche Touring (*see* above) or big city tourist offices.

All towns of any size operate their own local buses. For the most part, those link up with local trams (streetcars), electric railways services (S-bahn), and subways (U-bahn). Fares vary according to distance, but a ticket usually allows you to transfer freely between the various forms of transportation. Some cities issue 24-hour tickets at special rates.

By Bike   Information on all aspects of cycling in Germany is available from the **Bund Deutscher Radfahrer,** the Association of German Cyclists (Otto-Fleck-Schneise 4,6000 Frankfurt 71). There are no formalities governing the importation of bikes into Germany, and no duty is required. Bikes can also be carried on trains—though *not* on Intercity trains—if you buy a *Fahrradkarte,* or bicycle ticket. These cost DM 6.50 per journey and can be bought at any train station. Those under 26 with a "Tramper Ticket"—a monthly rover that costs DM 234—can take bikes free of charge. Full details are given in the German railway's brochure *Fahrrad am Bahnhof.*

Bicycles are also available for rental at more than 270 train stations throughout the country, most of them in south Germany. The cost is DM 10–DM 12 per day, DM 6–DM 8 if you have a valid rail ticket. They can be returned at any other station.

By Boat   River and lake trips are among the greatest delights of a vacation in Germany, especially along the Rhine, Germany's longest river. The Rhine may be viewed at a variety of paces: by fast hydrofoil, by express boat, by sedate motorship, or by romantic paddle steamer. For those in a hurry, there is a daily hydrofoil service from Düsseldorf right through to Mainz. It is advisable to book in advance for this. For gentler souls, there is a wide range of more leisurely cruises. German cruise ships also operate on the Upper Rhine as far as Basel, Switzerland; on the Main between Frankfurt and Mainz; on the Danube to Linz and on to Vienna; on the Europe Canal joining the Main and the Danube; on the Elbe and Weser and their estuaries; on the Inn and Ilz; and on the Ammersee, Chiemsee, Königsee, and Bodensee.

EurailPasses are valid on all services of the KD German Rhine Line and on the Mosel between Trier and Koblenz. (If you use the fast hydrofoil, a supplementary fee has to be paid.) DB Tourist Card holders are given a 50% reduction on KD ships. Regular rail tickets are also accepted, meaning that you can go one way by ship and return by train. All you have to do is pay a small surcharge to KD Rhine Line and get the ticket endorsed at one of the landing stage offices. But note that you have to buy the rail ticket first and *then* get it changed.

KD Rhine Line also offers a program of luxury tours ranging from a five-day cruise along the Rhine from Amsterdam to Basel to a four-day "Four-Country Cruise," which visits Amsterdam, Köln, Strasbourg, and Basel, among other cities, and costs from around DM 1,300 first-class. The ships cruise slowly to give you time to appreciate the landscape. The tours can be booked either for the cruise only to fit in with your own program, or as a complete vacation. One of the best and most attractive ways of seeing the glories of the Rhine and the Moselle is on one of the traditional KD old-time paddle steamers or on one of their large modern motor vessels. During the summer there are good services between Bonn and Koblenz and between Koblenz and Birgen; both trips take around five hours.

KD German Rhine Line now operates two luxury cruises on the Elbe River within Germany from May to October: a five-day trip from Bad Schandau to Magdeburg, and a seven-day journey from Bad Schandau to Hamburg. Ports of call include Dresden, Meissen, and Wittenberg. Other Elbe cruises continue into Czechoslovakia, with excursions to Prague, among other Czech cities.

KD has several budget deals, too; for example, on Sundays or holidays, children between 4 and 14 accompanied by adults pay only DM 5. Likewise, senior citizens pay only half price on Mondays. If it's your birthday, you travel free. For details of all KD services, contact the company in the United States at 170 Hamilton Avenue, White Plains, New York 10601–1788, tel. 914/948–3600, and at 323 Geary Street, San Francisco, California 94102–1860, tel. 415/392–8817; in Germany contact Köln-Düsseldorfer Deutsche Rheinschiffahrt AG, Frankenwerft 15, 5000–Köln 1, tel. 0221/20880.

By Car Entry formalities for motorists are few: All you need is proof of insurance, an international car-registration document, and an international driver's license. If you or your car are from an EC country, or from Austria, Norway, Switzerland, Sweden, or Portugal, all you need is your domestic license and proof of insurance. *All* foreign cars must have a country sticker.

Roads in the western part of the country are generally excellent, but many surfaces in eastern Germany, where an urgent improvement program is under way, are in poor condition.

There are three principal automobile clubs: **ADAC** (Allegmeiner Deutscher Automobil-Club, Am Westpark 8, 8000-Munich 70), **AvD** (Lyonerstr. 16, Frankfurt/Niederrad), and **DTC** (Amalienburgstr. 23, Munich 60).

ADAC and AvD operate tow trucks on all Autobahns; they also have emergency telephones every 1½ miles. On minor roads, go to the nearest call box and dial 19211. Ask, in English, for "road service assistance," if you have to use the service. Help is free, but all materials must be paid for.

Scenic Routes Germany boasts 26 specially designated tourist roads, all covering areas of particular scenic and/or historic interest. The longest is the **Deutsche Ferienstrasse,** the German Holiday Road, which runs from the Baltic to the Alps, a distance of around 1,070 miles. The most famous, however, and also the oldest, is the **Romantische Strasse,** the Romantic Road, which runs from Würzburg in Franconia to Füssen in the Alps, covering around 220 miles and passing some of the most historic cities and towns in Germany.

Among other notable touring routes—all with expressive and descriptive names—are the **Grüne Küstenstrasse** (Green Coast Road), running along the North Sea coast from Denmark to Emden; the **Burgenstrasse** (Castle Road), running from Mannheim to Nürnberg; the **Deutsche Weinstrasse** (German Wine Road), running through the heartland of German wine country; and the **Deutsche Alpenstrasse** (German Alpine Road), running the length of the country's south border. In addition, there are many other equally delightful, if less well-known, routes, such as the **Märchenstrasse** (the Fairy-tale Road); the **Schwarzwald Hochstrasse** (the Black Forest Mountain Road); and the **Deutsche Edelsteinstrasse** (German Gem Road).

Regulations As elsewhere in Western Europe, in Germany you drive on the right, and road signs give distances in kilometers. Political reunification did not bring a consensus to the rules of the road, however. In the western part of Germany, unlimited speeds on the autobahns continue, while in former East Germany—the five new states of Thüringia, Saxony, Saxony-Anhalt, Brandenburg, and Mecklenburg—a top limit of 130 kph (80 mph) remains in force (80 kph/50 mph on other country roads). Speed limits on non-Autobahn country roads in western areas vary from 80 to 100 kph (50 to 62 mph). On the former transit Autobahns linking Berlin and West Germany, there is still a speed limit of 130 kph (80 mph).

An absolute ban on alcohol is strictly enforced for drivers in the east, but drivers in the west can still legally sit behind the wheel after drinking two small beers or wine. These inconsistencies are expected to be resolved soon.

Note that seat belts must be worn at all times by front- *and* back-seat passengers.

Fuel Gasoline (petrol) costs are between DM 1.17 and DM 1.45 per liter. As part of antipollution efforts, many German cars now run on lead-free fuel. Some older cars may not run especially well on it, but it makes no difference at all to the performance of newer models. German filling stations are highly competitive and bargains are often available if you shop around, but *not* at Autobahn filling stations. Self-service, or *SB-Tanken*, stations are cheapest. Pumps marked *Bleifrei* contain unleaded gas.

Telephones

Eastern and Western Germany were recently united under a single country code, 49—formerly the code of West Germany only. Telephone connections to and from eastern Germany are still unpredictable because the telephone system inherited from the communist era remains overloaded.

Local Calls Local public phones charge a minimum 30 pfennigs per call (for five minutes). Public phones take 10 pfennigs and DM 1 coins. If you plan to make an out-of-town call, take along a good supply of DM 1 coins. Most phone booths have instructions in English as well as German; if yours doesn't, simply lift the receiver, put the money in, and dial. The area code for all of Berlin is 030.

International Calls These can be made from public phones bearing the sign "Inlands and Auslandsgespräche." They take 10 pfennigs, DM 1, and DM 5 coins; a four-minute call to the United States costs DM 15. To avoid weighing yourself down with coins, however, make international calls from post offices; even those in small country towns will have a special booth for international calls. You pay the clerk at the end of your call. Never make international calls from your hotel room; rates will be at least double the regular charge.

AT&T and MCI both have direct calling programs in Germany. AT&T's USADirect service, which charges $1.77 for the first minute, $1.09 for each additional minute, allows you to call collect or charge your calls to your AT&T calling card; either way, you pay AT&T rates and speak to an English-speaking operator. To make your call, dial 0130–0010 to access an AT&T operator. For additional information call 412/553–7458, ext. 314 (collect from outside the U.S.) or 800/874–4000. MCI charges $1.76 for the first minute, $1.09 for each additional minute, and works the same as AT&T; just dial 0130–0012 to get an MCI operator. For information call 800/950–5555, or 0130–81–5417 from Germany.

Operators and Information The western German telephone system is fully automatic, and it's unlikely that you'll have to employ the services of an operator. If you do, dial 1188, or 00118 for international calls. If the operator doesn't speak English (also unlikely), you'll be passed to one who does.

Mail

Postal Rates Airmail letters to the United States and Canada cost DM 1.90; postcards cost 90 pfennigs. All letters to the United Kingdom cost DM 1; postcards cost 60 pfennigs.

Receiving Mail You can arrange to have mail sent to you in care of any German post office; have the envelope marked "Postlagernd." This service is free. Alternatively, have mail sent to any American Express office in Germany. There's no charge to cardholders, holders of American Express traveler's checks, or anyone who has booked a vacation with American Express. Otherwise, you pay DM 2 per collection (not per item).

Tipping

The service charges on hotel bills suffice for most tips in your hotel, though you should tip bell hops and porters; DM 2 per bag or service is ample. Whether you tip the desk clerk depends on whether he or she has given you any special service.

Service charges are included in all restaurant bills (listed as *Bedienung*), as is tax (listed as *MWST*). Nonetheless, it is customary to round out the bill to the nearest mark or to leave about 5% (give it to the waiter or waitress as you pay the bill; don't leave it on the table).

In taxis, round out the fare to the nearest full mark as a tip. Only give more if you have particularly cumbersome or heavy luggage (though you will be charged 50 pfennigs for each piece of luggage anyway).

Opening and Closing Times

Banks Banks in Berlin are generally open 9–1:30 (until 5:30 on Tuesday and Thursday). Branches at airports and main train stations open as early as 6:30 AM and close as late as 10:30 PM.

Museums Most museums are open from Tuesday to Sunday 9–6. Some close for an hour or more at lunch, and some are open on Monday.

Shops Times vary slightly, but generally shops are open 9 or 9:15–6:30 Monday through Friday and until 2 PM on Saturday, except for the first Saturday in the month, when the bigger stores stay open until 4. Many shops also now remain open on Thursday evenings until 8:30.

National Holidays January 1; April 17 (Good Friday); April 19 (Easter); April 20 (Easter Monday); May 1 (May Day); May 28 (Ascension Day); June 8 (Pentecost Monday); October 3 (Day of German Unity); November 18 (Day of Repentance and Prayer); December 25, 26 (Christmas).

Sports and Outdoor Activities

The Germans are nothing if not sports-crazy, and there is practically no sport, however arcane, except perhaps cricket, that cannot easily be arranged almost anywhere in the country. A good number of sports packages—for sailboats, tennis, climbing, walking, horseback riding, to name only a few—are also available. Consult the German National Tourist Office or your travel agent for details. Below, we give details of some of the more popular participant sports. Details of important sporting events are also published every month by regional and local tourist offices.

Fishing Fishing is available at many locations in Germany, but a permit, valid for one year and costing from DM 10 to DM 20, available from local tourist offices, is required, as is a local permit to fish in a particular spot. These last are available from the owner of the stretch of water you plan to fish. Further details are available from local tourist offices or from **Verband der Deutschen Sportfischer** (Bahnhofstr. 35, 6050 Offenbach).

A number of hotels offer fishing for guests, but you will normally be expected to deliver your catch—if any—to the hotel.

Golf Golf in Germany is rapidly increasing in popularity, and there is a growing number of courses around the country. Clubs will usually allow nonmembers to play if they are not too busy; charges will be about DM 30 during the week and up to DM 60 on weekends and on public holidays. For information, write the **German Golf Association** (Leberberg 25, 6200 Wiesbaden).

Hiking and Mountaineering Germany's hill and mountain regions have thousands of miles of marked hiking and mountain-walking tracks. They are administered by regional hiking clubs and, where appropriate, mountaineering groups, all of which are affiliated with the **Verband Deutscher Gebirgs- und Wandervereine e.V.** (Reichs str. 4, 6600 Saarbrücken 3). It can provide information on routes, hiking paths, overnight accommodations, and mountain huts in western Germany. The former East German state-run hiking organization has collapsed. Local tourist offices in eastern Germany can provide information about trails and regional hiking clubs.

For Alpine walking, contact the **Deutsche Alpenverein** (Praterinsel 5, D–8000 Munich 22). It administers more than 50 mountain huts and about 9,500 miles of Alpine paths. In addition, it can provide courses in mountaineering and touring suggestions for routes in both winter and summer. Foreign members are admitted.

There are also various mountaineering schools that offer week-long courses ranging from basic techniques for beginners to advanced mountaineering. Contact the **Verband Deutscher Ski und Bergführer** (Lindenstr. 16, D–8980 Oberstdorf).

Local tourist offices and sports shops can usually supply details of mountain guides.

Horseback Riding Riding schools and clubs can be found throughout Germany. Rates are generally high, and most schools will insist on a minimum standard of competence before allowing novices to venture out. Alternatively, pony treks are available in many parts of the country. Contact the German National Tourist Office or local tourist offices.

Sailing A wide variety of sailing vacations and opportunities to rent sailboats is available throughout Germany. Most North Sea and Baltic resorts and harbors will have either sailing schools or sailboats of varying types to rent. Lake sailing is equally popular, particularly on Chiemsee in Bavaria and the Bodensee. For details, write **Verband Deutscher Segelschulen** (Graelstr. 45, 44 Münster).

Swimming Almost all larger towns and resorts have open-air and indoor pools, the former frequently heated, the latter often with wave or whirlpool machines. In addition, practically all coastal resorts have indoor seawater pools, as well as good, if bracing, beaches. Similarly, all German spas have thermal or mineral water indoor pools. Finally, Bavaria's Alpine lakes and a large number of artificial lakes elsewhere have marked-off swimming and sunbathing areas.

Note that swimming in rivers, especially the larger ones, is not recommended and in some cases is positively forbidden—look for the "Baden Verboten" signs—either because of shipping or pollution, or both.

Bathing caps are obligatory at all indoor and outdoor pools; if you don't have your own, you can rent one. It's hard not to notice that the Germans are keen on nudism. Many pools will have special days for nude bathing only, and on certain beaches nude bathing is also allowed. Signs that read "FKK" mean nudity is allowed.

Tennis Courts are available practically everywhere, summer and winter. Local tourist offices will supply details of where to play, charges, and how to book, the latter being essential in most areas. Charges vary from DM 16 to DM 25 for outdoor courts and DM 25 to DM 35 for indoor courts.

Windsurfing This has become so popular, particularly on the Bavarian lakes, that it has had to be restricted on some beaches as a result of collisions between Windsurfers and swimmers. Nonetheless, there are still many places where you can windsurf and where Windsurfers can easily be rented. Lessons, at around DM 25 per hour, are also generally available. For further information, contact the German National Tourist Office or **VDWS** (Fasserstr. 30, 8120 Weilheim, Oberbayern).

Winter Sports   South Bavaria is the big winter-sports region, with Garmisch-Partenkirchen the best-known center. There are also winter-sports resorts in the Black Forest, the Harz region, the Bavarian Forest, the Rhön Mountains, the Fichtelgebirge, the Sauerland, and the Swabian mountains. The season generally runs from the middle of December to the end of March, but at higher altitudes, such as the Zugspitze (near Garmisch), you can usually ski from as early as the end of November to as late as the middle of May. There's no need to bring skis with you—you can rent or buy them on the spot. Look for the special winter off-season rates (*Weisse Wochen*) offered by most winter sports-resorts for cross-country and downhill skiing vacations. Prices include seven days' bed and breakfast (or half-board) plus ski lessons.

For cross-country (or *Langlauf*) skiing, which is becoming increasingly popular—the equipment is considerably cheaper than downhill (or *Alpin*) equipment, and there is no waiting at ski-lifts—there are stretches of prepared tracks (or *Loipen*) to be found in the valleys and foothills of most winter-sports centers, as well as in the suburbs of larger towns in south Bavaria.

Ski-bobbing is on the increase. There are runs and schools at Bayrischzell, Berchtesgaden, Garmisch-Partenkirchen, Füssen, and Oberstdorf in the Alps, as well as at Altglashütten, Bernau, and Felberg in the Black Forest. Ice rinks, many open all year, can be found everywhere.

Dining

Berlin has an enormous variety of eating places, ranging from street-corner hamburger stands to international-class restaurants, from traditional German taverns to exotic establishments offering every kind of ethnic food. Virtually every street corner in Berlin has its *Gaststätte*, a sort of combination diner and pub. There are 6,000 of them in Berlin, one for every 400 inhabitants. Here the emphasis is on the characteristic German preference for *gut bürgerliche Küche*, or good home cooking, with simple food, wholesome rather than sophisticated, at reasonable prices. These are also places where people meet in the evening for a chat, a beer, and a game of cards, so you needn't feel compelled to leave as soon as you've eaten. They normally serve hot meals from around 11 AM to 9 PM or later; many places stop serving hot meals between 2 and 6 PM, although you can still order cold dishes. Lunch rather than dinner is the main meal of the day, accounting for the general practice of offering a *Tageskarte*, or suggested lunchtime menu. For less than DM 20 you can tuck into a soup and main course and perhaps a dessert. Some, although not all, expensive restaurants also offer a table d'hote (suggested or special) daily menu. Prices will be much higher than in a Gaststätte but considerably cheaper than à la carte.

A specialty of the Berlin dining scene is the abundance of "breakfast cafés," where you can order a filling breakfast and unlimited coffee virtually all day. On Sunday mornings they are the scene of *Frühschoppen*, when live jazz is played as the breakfast buffet is served. In eastern Berlin, the variety of fare is smaller but this is changing as new businesses find their footing.

Budget Eating Tips
Foreign Restaurants

Berlin has a vast selection of moderately priced Italian, Greek, Chinese, and—largely as a result of the number of Turkish workers in Germany—Turkish restaurants. All are good value. Italian restaurants are about the most popular of all specialty restaurants in Berlin. One restaurant in ten in Berlin is Italian—the pizza-to-go is as much a part of the average German's diet as *Bratwurst* or a hamburger. You'll find that Chinese restaurants in particular offer special tourist and lunch menus.

Stand-up Snack Bars

Often located in pedestrian zones, *Imbiss* stands can be found in almost every busy shopping street, in parking lots, train stations, and near markets. They serve *Wurst* (sausages), grilled, roasted, or boiled, of every shape and size, and rolls filled with cheese, cold meat, or fish. Prices range from DM 3 to DM 6 per portion.

Department Stores

For lunch, restaurants in local department stores (*Kaufhäuser*) are especially recommended for wholesome, appetizing, and inexpensive food. **Karstadt, Wertheim,** and **KaDeWe** have particularly good restaurants.

Fast Food

A number of fast-food chains exist all over the country. The fast-food chains such as **McDonald's** and **Burger King** are well established in the area that was West Berlin and are now extending into the eastern part of the city.

Picnics

Buy some wine or beer and some cold cuts and rolls (*Brötchen*) from a department store, supermarket, or delicatessen and turn lunchtimes into picnics. You'll not only save money, but you'll also be able to enjoy Berlin's beautiful parks and riverside greenery. Be aware, however, that picnics are not typically German and you might be examined by many with amusement.

Ratings

The restaurants in our listings are divided by price into four categories: Very Expensive; Expensive; Moderate; and Inexpensive. *See* Dining in individual chapters for specific prices. Nearly all restaurants display their menus, with prices, outside; all prices shown will include tax and service charge. Prices for wine also include tax and service charge.

Lodging

Berlin has the wide range of hotel accommodations you'd expect to find in such a metropolis, although eastern Berlin is desperately short of medium-priced and inexpensive rooms. The luxury hotels in the eastern part of the city are just as modern and well appointed as those in the west—and equally pricey. Unification has been followed by a building boom in the east, and the number of hotels there is expected to double in the next five years. Eastern Berlin's top hotels are all situated around the historic city center, while western Berlin's tend to be grouped within a few steps of the Kurfürstendamm. For reasonably priced accommodations try outlying areas such as Charlottenburg or Schöneberg. The tourist offices in both parts of Berlin will make reservations for a nominal fee, but to be sure of securing a room, use their services before 4 PM.

The standard of German hotels—from sophisticated luxury spots (of which the country has more than its fair share) to the humblest country inn—is excellent. Rates vary enormously, though not disproportionately so in comparison with other north European countries. You can nearly always expect courteous and polite service and clean and comfortable rooms.

In addition to hotels proper, the country also has numerous Gasthöfe or *Gasthäuser,* which are country inns that serve food and also have rooms; pensions, or *Fremdenheime* (guest houses); and, at the lowest end of the scale, *Zimmer,* meaning simply "rooms," normally in private houses (look for the sign reading *Zimmer frei* or *zu vermieten* on a green background, meaning "to rent"; a red sign reading *besetzt* means that there are no vacancies).

Lists of German hotels are available from the German National Tourist Office and all regional and local tourist offices. (Most hotels have restaurants, but those listed as *Garni* will provide breakfast only.) Tourist offices will also make bookings for you at a nominal fee, but they may have difficulty doing so after 4 PM in high season and on weekends, so don't wait until too late in the day to begin looking for your accommodations. (If you do get stuck, ask someone who looks local—a postman, policeman, or waitress, for example—for a Zimmer zu vermieten or Gasthof; in rural areas especially you'll find that people are genuinely helpful). A hotel reservation service is also operated by **ADZ** (Corneliusstr. 34, W–6000 Frankfurt/Main, tel. 069/740767). It is able to make reservations in many hotels throughout the country for a small fee.

Many major American hotel chains—Hilton, Sheraton, Holiday Inn, Arabella, Canadian Pacific, Ramada, Preferred— have hotels in the larger German cities. Similarly, European chains are well represented.

Romantik Hotels Among the most delightful places to stay—and eat—in Germany are the aptly named Romantik Hotels and Restaurants. The Romantik group now has establishments throughout north Europe (and even a few in the United States), including around 60 in Germany itself. All are in atmospheric and historic buildings—an essential precondition of membership—and are personally run by the owners, with the emphasis on excellent food and service. Prices vary considerably from Very Expensive to Moderate (*see* Ratings, below), but in general represent good value, particularly the special-weekends and short-holiday rates. A three- or four-day stay, for example, with one main meal, is available at about DM 250 to DM 400 per person.

In addition, German Railways offers a special "Romantik Hotel Rail" program, which, in conjunction with a GermanRail Tourist Ticket, gives nine days' unlimited travel. You don't need to plan your route in advance—only your first night's accommodation needs to be reserved before you leave. The remaining nights can be reserved as you go. The package also includes sightseeing trips, a Rhine/Mosel cruise, bicycle rentals, and the like.

A detailed brochure listing all Romantik Hotels and Restaurants which costs $7.50 (including mailing) and a free miniguide are available from **Romantik Hotels Reservations** (Box 1278, Woodinville, WA 98072, tel. 206/485–6985; for reservations, tel. 800/826–0015).

Castle Hotels Of comparable interest and value are Germany's castle, or *Schloss*, hotels, all privately owned and run and all long on atmosphere. A number of the simpler ones may lack some amenities, but the majority combine four-star luxury with valuable antique furnishings, four-poster beds, stone passageways, and baronial atmosphere. Some offer full resort facilities, too (tennis, swimming pools, horseback riding, hunting, and fishing). Nearly all are located away from cities and towns.

The German National Tourist Office issues a *Castle Hotels in Germany* brochure. They, and your travel agent, can also advise on a number of packages available for castle hotels, including four- to six-night tours.

Spas Taking the waters in Germany, whether for curing the body or merely beautifying it, has been popular since Roman times. There are about 250 health resorts and mineral springs in the country—the word *Bad* before the name of a place is a sure sign that it's a spa—offering treatments, normally at fairly high prices. Beauty farms are normally found only in Very Expensive spa hotels. Although spas exist in eastern Germany, most are rundown and not highly recommended.

There are four main groups of spas and health resorts: (1) the mineral and moorland spas, where treatments are based on natural warm-water springs; (2) those by the sea on the Baltic and North Sea coasts; (3) hydropathic spas, which use an invigorating process developed in the 19th century; and (4) climatic health resorts, which depend on their climates—usually mountainous—for their health-giving properties.

The average cost for three weeks of treatment is from DM 800 to DM 2,100; for four weeks, DM 1,300 to DM 3,200. This includes board and lodging, doctor's fees, treatments, and tax. A complete list of spas, giving full details of their springs and treatments, is available from the German National Tourist Office, or from **Deutsche Bäderverband,** the German Health Resort and Spa Association (Schumannstr. 111, 5300 Bonn 1).

Rentals Bungalows or apartments (*Ferienwohungen* or *Ferienapartments*), usually accommodating two to eight people, can be rented throughout Germany. Rates are low, with reductions for longer stays. There is usually an extra charge for gas and electricity, and sometimes water. There is also normally a charge for linen, though you may also bring your own.

Details of rentals in all regions of the country are available from the regional and local tourist offices. In addition, the German Automobile Association issues listings of family holiday apartments; write **ADAC Reisen** (Am Westpark 8, 8000 Munich 70).

Farm Vacations *Urlaub auf dem Bauernhof,* or vacations down on the farm, have increased dramatically in popularity throughout Germany over the past five years, and almost every regional tourist office now produces a brochure listing farms in its area that offer bed and breakfast, apartments, and entire farmhouses to rent. In addition, the German Agricultural Association (DLG) produces an illustrated brochure listing over 1,500 farms, all inspected and graded, from the Alps to the North Sea, that offer accommodations. It costs DM 7.50 (send an international reply coupon if writing from the United States) and is available from **DLG Reisedienst, Agratour** (Zimmerweg 16, D–6000 Frankfurt/Main 1).

Camping Campsites—some 2,000 in all—are scattered the length and breadth of Germany. The **DCC,** or German Camping Club (Mandlstr. 28, D–8000 Munich 40) produces an annual listing of 1,600 sites; it also details sites where trailers and mobile homes can be rented. Similarly, the German Automobile Association (*see* Rentals, above, for address) publishes a listing of all camp-sites located at autobahn exits. In addition, the German National Tourist Office publishes a comprehensive and graded listing of campsites.

Sites are generally open from May to September, though about 400 are open year-round for the very rugged. Most sites get crowded during high season, however. Prices range from around DM 10 to DM 15 for a car, trailer, and two adults; less for tents. If you want to camp elsewhere, you must get permis-sion from the landowner beforehand; ask the police if you can't track him or her down. Drivers of mobile homes may park for one night only on roadsides and in autobahn parking-lot areas, but may not set up camping equipment there.

Youth Hostels Germany's youth hostels—*Jugendherbergen*—are probably the most efficient, up-to-date, and proportionally numerous of any country's in the world. There are more than 700 in all, many located in castles that add a touch of romance to otherwise utili-tarian accommodations. Since unification, many eastern German youth hostels have closed down. An effort is being made, however, to keep as many open as possible, and renova-tions are currently underway to bring eastern hostels up to the standards of their western counterparts.

Apart from Bavaria, where there is an age limit of 27, there are no restrictions on age, though those under 20 take preference when space is limited. You'll need an International Youth Hos-tel card, valid for one year, for reduced rates, usually about DM 12 to DM 18 for youth under 27 and DM 13.50 to DM 22 for adults (breakfast included). Cards are available from the **Amer-ican Youth Hostels Association** (Box 37613, Washington, DC 20013) and the **Canadian Hostelling Association** (333 River Rd., Ottawa, Ontario K1L 8H9). For listings of German youth hos-tels, contact the **Deutsches Jugendherbergswerk Hauptverband** (Bismarckstr. 8, D–4930 Detmold, tel. 05231/74010) or the German National Tourist Office.

Ratings The hotels in our listings are divided by price into four catego-ries: Very Expensive; Expensive; Moderate; and Inexpensive. *See* Lodging in individual chapters for specific prices. Note that there is no official grading system for hotels in Germany. Rates are by no means inflexible, and depend very much on supply and demand. Many resort hotels offer substantial re-ductions in winter, except in the Alps, where rates often rise in winter. Likewise, many Very Expensive and Expensive hotels in cities offer substantial reductions on weekends and when business is quiet. It's always worth checking to see if reduc-tions are available; the savings can be considerable. Rooms booked after 10 PM are often cheaper, too, on the basis that an occupied room at a reduced rate is better than an empty one. You should be careful about trying to book late in the day at peak times, however. During trade fairs (most seem to be held in the spring and fall), rates in city hotels can rise appreciably. Break-fast is usually but not always included in room rates; be sure to check before you book. Check, too, to see if your room has a show-er or a tub—some of the cheaper rooms have neither—as a room with a shower will be a little less expensive than a room with a tub. Finally, if you don't like the room you're offered, ask to see another.

Credit Cards

The following credit card abbreviations are used: AE, American Express; DC, Diners Club; MC, MasterCard; V, Visa.

2 Portrait of Berlin

Seeing Is Believing

By Christopher
Hope

*South
African–born
novelist
Christopher Hope
happened to be
visiting West
Berlin when the
Wall fell; his
eyewitness
account appeared
in* The New
Republic *one
month later, in
December 1989.
His new novel,*
Serenity House,
*was published in
1992, as was a
collection of short
stories,* Swirsky
Aloft.

You know that things are serious when the TV news stations start flying in their anchor men and women. Chattering groups of them thronged Berlin Airport when I arrived on November 12, father figures and mother confessors from the news desks of the American networks, the British Broadcasting Corp., Japanese TV, and the European pop and sports satellite channels. They were eager to present the news in situ, beside the Berlin Wall, in front of the Brandenburg Gate. They were attended by baggage bearers, drones, and soldiers who formed a kind of protective scrimmage, easing their costly charges through passport control, incredulous that mere officials should obstruct the faces welcomed into millions of homes each night.

Berliners have always displayed disrespect when faced with power or privilege. And household names become very parochial the moment they leave the house. The famous faces, it must be said, are paler than expected, the eyes flutter restlessly as if searching for makeup and the auto-cue. As the Berliners well knew, these were people who a few weeks ago could not have picked out their divided city on a map. Berlin flickered in the memory, if at all, mixed with images of Liza Minnelli belting out her stuff in *Cabaret*. Indeed, for most people Berlin was an improbable oasis in the East German wilderness, cut in two by the Wall, surrounded by Russian troops, a stump of a city crowded with allied soldiers, spiked with missiles, lined with steak houses.

Berlin was last in the news in a big way during the Berlin airlift, and during the building of the Wall in 1961. It was featured vividly when President Kennedy gazed out across the Wall and proclaimed: "I am a Berliner." But thereafter it was simply a schizophrenic city. A remnant of a vanished metropolis, occupied by its conquerors—in the West a prosperous fortress of 2 million people; in the East a prison house its masters called paradise, a place of outer darkness. Berlin was not a place—it was an issue. It never quite seemed to be part of modern Germany. When people thought of West Germany they tended to think of Bonn, the apologetic federal capital, of Mercedes and BMW, and of the strength of the deutsche mark. It was devoutly to be hoped that the two Germanys would one day be reunited, but outside the circles of the devout, no one was putting any money on it.

Since the erection of the Wall 30 years ago, Berlin has become a kind of distant theater of the cold war. A fine place for spy stories, the scene of memorable exchanges of secret

You've Let Your Imagination Go, Now Get Up And Follow Your Dreams.

For The Vacation You're Dreaming Of, Call American Express® Travel Agency At 1-800-YES-AMEX.*

American Express will send more than your imagination soaring. We'll fly you, sail you, drive you to any Fodor's destination and beyond. Because American Express believes the best vacations happen from Europe to the Orient, Walt Disney® World to Hawaii and everywhere in between.

For dependable service, expert advice, and value wherever your dreams take you, call on American Express. After all, the best traveling companion is a trustworthy friend.

Travel Agency

It's easy to recognize a good place when you see one.

American Express Cardmembers have been doing it for years.

The secret? Instead of just relying on what they see in the window, they look at the door. If there's an American Express Blue Box on it, they know they've found an establishment that cares about high standards.

Whether it's a place to eat, to sleep, to shop, or simply meet, they know they will be warmly welcomed.

So much so, they're rarely taken in by anything else.

Always a good sign.

agents; daring escapes by hugely brave men and women hidden in the cunning compartments of trucks and automobiles; flights by hot air balloon; midnight dashes through the sewers beneath the city. And of abortive escapes that ended in gunfire and bleeding bodies. Along the length of the Wall small tabernacles remember with a name or a photograph those who did not get away.

Then suddenly the world was stood on its head. The night of Friday, November 10, the East Germans began smashing through the Wall. By November 14 there were 22 new crossing points, with promises of more to come. And through these gaps poured the grateful tens of thousands. The invasion so long predicted was coming true. Even the direction was right—the invaders came from the East. But they carried not rifles but shopping bags, and they arrived not in tanks but on foot, or in tiny two-stroke motorcars called Trabants, belching fumes, their fiberglass frames shivering on their uncertain chassis. To watch the tiny Trabant cross the Wall and go chugging along the broad West Berlin boulevards, impatiently followed by a gas-guzzling, absurdly fast turbo triumph of German automotive engineering, is to be present at a motorized street theater. The way into the future might be summed up by a single stage direction: "Exit a Trabant, pursued by a Porsche."

West Berliners, usually so laconic, acerbic, irreverent, melted in the face of this invasion. The Opera House offered free performances of Mozart's *Magic Flute*. The city fathers allowed free travel on the subway, the U-Bahn. They gave each new arrival 100 marks to spend. The department stores hung out welcome signs and exchanged the visitors' dud currency at the rate of ten East German marks for one West German mark. Around the square at the top of the Kurfürstendamm, beside the ruins of the Kaiser Wilhelm Memorial Church commemorating the destruction of Berlin, sausage stalls appeared, trestle tables, beakers of beer, mobile toilets, street musicians, and unbounded conviviality. The visitors were quickly dubbed the *"Ossies"* to distinguish them from the West Berliners, who became, naturally, the *"Wessies."* When *Ossies* met *Wessies*, there took place in West Berlin the biggest damn family reunion Europe has seen since the War.

True, there were also a few party poopers about. Taxi drivers worried aloud about the cost of it all. After all, there were at least 1.2 million East Berliners (or were the last time any had been brave enough or foolhardy enough to count them), and at 100 marks a head, the overall subsidy for this invasion, in every sense, was not small beer. Similarly, guest workers employed to do the work that West Berliners disdain took a rather dim view. "What will happen to me?" the Turkish cleaning attendant of a block of flats asked her employer, "when the *Ossies* undercut me?"

Her employer appeared happily unconcerned. "I know, I've had three offers already."

And what of the thousands of troops that the Western allies and the Russians have kept massed along this crucial border? More worrying still, to the Poles and others—with sad memories of the last united Germany—where were the borders of Germany itself? Why had the West German chancellor, on a visit to Poland, declined to state that the postwar boundaries were immovable? And what on earth was one to make of a German people who, it seemed, were no longer preparing for the war but mounting shopping expeditions instead?

I t was all very confusing and very euphoric and vaguely troubling all at once. Anyone who imagined that things would settle down did not, as they say in Berlin, have all his cups in the cupboard. Such people also mistook the significance of symbols. A Wall had once stood between East and West, built of stone and stained with blood. One night, without warning, it fell down. And only the rich bird life, thriving along its empty, eerie length, would mourn its passing. No one was surprised by the news that three Communist mayors from the East had committed suicide. It was the opinion of otherwise pacific matrons taking coffee in the Kempinski Eck, the famous plush, glass-fronted observatory on the Kurfürstedamm, that the disgraced former leader of East Germany, Erich Honecker, should "do the decent thing" and follow suit.

West Berliners have always detested the Wall, but they learned to live with it. They have jogged along its length and have daubed it with graffiti from end to end, but except on rare occasions when it thrust itself into view with a spectacular escape, or some important politician came to call and made a speech, they forgot about it. What West Berlin has never allowed anybody to forget is the War itself. Bullet holes are still to be seen, spattering the sides of buildings. Fragments of the portals of the old Berlin synagogue are cemented into the porch of the Jewish Community Center in Fasanenstrasse. West Berlin is a city loud with ghosts.

The area around the Wall added to the sense of war-torn desolation. Once it was the site of the Potsdamer Platz, among the busiest intersections in Europe, the very heart of Berlin. Since the War ended it has been a muddy, disconsolate slum. Taxi drivers assured visitors with laconic understatement that it was not "a development area." The deserted embassies look like the victims of some belowstairs revolt by the lower vegetable orders. Creepers spread across their facades and reach through open windows into empty rooms.

Reminders of the cataclysms are everywhere: the Hitler bunker; the site of the Gestapo torture chambers in Wilhelmstrasse; the fragmentary remains of the old Anhalter station, a crumbling facade and a few headless statues on a roof out of which trees have sprouted. Before the War the Anhalter dispatched 60 trains a day to Dresden, Rome, Vienna. Nearby is Friedrichstrasse, now a gray shadow of its pre-war, tinselly self. It sputters out in a pizzeria and a rash of bars, ending abruptly when it runs up against Checkpoint Charlie. The graffiti on the Wall reveals the genial derision in which West Berliners hold the foreigner's tender fascination with this monstrous monument: "What are you staring at? Have you never seen a wall before?"

There has always been something inconsolably sad in the air of West Berlin. East Berlin, by contrast, has always pretended otherwise. East Berliners never spoke of their city as "East Berlin," but always and only as Berlin, the capital of the only legitimate Germany. They preferred to ignore the existence of the imposter stuck away in the middle of 110 miles of East German territory. East German soldiers were to be seen regularly changing the guard on Unter Den Linden, still doing the goose step, wearing helmets like soup plates.

Naturally I crossed the Wall into the East for the simple pleasure of witnessing East Germans moving the other way. They waited patiently in long lines, helped by the border guards to fill in their travel forms. It must be strange to ask directions from a man who a week earlier would have shot you for trying to leave the country. It must have been even stranger for the guards themselves, trained to snarl, shoot, and inspect the undersides of tourist buses with giant dentist mirrors. Overnight they had become part of the courtesy staff, obliging, efficient, seemingly delighted that most of the population planned a trip abroad.

I traveled to the East with a British novelist who had never made the crossing before. She had a theory that you could tell you were getting older when the popes started looking younger. But in Berlin, that test seemed really to apply to border guards. They appeared to have shed years overnight. "Please step this way to exchange your money," a smiling fellow invited toothily, holding the door. Only those used to making this dreary crossing would understand the novelty of his demeanor. I exchanged good West German marks for bad, an obligatory transfer, a tax on curiosity. One day East German banknotes will, like the Wall itself, become collectors' items. On the face of the 20-mark note Goethe stares back quietly, as if disturbed to find himself so framed.

There has never been much to see in the streets of East Berlin, or in the shops. A smart new coffeehouse adorns the corner of Friedrichstrasse, in its continuation on the other side of the Wall. It is always packed to capacity. Most of the customers appear to have taken up their seats soon after the building was completed and show no signs of leaving. In a nearby supermarket, food is more plentiful than it is, say, in Moscow. But a German economy, *any* German economy, must be in deep trouble if it cannot make even bottles of sauerkraut look attractive. But what lightens everything in a lovely, astonishing fashion are the chattering crowds of East Berliners at the crossing points, waiting to leave as if it were the most natural thing in the world. Most are going for the day, complete with bags, babies, and beaming smiles, heading for the bright lights of West Berlin.

And for citizens of a regime known for its prim moralizing, its political piety, and it claims to be untainted by the lures of Western junk, the *Ossies* show themselves to be endearingly human. They crowd the non-stop strip shows on Kant Strasse. The unexpected connection between vice and philosophy is a feature of West Berlin. After all, the crown (if that is the word) of Martin Luther Strasse happens to be an emporium known as Big Sexy Land. The clip joints reduced their entry fee and offered two free beers to our "Eastern guests" and reported that the crowds were "good-humored."

And so they were. They were also "different," a word that kept cropping up among West Berliners who observed the visitors closely. The *Ossies* manifest that special sort of raging docility that distinguishes Eastern European crowds, people accustomed to standing in line and monitoring their expectations every wish of the way. The *Wessies* looked upon the *Ossies* with a benign complexity attended by gentle satisfaction. They were, quite simply, as pleased as punch to see them in West Berlin—though not quite sure what to do with them.

And thus it was with a certain relief that the *Wessies* sought refuge in their bars, restaurants, and watering holes where the *Ossies* could not follow and sat talking excitedly over meals that only they could afford. And the *Ossies* would press their noses to the windows of the Paris Bar like gentle ghosts. Yet there was no discernible resentment in their stares. *Ossies* were to be seen striding through the most distant suburbs, stopping to stare at children playing in the park, or a man washing his car, or gathering in great crowds outside the windows of the BMW showrooms. After all, what qualitative difference is there among the objects of your fascination when you are seeing it all for the first time? It is all very natural, and not a little sad.

At the entrance to a large department store I watched a family of East Berliners, freshly arrived, wide-eyed and eerily silent. Father, mother, and a boy of about six were passing the chocolate counter. Suddenly the little boy stopped dead. He had seen the chocolates, homemade and gleaming darkly under the lights, perfection behind the glass, a costly pyramid, profligate, tempting, untouchable. His adoration passed like an electric current into his mother and father and rooted them to the spot. No one spoke.

After a while, like sleepers awakening, they shook themselves and went on their way. Seeing is believing. It's not the same as having, but it will do, for a while at least.

3 Berlin

Since autumn 1989 Berlin has been in the headlines as the focal point and touchstone of a reuniting Germany, culminating in the historic vote on June 20, 1991, by the German Parliament to make the city once again the full-time seat of the German government. Thus ends one of the great geographic and political anomalies of the 20th century: a city split in two by a 10-foot-high concrete wall, with its larger western half an island of capitalist democracy, surrounded by an East Germany run by hard-line Stalinist Communists. Built in 1961 at the height of the Cold War, the Berlin Wall symbolized the separation of two distinctly different political and economic systems. Ironically, though, it also became a major tourist attraction, where viewing platforms along the western side enabled visitors to see the battlefront-like No Man's Land, guarded by soldiers and peppered with deadly mines and booby traps. The Wall's demolition cast it once more as a symbol: this time, though, a symbol of the change sweeping over former Iron Curtain countries. Two large chunks of the Wall have been left standing as reminders of the grim past.

Berlin actually began as two cities, more than 750 years ago. Museum Island, on the Spree River, was once called Cölln, while the mainland city was always known as Berlin. As early as the 1300s, Berlin prospered from its location at the crossroads of important trade routes, and it became filled with merchants and artisans of every description. After the ravages of the Thirty Years' War (1618–48), Berlin rose to power as the seat of the Brandenburg dynasty, and 200 years later when the Brandenburgian and Prussian realms united under the Hohenzollerns, Berlin was the chosen capital. The 1701 coronation of the enlightened ruler King Friedrich II—also known as Frederick the Great—set off a renaissance in the city, especially in the construction of academic institutions such as the Academy of Arts and the Academy of Sciences.

The Prussian empire, especially under Count Bismarck in the late 19th century, proved to be the dominant force in unifying the many independent German principalities. Berlin maintained its status as the German capital throughout the German Empire (1871–1918), the post-World War I Weimar Republic (1919–33), and Hitler's Third Reich (1933–45). In the 1920s and early '30s the city also served as an important European social and cultural capital, tinged with a reputation for decadence. But during World War II, acting as the Nazi headquarters, it was bombed to smithereens—at the end of hostilities there was more rubble in Berlin than in all other German cities combined. Most of what you see there today has been built, or rebuilt, since 1945.

With the division of Germany after World War II, Berlin also was partitioned, with American, British, and French troops in the districts to the west, the Soviet Union's forces to the east. After the Potsdam Agreement in 1945, the three western zones of occupation gradually merged into one, becoming West Berlin, while the Soviet-controlled eastern zone defiantly remained separate. In 1948, in an attempt to force the Western Allies to relinquish their stake in the city, the U.S.S.R. set up a blockade cutting off all overland supply routes from the West. The Western Allies countered by mounting the Berlin Airlift, during which some 750,000 flights delivering 2 million tons of goods kept Berlin alive for most of a fateful year, until the

Soviets finally lifted the blockade. As peace conferences repeatedly failed to resolve the question of Germany's division, the Soviets in 1949 established East Berlin as the capital of its new puppet state in East Germany. West Berlin was not technically part of the West Germany republic, though it was clearly tied to its legal and economic system. The division of the city was emphasized even more in 1961 when the East Germans constructed the infamous Berlin Wall.

Reunited Berlin is much more than two halves of a large city stitched together again after decades of painful separation. With surprising speed this amazing metropolis has grown together to reemerge as the largest city on the Continent. You can walk now with ease across a former fortified frontier without realizing it, and you have to look hard to find the ugly traces of the Wall that divided the city for so long. Berlin really is one city again, and there's not much point now in clinging to the old comparisons between east and west. Gone, too, is the cheap, first-time thrill of venturing through the Wall and into the forbidden territory of the East. Those who did it have their memories; those who visit Berlin for the first time in these post-unification years are deprived of a frisson or two—but they are rewarded with the sight of a city in the exciting phase of renewal and self-recognition. The visible signs of this are almost all to be found in eastern Berlin, much of which in 1992 resembled one huge construction site, with whole blocks either being razed to make way for dazzling new department stores, hotels, and commercial centers, or returned to their long-neglected historical appearance.

With the Wall now on the junk pile of history, visitors can at last appreciate the qualities that mark the city as a whole. Its particular charm always lay in its spaciousness, its trees and greenery, its racy atmosphere, and the ease with which you could reach the lakes and forests within its perimeter. It is a vast city, laid out on an epic scale—western Berlin alone is four times the size of Paris. Whole towns and villages are inlaid into the countryside beyond the downtown area. The really stunning parts of the prewar capital are in the eastern sector, with its grand boulevards and monumental buildings, the classical Brandenburg Gate, and the stately tree-lined avenue of Unter den Linden.

What really makes Berlin special, however, are the intangibles—the spirit and bounce of the city. Here is life in a pressure cooker, life on the edge—literally and figuratively. Berliners of whatever age are survivors; they have lived with adversity all their lives, and have managed to do so with a mordant wit and cynical acceptance of life as it is rather than the way one hopes it might be.

Berliners are brash, no-nonsense types, who speak German with their own racy dialect. Their high-voltage energy is invariably attributed to the bracing Berlin air, the renowned *Berliner Luft*. Crisis has been a way of life here for as long as anyone can remember. "To survive with a measure of style and humor" could serve as the city's theme.

Essential Information

More than three years after the official unification of the two Germanies, the nuts-and-bolts work of joining up the two halves is by no means complete, and uncertainties still abound. We have given addresses, telephone numbers, and other logistical details based on the best available information, but please understand that changes are taking place at a furious pace in everything from postal codes and telephone numbers to street names. Eastern Berlin's separate telephone code (02) has been phased out; the code for the whole city is now 030 (formerly only western Berlin's code). Public museums in western Berlin, once free, are starting to charge admission.

Important Addresses and Numbers

Tourist Information

The **Verkehrsamt Berlin** (main tourist office) is located in the heart of the city in the Europa Center (tel. 030/262–6031). If you want materials on the city before your trip, write **Verkehrsamt Berlin** (Martin-Luther-Strasse 105, D-1000 Berlin 62). For information on the spot, the office is open daily 8 AM–10:30 PM. There are also offices at **Tegel Airport** (tel. 030/410–13145; open daily 8 AM–11 PM); **Bahnhof Zoo** train station (tel. 030/313–9063; open daily 8 AM–11 PM); and at the **Alexanderplatz Television Tower** (tel. 030/242–4675; open daily 8–5). Berlin has an information center especially for women, offering help with accommodations and information on upcoming events. Contact **Fraueninfothek Berlin,** c/o Frauennetzwerk (Potsdamerstr. 139, tel. 030/282–3930; open Tues.–Sat. 9–9, Sun. and public holidays 9–3).

For information on all aspects of the city, pick up a copy of *Berlin Turns On,* free from any tourist office. Also, the listings in *Berlin Programm* (DM 2.50), a monthly guide to Berlin arts, provide the latest information about concerts, opera, and theater.

Embassies and Consulates

United States Consulate (Clayallee 170, tel. 030/832–4087); **British Consulate** (Uhlandstr. 7–8, tel. 030/309–5292).

Following the unification of the city, the American and British embassies in former East Berlin have taken on the character of information centers. The **American** office is still at Neustädtische Kirchstrasse 4–5 (tel. 030/220–2741) and the **British** office remains at Unter den Linden 32–34 (tel. 030/220–2431). **Canada** has a Consulate-General at the Europacenter (tel. 030/2611161).

Emergencies

Police: tel. 030/110. **Ambulance and emergency medical attention:** tel. 030/310–031. **Dentist:** tel. 030/1141 or after 9 PM, tel. 030/892–0379. **Pharmacies:** Berlin pharmacies offer late-night service on a rotation basis. Every pharmacy displays a notice indicating the location of the nearest shop with evening hours. For emergency pharmaceutical assistance, call 030/1141.

Changing Money

Berlin banks are open Monday, Wednesday, and Friday 9–1:30, Tuesday and Thursday 3:30–5:30. You can change money or cash checks at the Wechselstube at the Bahnhof Zoo (Mon.–Sat. 8 AM–9 PM, Sun. and public holidays 10–6) and at the Berlin Bank City Service's Tegel Airport office (open daily 8 AM–10 PM).

English-Language Bookstores	**Marga Schoeller,** Knesebeckstr. 33, tel. 030/881–1112. **Buchhandlung Kiepert,** Hardenbergstr. 4–5, tel. 030/331–0090. **The British Book Shop,** Mauerstr. 83–84 or Herder Tauntzienstr. 13, tel. 030/212440.
Travel Agencies	**American Express,** Friedrichstr. 172, tel. 030/238–4102. **American Express Reisebüro,** Kurfürstendamm 11, tel. 030/882–7575.
	American Lloyd, Kurfürstendamm 36, tel. 030/883–7081.
Car Rental	**Avis:** Tegel Airport, tel. 030/410–13148; Budapesterstr. 43, Europa Center, tel. 030/261–1881; Haus der Reise, Alexanderpl. 5, tel. 02/2125575. **Europcar:** Kurfürstenstr. 101, tel. 030/213–7097. **Hertz:** Tegel Airport, tel. 030/410–13315; Budapesterstr. 39, tel. 030/261–1053. **Sixt-Budget:** Tegel Airport, tel. 030/41012886; Budapesterstr. 16, tel. 030/261–1357.
Luxury Cars	For chauffeured limousines and luxury sports cars, try **Autohansa** (Bundesallee, tel. 030/851–4061), **Bothy Rent a Car** (Stralauer Platz, tel. 02/436–2330; Karl-Marx-Str. 36, tel. 02/623–5066), **First Class Car** (in the Hotel Steigenberger, Los-Angeles-Platz, tel. 030/213–9634 or 030/213–9600), **Chauffeur & Limousine Service** (Kaisderdamm 28, tel. 030/301–7027), and **Janisch Limousinen Service** (Uhlandstr. 185, tel. 030/883–3079). **Sixt-Budget** (*see* above) has Berlin's biggest fleet of Mercedes and Porsches.

Arriving and Departing by Plane

Airlines flying to western Berlin's **Tegel Airport** from major U.S. and European cities include Delta, TWA, United, Iberia, Alitalia, SwissAir, Air France, British Airways, Lufthansa, Euro-Berlin, and some charter companies. Because of increased air traffic following unification, the former military airfield at **Tempelhof** is being used increasingly. Despite substantial government subsidies, domestic fares are high. Tegel Airport is only 6 kilometers (4 miles) from the downtown area, and Tempelhof is even closer. For information on arrival and departure times, for Tegel, call 030/41011.

Eastern Berlin's **Schönefeld Airport** is about 24 kilometers (15 miles) outside the downtown area. It is used principally by Soviet and eastern European airlines, although with the increase in flights to Tegel, it's been taking more and more charter traffic. For information on arrival and departure times call 030/672–4031.

Between the Airport and Downtown	Blue airport bus No. 9 runs at 10-minute intervals between Tegel and downtown via Kurfürstendamm (the main avenue), Bahnhof Zoologischer (the main train station), and Budapesterstrasse. The total trip is 30 minutes; fare is DM 3. Expect to pay about DM 20 for the same trip by taxi. If you rent a car at the airport, take the Stadtautobahn (there are signs), the highway into Berlin. The Halensee exit leads to Kurfürstendamm (Ku'damm for short).

From Schönefeld, a shuttle bus leaves every 10–15 minutes for the nearby S-bahn station; S-bahn trains leave every 20 minutes for the Friedrichstrasse station downtown. A taxi ride from the airport takes about 40 minutes. By car, follow the signs for "Stadtzentrum Berlin."

Arriving and Departing by Train, Bus, and Car

By Train There are five major rail routes to Berlin from the western half of the country (from Hamburg, Hannover, Köln, Frankfurt, and Nürnberg) and the network is set to expand to make eastern German territory more accessible. At press time, trains are jointly run by the former East German Deutsche Reichsbahn (DR) and former West Germany's Deutsche Bundesbahn (DB), and reduced-price DB tickets are accepted. Check out the 10-day "Berlin Saver Ticket," sold at western German stations; it offers reductions of 33%. Trains from western Germany arrive at Berlin's main terminus, Bahnhof Zoologischer Garten (Bahnhof Zoo). The U-bahn (subway) and S-bahn (suburban railroad) stop here, too. Eastern Berlin's chief stations are at Friedrichstrasse or the Ostbahnhof. For details, call **Deutsche Bundesbahn Information** (tel. 030/19419) or **Deutsche Reichsbahn** (tel. 030/31102116); **reservations** (tel. 030/311–022112).

By Bus Buses are slightly cheaper than trains; Berlin is linked by bus to 170 European cities. The main station is at the corner of Masurenallee and Messedam. Reserve through DER (state), commercial travel agencies, or the station itself. For information, call 030/301–8028.

By Car The "transit corridor" roads linking former West Germany with western Berlin are still there, but the strict restrictions that once confined foreign motorists driving through East Germany have vanished, and today you can travel at will through the country. Expressways link Berlin with the eastern German cities of Magdeburg, Leipzig, Rostock, Dresden, and Frankfurt an der Oder. At press time, speed restrictions of 130 kph (80 mph) still applied, and you must carry your driver's license, car registration, and insurance documents.

Getting Around

By Public Transportation Berlin is too large to be explored on foot. To compensate, the city has one of the most efficient public transportation systems in Europe, a smoothly integrated network of subway (U-bahn) and elevated (S-bahn) train lines, buses, trams (in eastern Berlin only), and even a ferry (across the Wannsee Lake), making every part of the city easily accessible. There's also an all-night bus service, indicated by the letter "N" next to route numbers. In summer, there are excursion buses linking the downtown area with the most popular recreation areas.

A DM 3 ticket (DM 2 for children) covers the entire system for two hours and allows you to make an unlimited number of changes between trains and buses. A pack of four tickets costs DM 10.40 (DM 6.40 for children). The best deal for visitors who plan to travel extensively around the city is the **Berlin Ticket,** valid for 24 hours and good for all trains and buses; it costs DM 12 (DM 6 for children). A six-day pass allowing unlimited travel on all buses and trains within Berlin between Monday and Saturday costs DM 28. If you plan to visit the Wannsee Lake, buy the **combined day ticket,** good for the entire network and the excursion boats of the Stern- und Kreisschiffahrt line; it costs

Berlin Public Transit System

DM 18.50 (DM 9.30 for children). If you are just making a short trip, buy a Kurzstreckentarif. It allows you to ride six bus stops or three U-bahn or S-bahn stops for DM 2 (DM 1.50 for children). Buy it in packs of four for the best value (DM 6.40 adults, DM 4.80 children). Finally, there's a ticket good only for rides along the Ku'damm on buses 119 and 129: it costs DM 1. The fare structure now covers transportation systems for both parts of Berlin.

All regular tickets are available from vending machines at U-bahn and S-bahn stations. Punch your ticket into the red machine on the platform. The Berlin Ticket and the combined day ticket can only be bought from the main BVG ticket offices at the Bahnhof Zoo station and at the Kleistpark U-bahn station. For information, either call the **BVG** (Berliner Verkehrsbetriebe, tel. 030/216–5088) or go to the information office on Hardenbergplatz, directly in front of the Bahnhof Zoo train station.

By Taxi Fares start at DM 3.40 and increase by DM 1.69 per kilometer (DM 2.69 after midnight). There's an additional charge of 50 pfennigs per piece of luggage. Figure on paying around DM 10 for a ride the length of Ku'damm. Hail cabs in the street or order one by calling tel. 030/6902, 030/216–60, 030/261–026, 030/240024, or 030/240–202, or 030/3646 in eastern Berlin.

By Bike Bicycling is popular in Berlin. While it's not recommended in the downtown area, it's ideal in outlying areas. Some bike paths have been set up and many stores that rent bikes carry the Berlin biker's atlas to help you find them. Outfits renting bicycles include: **Fahrradbüro** Berlin (Hauptstr. 146, tel. 030/784–5562), and **Räderwerk** (Körtestr. 14, by U-bahn station Südstern, tel. 030/691–8590), which offers a week's rental for only DM 40; for bike rental in the Grunewald forest go to the S-bahn station Grunewald, tel. 030/8115829.

Guided Tours

Orientation Tours There's no shortage of companies offering orientation tours (in English) covering all major sights in both eastern and western Berlin. They range in length from two and a half hours to four hours, with fares from DM 30 to DM 45. All operators also offer excursions to Potsdam (DM 50–DM 70) and Dresden (DM 50–DM 100), and tours of Berlin by night (the DM 95 fare includes two or three drinks at nightclubs). These general tours are more or less identical in program and price.

Tour Operators **Berliner Bären Stadtrundfahrten** (BBS, Rankestr. 35, tel. 030/213–4077). Groups depart from the corner of Rankestrasse and Kurfürstdendamm.

Berolina Stadtrundfahrten (Meinekestr. 3, tel. 030/8822001). Groups depart from the corner of Kurfürstendamm and Meinekestrasse, and, in eastern Berlin, from the corner of Unter den Linden and Universitätstrasse.

Bus-Verkehr-Berlin (BVB, Kurfürstendamm 225, tel. 030/8826847). Tours leave from Kurfürstendamm 225.

Severin & Kühn (BVB, Kurfürstendamm 216, tel. 030/883–1015). Groups leave from clearly marked stops along the Kurfürstendamm, and in eastern Berlin, at the corner of Unter den Linden and Universitätstrasse.

Special-Interest Tours Sightseeing tours with a cultural/historical bias are offered by **Kultur Kontor** (Savignypl. 9–10, tel. 030/310–888). Tours include "Berlin Becoming Berlin," "Berlin 1933–45," and "The Roaring '20s." Departures are from the corner of Savignyplatz and Kantstrasse. **Berliner Geschichtswerkstatt** (Goltzstr. 49, tel. 030/215–4450) also offers historical tours and tours on foot, starting from the Naturkundemuseum, at Invalidenstrasse 43. Bus excursions to the countryside around Berlin and as far as Magdeburg are offered by **Pluspunkt e.V.** (Hohenzollerndamm 188, tel. 030/862–1260).

Boat Trips Berlin not only has more water than any other inland European city but also Europe's biggest inland resort lake, so a tour by boat is as good a way of seeing the city as by bus. There are several operators offering cruises ranging from a pleasure trip around the Wannsee to a cultural tour of the canals of the inner city.

A tour of the **Havel lakes** is the thing to do in summer. Trips begin at Wannsee (S-bahn: Wannsee) and at the Greenwich Promenade in Tegel (U-bahn: Tegel). You'll sail on either the whale-shaped vessel *Moby Dick* or the *Havel Queen*, a Mississippi-style boat, and cruise 17 miles through the lakes and past forests. Tours last 4½ hours and cost between DM 10 and DM 15. There are 20 operators. *See* below for the leading ones.

Tours of downtown Berlin's **canals** take in sights such as the Charlottenburg Palace and the Congress Hall. Tours depart from Kottbusser Bridge in Kreuzberg and cost around DM 10.

Two companies concentrate on cultural tours in which Berlin's history and architectural development can be followed from the deck of a boat. They are: **Kultur-Kontor** (Savignyplatz 9–10, tel. 030/310–888) and **Berliner Geschichtswerkstatt** (Goltzstr. 49, tel. 030/215–4450).

Tour Operators **Stern- und Kreisschiffahrt** (Sachtlebenstr. 60, tel. 030/810–0040).

Reederei Bruno Winkler (Levetzowstr. 16, tel. 030/391–7010).

Reederei Heinz Riedel (Planufer 78, tel. 030/6913782 or 030/6934646). Included in its large itinerary of lake and river cruises is a tour of the central city canals, starting from the Kottbusser Bridge near the Kottbusser Tor U-bahn station.

Die Weisse Flotte (Haupthafen Treptow, tel. 030/271–2327 or 030/271–2328). This is former East Germany's state-run pleasure-boat company, and no line knows the eastern Berlin waters better. Boats depart from the Haupthafen Treptow (Treptow S-bahn station).

Personal Guides The Verkehrsamt Berlin (tel. 030/262–6031) at Europa Center can provide you with a list of reputable guides who are fluent in English.

Walking Tours Walking tours of Berlin are organized by several companies and walking clubs, among them:

Berliner Wanderclub (Geschäftsstelle Berliner Strasse 40–41, tel. 030/875175). This club also conducts hiking, cycling, and skiing tours in the Berlin and Brandenburg areas.

Historische Statt Reisen Berlin (Stephanstr. 24, tel. 030/395–3078).

Wanderkreis Berlin (Marschnerstr. 12, tel. 030/8349977) features different tours that emphasize culture, history, architecture, and politics.

Exploring Berlin

Orientation

The Berlin familiar to Western visitors was already a huge city before reunification. After the Wall fell and the two halves of the long-divided city joined up, Berlin became an enormous metropolis. By the year 2005 it's expected to become the biggest European continental city between the Atlantic and the Urals. It's already the largest in area. Paris, with twice the population, could fit six times within its borders, which enclose an urban area of nearly 900 square kilometers.

Berlin is a remarkably green city, with forests, rivers, lakes, 60 parks, and even large tracts of farmland covering more than 30% of its surface. It has Europe's largest inland stretch of recreational lakeland and the Continent's biggest inland beach; a boat tour of its canals and Havel lakes covers a greater distance than the Middle Rhine between Koblenz and Rüdesheim. You can walk 70 kilometers from the inner city Zoo to Berlin's outermost community, Lübars, without touching more than a few hundred yards of main road. And Lübars really is a community, one of 59 villages and 27 estates and farms that were absorbed to create Greater Berlin in 1920.

Seventy years later, Berlin still has the character of a collection of disparate parts, more like a country than a metropolis. The bells of no fewer than 55 village parish churches ring out on Sunday mornings. Visit Spandau, Schöneberg, or Köpenick on market day and you'll be excused for checking your map to make sure you're still in Berlin. Go on an outing to the Wannsee or Müggelsee lakes on a summer day and you'll think the Baltic coast has moved overnight.

This sense of a multifaceted city-state has its fascination—but also its frustrations. Berlin is a very difficult city for the visitor to get to know comfortably. You can't walk around it in a day, and even if you have the luxury of a week's stay you'll still return home with the nagging certainty that you've only just touched the surface. You'll also find a city again united but with its old prejudices still lingering like a Trabbi's poisonous exhaust fumes hanging in the air. You'll still sense the divide as you cross the largely invisible but still emotionally perceptible line that was once the Wall. The only really visible division is now the River Spree that winds an east–west course between green banks and gray wharves and warehouses. In the eastern section of the city, the Spree is identified with the only part of Berlin that could be described as its "old town," the picturesque Nikolaiviertel. In the west, it skirts the city's biggest park, the Tiergarten, which means "Zoological Garden." (Don't be alarmed—the only wild animals you'll find there are safe behind bars and deep ditches in the Zoo, which slots into the park's southwestern corner.) The chances are that you'll be staying in this area, for this is Berlin's premier hotel territory, the point where the celebrated Kurfürstendamm starts on its arrow-straight journey westward to Berlin's other great, green playground, the Grunewald forest. Here you'll find Berlin's other river, the Havel, and its lakes. Eastern Berlin claims the city's largest lake, the Müggelsee, and if you're seeking a swim on a hot day, that's the one to head for; the Grunewald lakes can get very crowded. You can escape the crowds just about anywhere in eastern Berlin, for much of that part of the city is still off-the-beaten-track territory. You'll find few tourists in areas such as Prenzlauerberg and Köpenick, although Berlin is changing with such speed that they could soon be rivaling the "in" suburbs of the western half. And, who knows, by the time you visit you may really discover a truly united city. You'll certainly discover a fascinating one.

Highlights for First-Time Visitors

Kaiser Wilhelm Gedächtniskirche
Kaufhaus des Westens department store (the KaDeWe)
Zoologischer Garten
Haus am Checkpoint Charlie (Wall Museum)
Brandenburger Tor
Reichstag
Pergamonmuseum
Gemäldegalerie, Dahlem
Schloss Charlottenburg
Ägyptisches Museum
Alexanderplatz

Tour 1: From Checkpoint Charlie to Alexanderplatz

Numbers in the margin correspond to points of interest on the Inner Berlin map.

The contrast between the bustling, cement-mixing activity in the streets and squares of eastern Berlin and the solid, established scene in the west is striking, and the first of our recommended tours plunges you directly into the paradox that Berlin still presents.

① If you begin at western Berlin's glittering **Kurfürstendamm**—nicknamed the Ku'damm—the contrast with what's ahead will be all the more striking. Catch the U-1 subway line east from Wittenbergplatz, catty-corner from that symbol of abundance, the KaDeWe department store. Change at Hallisches Tor to the northbound U-6 line heading toward Tegel. Get out at Kochstrasse. Here on the corner of Kochstrasse and Friedrichstrasse was the most famous of the Berlin **②** Wall crossing points, **"Checkpoint Charlie,"** setting of many memorable spy novels and films.

The physical checkpoint, a wooden pavilion, was hoisted away by crane in an emotional ceremony shortly after the Wall crumbled, but the red-and-white barrier and threatening gray watchtower are still there, kept as a reminder of this particular chapter of Berlin's history. The watchtower is being taken over by the nearby **Haus am Checkpoint Charlie,** a museum tracing the history of the Wall and vividly describing the most ingenious of the successful escapes. Here you'll find a miniature submarine that brought one East German unscathed through the river frontier, and a coffinlike assembly of two hollowed-out surfboards in which a West German smuggled his girlfriend west. Keeping up with the times, the museum also has some

Inner Berlin

spectacularly decorated pieces of the Wall on display. *Haus am Checkpoint Charlie, Friedrichstr. 44, tel. 030/2511031. Admission: DM 7.50 adults, DM 4.50 children. Open daily 9 AM– 10 PM.*

A drab, gray section of the Wall still stands as a memorial just beyond the Checkpoint Charlie barrier. On the corner, at the barrier itself, is the famous Cafe Adler, once a lonely outpost of Western hospitality in the shadow of the Wall but now just part of the general city scene.

Heading north on Friedrichstrasse, you can observe the burgeoning commercial development of eastern Berlin in microcosm. An attempt is being made to return this wide shopping boulevard to something approaching the flair it had in its prewar days. Large, fashionable stores will soon be lining the street again. By spring 1992, designer Escada, the jewelers Christ, and Mercedes Benz had moved in.

Turn right from Friedrichstrasse into Johannes-Dieckmann-Strasse and straight ahead two prominent cupolas beckoning
❸ you into one of the finest squares in all Europe, the **Gendarmenmarkt.** The cupolas belong to two monumental churches, the 18th-century **Deutscher Dom** (German Cathedral) and the **Französischer Dom** (French Cathedral), flanking in perfect harmony the beautiful Neoclassical **Schauspielhaus,** one of the greatest works of the Berlin architect Karl Friedrich Schinkel and now home to the Berlin Symphony Orchestra. (Don't confuse the Deutscher Dom with the massive Berliner Dom, the city's own cathedral, which sits squarely beside the Spree River, a short walk away.) The Deutscher Dom, at press time closed for restoration, is an earlier cathedral, but by no means as important. It was built by Berlin's Lutherans in 1701–08, and although it commands no great place in Berlin history, the broad steps you see before the church once displayed the coffins of revolutionaries who died in the uprisings of March 1848.

Immediately north of the Deutscher Dom is the Schauspielhaus, which opened again to the public as recently as 1984 after laborious reconstruction. "Schauspielhaus" means "theater," but now only concerts are performed here (*see* The Arts, below), possibly explaining the rather concerned look on the face of Friedrich von Schiller, who stands in statue form in the middle of the square. Completing the harmonious trio of classically proportioned buildings is the Französischer Dom, built at the same time as its almost twin, the Deutscher Dom, for Huguenot settlers who found refuge in Berlin. The nostalgic Huguenots built it as a copy of their home church in Charenton, France; today it houses a Huguenot museum and a restaurant-in-the-round, 70 feet up under the dome. There are 254 steps to climb before you reach the restaurant (Französischer Hof), but there's a refreshing glass of wine or beer waiting at the top. *Hugenottenmuseum, Gendarmenmarkt. Admission: DM 2 adults, DM 1 children. Open Tues., Wed., Thurs., Sat. 10–5; Sun. 11:30–5.*

Time Out   Save the Französischer Hof for a leisurely lunch or dinner before or after a concert. For a quick snack, try one of these nearby café/restaurants: the **Cafe Arkade** (Französischerstr. 25), on the northwest corner of the square, or the **Cafe zur Laube** (Otto

Nuschkestr. 20), a local favorite that boasts its own *Konditorei* (pastry shop).

Leave the Gendarmenmarkt by Französischerstrasse and follow it west into Werderstrasse. The red-brick, neo-Gothic church on your left, the **Friedrichswerdersche Kirche,** was designed by Schinkel in 1824–30 in a style that combines vertical Gothic lines with a heavy solidity. You'll either hate the building's rather dirty red appearance and frivolous brass-ball-capped turrets or be fascinated by them; it was quite the rage at the time, and became a model for many churches in Prussia. The interior, no longer a church but a museum dedicated to the work of Schinkel and his contemporaries, is surprisingly light and airy, with a very delicate ribbed ceiling. *Schinkelmuseum, Friedrichswerdersche Kirche, Werderstr., tel. 030/208–1323. Admission: DM 1 adults, 50 pf children. Open Wed.–Sun. 10–6.*

Cross the Spree by the Schleusen bridge (there's a fine view from either side) and into vast **Marx-Engels-Platz.** On this windy, barren square once stood the Berliner Schloss (Berlin Palace), an Italian Baroque royal and imperial residence that grew from a 15th-century castle. The palace was bombed out in the war, and instead of attempting to rebuild it East Berlin's Communist rulers blew up the remaining walls, cleared the ground, and erected the bombastic bronzed glass and concrete **Palast der Republik** (Palace of the Republic), which dominates the square today. The Palast was the seat of the Volkskammer, the East German parliament, but it also gave space to several restaurants, a theater, dance hall, and even a bowling alley. The locals call it the Palazzo Prozzo (a play on the German word *protzen*, meaning to show off in a gaudy way). Mercifully, the fine Baroque portal of the former palace was saved, carted off stone by stone across the square and inserted into the facade of the government building on your right, a particularly jarring juxtaposition.

Further along this side of the Marx-Engels-Platz are the former royal stables, the **Marstall,** a grand complex in imperial Prussian style. The Neue Marstall is now the city library, and the Alte Marstall hosts special loan exhibitions. On the corner of the Marstall you'll see one of the still-existent representations of Marx himself, a bronze relief showing the father of international socialism watching benignly over participants in the 1918–19 communist uprisings. Your attention is bound to be drawn by the starkly contrasting Renaissance facade of the house directly bordering the Marstall in Breitestrasse. This is the **Ribbeckhaus,** Berlin's only remaining Renaissance building. It was built for businessman Hans Georg von Ribbeck in 1624 and now serves as a government office.

From Breitestrasse return to Rathausstrasse, named after the former East Berlin city hall standing on the corner of Spandauerstrasse. It's called the **Rotes Rathaus**—the Red City Hall—not because of its communist associations but for its red-brick construction. Erected in 1861–70 on the site of Berlin's original, medieval town hall, in what was considered a suitably historical style—neo-Renaissance—the Rotes Rathaus looks oddly Venetian. A novel touch is the tiled frieze running along its facade, representing scenes from Berlin's history. If you're hungry, you can duck down into the cellar, where you have your choice of two restaurants (*see* Dining, below).

The ultimate destination of this first tour is clearly visible from here: the 365-meter-high (1,198-foot-high) Fernsehturm, the television and radio tower that was once the futuristic symbol of East Berlin. The tallest structure in the entire city, it soars **⑧** into the sky from the center of vast **Alexanderplatz** (nicknamed Alex), in prewar days a stylish piazza (named for the Russian czar Alexander I) but now a jumble of fast-food stands, nondescript 1950s high rises, Kaufhof department store, and the ugly Hotel Stadt Berlin. Architecture buffs will want to note the two 1930s buildings opposite the railroad bridge, on the southwest side of Alexanderplatz, by Peter Behrens, an early modernist who employed the young Walter Gropius and Mies van der Rohe as junior partners in his firm. These Bauhausian structures, strikingly abstract in their day, are in a sad state of disrepair. To get away from it all, take a high-speed elevator to the tower's observation platform and soak up the best view of Berlin you can have short of buying a plane ticket. *Fernsehturm, Alexanderplatz. Elevator: DM 5 adults, DM 2.50 children. Open daily 9 AM–midnight.*

It's no small irony that one of Berlin's oldest churches, the Gothic **Marienkirche** (open daily 9–5), stands on the edge of Alexanderplatz, almost in the shadow of the soaring television tower. The modest brick church shelters several treasures, including a 15th-century bronze baptismal font, a beautiful pulpit created in 1701 by Andreas Schluter, and the remarkable *Totentanz* fresco, a vivid, nightmarish representation of the "dance of death" theme, dating from 1450. Guided tours of the church are conducted daily at 1 PM, and organ recitals regularly take place Saturdays at 4:30 PM.

Time Out If it's chilly outside, you might want to warm up with a steaming hot bowl of soup at the **Suppenterrine** on Alexanderplatz. You'll rub shoulders at a communal zinc-topped bar with eastern Berliners sipping cabbage broth and local beer. It's not very classy, but it's cheap and cheerful. Alternatively, snack outdoors on a bulging *Dönnerkebab* sandwich, stuffed with succulent grilled lamb slices, onions, tomatoes, and cooked red cabbage. You'll find several food and beer stands near the Alexanderplatz S-bahn, where Rathausstrasse leads into the square.

Tour 2: Tiergarten, Brandenburger Tor, Kulturforum

Numbers in the margin correspond to points of interest on the Inner Berlin map.

For such a central Berlin attraction, the Brandenburger Tor (Brandenburg Gate) is not so easy to reach by public transport, and only a handful of hotels in eastern Berlin (and none in western Berlin) are within walking distance. If you're staying in the western part of the city, and anywhere near the Ku'damm, jump onto a number 129 bus, claim an upstairs seat, and travel to the Tor in style. You'll take in some sights on the way and be **⑨** tempted to break your journey—at the **Siegessäule,** for instance, the victory column in the middle of the traffic circle known as the Grosser Stern (Big Star). Several main roads

meet here, including Strasse des 17 Juni, the east–west axis of
the park, named for the date of the unsuccessful 1953 uprising
of East Berlin workers against the Soviets.

The 69-meter-high (227 feet) granite, sandstone, and bronze
monument, built in 1873 to celebrate three illustrious Prussian
military campaigns, originally stood before the Reichstag, on
the former Königsplatz (King's Square), today's vast, grassy
Platz der Republik (Republic Square). It was moved to its present position in 1938 during Hitler's ill-fated efforts to remodel
Berlin to his own megalomaniacal plans. There's an observation platform at the top, reached by a giddy climb of 285 steps.
A warning: Don't visit the Siegessäule at night unless you're
looking for erotic adventure; it's the haunt of Berlin's very-af-
ter-dark set. *Admission: DM 1.20 adults, 70 pf children. Open
Apr. 1–Oct. 31 Mon. 3 PM–6 PM, Tues.–Sun. 9–6.*

🔟 The next stop on the number 129 is the **Schloss Bellevue,** an exquisite palace built on the banks of the Spree for Frederick the
Great's youngest brother, Prince Augustus-Ferdinand. Today
the palace serves as the German president's official Berlin residence, but there is talk of relocating him. The stately gray- and
cream-colored building is set in 50-acre grounds containing a
small park called the English Garden, which was dedicated by
Britain's prime minister Anthony Eden, who followed up the
gesture shortly afterward by declaring war on Germany. Most
of the trees there were later chopped down to provide fuel in
the hard wartime winters. There are no hard feelings now on
either side: Britain's Queen Elizabeth donated some of the
park's new trees, and the Berliners refer affectionately to one
of their favorite parks as the "Garden of Eden." *Schloss Bellevue Park: open daily 8–dusk.*

Soon you'll be passing the weirdest assembly hall you'll encoun-
⓫ ter in Berlin, the **Kongresshalle,** a conference center built in
1957 as the American contribution to the International Building Exhibition, Interbau. It was designed by Hugh Stubbins.
The shock effect of its modernistic architectural style—it resembles an open oyster shell (or a giant, toothy grin—
Berliners dubbed it "Jimmy Carter's Smile" when the American president came to Berlin on an official visit)—was increased when the roof fell in in 1980. The building has since
reopened. You don't have to attend a meeting to inspect this
oddity; temporary exhibitions there are open to the public.

⓬ The massive bulk of the **Reichstag** (Imperial Parliament) will
then loom into sight. The bus stops right next to it. This imposing example of Prussian architectural grandeur was built in the
1890s to house the Prussian Parliament, and 30 years later it
performed a similar function for the ill-fated Weimar Republic.
The Reichstag was burned to a shell under mysterious circumstances on the night of February 28, 1933. The Nazis blamed
the communists and thus found a convenient pretext for sus-
pending the constitution and outlawing all opposition parties.
After reconstruction, the Reichstag was again badly damaged
in 1945 in the last Allied offensive of the war. The Reichstag
will once again house the Bundestag, the German Parliament,
but at press time the timetable for the move from Bonn to Berlin had not been set. (What *is* certain is that the area around the
Reichstag will become one huge construction site, as new offices are built for parliamentary members and their staffs.)
Currently, the west wing of the building houses a comprehen-

sive and very interesting exhibition entitled "Questions on German History," covering German history since 1800. The sections dealing with the Third Reich are especially fascinating. Although it's likely that the display will remain in the Reichstag through 1993, visitors should contact the Berlin Tourist Office for the latest information. *Admission free. Open Tues.–Sun. 10–5.*

Time Out You can break your tour at this point (and still catch the next bus, using your current ticket) with a refresher at the Reichstag café. It's light, airy, and the prices are not ceiling-high.

Before moving on, stroll to the nearby Spree River bank for a sad reminder of the most recent painful phase of German history. You'll see several crosses on the riverbank, each commemorating someone who died trying to cross the river frontier to the West. The closely guarded frontier between East and West, which ran down the center of the river, skirted the back of the Reichstag and around the next monument in your tour, the nearby Brandenburger Tor.

Just south of the Reichstag, where Strasse des 17 Juni meets Unter den Linden, is a monumental symbol of German unity and of the long division of Berlin—the mighty **Brandenburger Tor.** Ever since the Wall was built the Brandenburger Tor, once the pride of imperial Berlin, was stranded in the eerie No Man's Land. When the Wall came down, it was the focal point of much celebrating, for this evocative symbol of Berlin was finally restored to all the people of the newly united city. The Brandenburger Tor is the only remaining gate of an original group of 14 built by Carl Gotthard Langhans in 1788–91, in virile classical style, as a triumphal arch for King Frederick Wilhelm II. The Quadriga, a chariot drawn by four horses and driven by the Goddess of Peace, was added in 1793. The goddess was originally naked, but puritanical protesters persuaded the city fathers to clothe her in a sheath of sheet copper. Troops paraded through the gate after successful campaigns, the last time being in 1945 when victorious Red Army troops took Berlin. The upper part of the gate, together with its chariot and Goddess of Peace, were destroyed in the war, but in 1957 the original molds were discovered in West Berlin and a new quadriga was cast in copper and presented as a gift to the people of East Berlin—a remarkable, rare instance of Cold War–era East-West cooperation.

A short distance west, walking along Strasse des 17 Juni, you will reach the **Soviet Victory Memorial,** until 1990 a Russian enclave in the West. Built directly after the end of World War II, before power plays between opposing sides had been set in motion, it was located in the western rather than the eastern sector. Through an East-West arrangement it has been allowed to remain there, although no longer guarded by Soviet troops, and now serves as a major attraction. The semicircular monument, which shows a bronze statue of a soldier, rests on a marble plinth taken from Hitler's former Berlin headquarters, flanked by what are said to be the first two tanks to have fought their way into Berlin in 1945.

Continuing on foot, turn south from the memorial and cross the tip of the Tiergarten to **Potsdamerplatz,** a somewhat dull-looking expanse that was once among the busiest squares in prewar

Berlin. Potsdamerplatz is the point where the British, American, and Russian sectors met and is often referred to as the three-sector corner. The Wall cut through the center of the square. Not far from the square, on part of the wasteland on the other side of the dividing border, is a little knoll marking the remains of Hitler's reinforced concrete bunker where he spent his last days. At press time, discussions were under way on what to do with the site.

On nearby Potsdamerstrasse, on Heinrich-von-Kleist-Park, is the former **Alte Kammergericht** (Prussian Court Building), in which many Nazi show trials were held before the infamous Judge Roland Freisler. The building was taken over by the Allies in 1945 and is still used by the Allied forces. It was here that the four-power agreement, which set the rules governing communication between the two halves of the city, was signed in 1971.

Several blocks north, in Kemperplatz, lies the **Kulturforum** (Cultural Forum), a large square where you'll find a series of museums and galleries. Their contents will be shifting as state collections that were split in the war and stuck on opposite sides of the Wall are finally reunited. Two new buildings will join the complex. One, opening in summer 1993, will house the collection of drawings and prints currently at Dahlem (*see* Outlying Sights and Attractions, below) and an arts library. The other, slated for completion in 1996, will display paintings dating from the late Middle Ages to 1800, many of them now at the Gemäldegalerie at Dahlem and at the Bodemuseum on Museumsinsel (*see* Tour 4, below). Contact the Berlin Tourist Office for word on inevitable closings.

The roof that resembles a great wave belongs to the **Philharmonie** (Philharmonic Hall). Built in 1963, it is home to the renowned Berlin Philharmonic Orchestra. The functional design of the concert hall allows an audience of 2,000 to sit on all sides of the orchestra. The brilliant acoustics more than make up for ticketholders who face the backs of the orchestra. The main hall reopened in the spring of 1992 after an ambitious renovation. *Philharmonie ticket office: Matthäikirchstr. 1. Open weekdays 3:30–6 and weekends 11–2.*

The Philharmonie added the **Musikinstrumenten-Museum** (Musical Instruments Museum) to its attractions in 1984. It is well worth a visit for its fascinating collection of keyboard, string, wind, and percussion instruments. *Tiergartenstr. 1, tel. 030/254–810. Admission free. Open Tues.–Fri. 9–5, weekends 10–5. Guided tours on Saturdays at 11 with a noon presentation of the Wurlitzer organ. Tour admission: DM 3.*

Opposite the Philharmonie is the **Kunstgewerbemuseum** (Museum of Decorative Arts). Inside this three-story building you'll find a display of the development of the arts and crafts in Europe from the Middle Ages to the present day. Among its treasures is the Welfenschatz (Guelph Treasure), a collection of 16th-century gold and silver plate from Nürnberg. The most impressive single piece is a reliquary in the form of a domed Byzantine church. Made in Köln in 1175, it is believed to have held the head of St. Gregory when it was brought back from Constantinople in 1773. Other displays of particular interest are the ceramics and porcelains. *Matthäikirchstr. 10, tel. 030/*

266–2911. Admission: DM 4 adults, DM 2 children. Open Tues.–Fri. 9–5, weekends 10–5.

Leave the museum and walk south past the mid-19th-century church of St. Matthaeus to the **Neue Nationalgalerie** (New National Gallery), a modern glass and steel building designed by Mies van der Rohe and built in the mid-1960s.

The gallery's collection comprises paintings, sculptures, and drawings from the 19th and 20th centuries, with an accent on works by Impressionists such as Manet, Monet, Renoir, and Pissarro. Other schools represented are German Romantics, Realists, Expressionists, Surrealists, and the Bauhaus. The gallery also has a growing collection of contemporary art from Europe and America. *Potsdamerstr. 50, tel. 030/266–2666. Admission: DM 4 adults, DM 2 children. Open Tues.–Fri. 9–5, weekends 10–5.*

The last stop on the tour of the Cultural Forum is the **Staatsbibliothek** (National Library), opposite the Neue Nationalgalerie. This modern building, housing one of the largest libraries in Europe, with four million volumes, was designed by Hans Scharoun, the architect of the Philharmonie. *Potsdamerstr. 33, tel. 030/2661. Admission free. Open Mon.–Fri. 9–9, Sat. 9–5.*

From here you can walk back to the Zoologischer Garten station or the Ku'damm along Tiergartenstrasse heading west into Budapesterstrasse.

Tour 3: Kurfürstendamm to Zoologischer Garten

Numbers in the margin correspond to points of interest on the Inner Berlin map.

Every city has its "main street," and sometimes the thoroughfare acquires such a central place in its history, tradition, and everyday life that the two become almost interchangeable. Mention western Berlin and the name "Ku'damm" springs automatically to mind. Newly unified Berlin has two such streets now, of course, with Unter den Linden doing for eastern Berlin what the Ku'damm performs for the western part of the city (*see* Tour 4, below). That was an additional bonus bestowed by unification, and who can begrudge the long-beleaguered Berliners the pleasure?

The odd name is short for **Kurfürstendamm,** meaning the "Elector's Causeway." The Elector Joachim II of Brandenburg laid it out in the 16th century as his personal highway to connect his riverside palace in central Berlin to his hunting lodge in the Grunewald (*see* Excursions, below). Bismarck, the "Iron Chancellor" and the force behind Germany's 19th-century unification, widened it to a stately 55 yards in order to give Berlin a boulevard to compare with the grand avenues of Paris, but it was still some years before the Ku'damm developed into anything like the glittering avenue you see today. In fact, during Berlin's heydays of the turn of the century and the Roaring Twenties, the Ku'damm was outshone by Unter den Linden and other streets of what was to become drab postwar East Berlin. That was where the real heart of Berlin lay, and the Ku'damm was off the beaten track for many society types. The Ku'damm's prewar fame was based on its sometimes sordid nighttime scene, dominated by bars, dance halls, prostitutes, and all the gaudy rag tag and bobtail of the city's "alternative" lifestyle.

The Ku'damm shared the wartime fate of the rest of Berlin and suffered severe bomb damage. Nearly half the 245 Bismarck-era buildings were destroyed and the rest were damaged in varying degrees. What you see today (as in most of Berlin) is either restored or was constructed since the war. The result is a garish clash of styles, with fin-de-siècle mansions rubbing fine shoulders with cheap department stores, exclusive cafés sharing the sidewalk with seedy clubs. Some Berliners hate the street and try to avoid it at any hour. But there can't be many of them, because the Ku'damm throbs with life 24 hours a day—and certainly not all who pack its wide pavements are visitors. Whatever you think about the street, you'll admit it would be difficult to imagine Berlin without it.

The Ku'damm is two miles long and every block offers a contrast of one kind or another, so you can begin your tour at any point. If you stroll the length of it on one side and return on the other you've covered a literally blistering distance, but if you tire there are several bus lines traveling the route and a specially reduced Ku'damm ticket.

The Ku'damm is at its most impressive at its eastern end. Starting out at **Breitscheidplatz,** a large, untidy square partly ruined by high rises (including the Europa-Center), you'll find this stretch redeemed by the presence of western Berlin's most famous memorial, the bombed-out church tower of the **Kaiser Wilhelm Gedächtniskirche.** The church was built in a curious neo-Romanesque style and dedicated not to a saint but to Kaiser Wilhelm I, who attended the consecration in 1895. Allied bombers destroyed all but the bell tower, which was kept in its war-scarred state as a memorial. A permanent exhibit inside the base of the tower includes a collection of photographs and documents tracing the history of the church and items stressing the theme of forgiveness and reconciliation, including a cross of four medieval nails recovered from the ruins of Coventry Cathedral in England after German bombers destroyed that historic church. On the ceiling of the tower's interior you'll see 19th-century mosaics portraying not only religious scenes but also German imperial pageantry. The imperial character of the church is musically underscored by a carillon that peals from the tower on the hour, playing a jaunty tune composed by Kaiser Wilhelm's grandson, Prinz Ludwig Ferdinand von Hohenzollern. *Admission free. Open Tues.–Sat 10–6, Sun. 11–6.*

In 1961–63 a new church was built next to the Gedächtniskirche ruins. Paired with a hexagonal bell tower, it's a modern, octagonal structure with honeycomb walls of vivid stained glass (imported from Chartres in France), which burst magically into life after dark with an indigo light that acts as a beacon in the night sky of central Berlin. (The two have been dubbed the "Lipstick" and "Compact.") Inside, you'll find a very moving representation of Mary and the infant Jesus—the *Stalingrad Madonna*—drawn in charcoal by a German army doctor shortly before Christmas, 1942, at the height of the siege of Stalingrad. Next to it is a 13th-century Spanish crucifix that forms the centerpiece of a memorial to the men and women of the July 1944 plot to overthrow Hitler.

Time Out Set some time aside for coffee in the nearby **Einstein Stadtcafe** (Kurfürstendamm 67), where you can choose from an array of exotic coffees. There's also an interesting art gallery on the first floor of this fine 19th-century mansion.

Vying with the Gedächtniskirche for attention on Breitscheid-
㉕ platz is the 22-story **Europa Center,** a vast complex that makes up in variety what it lacks in surface beauty. This 1960s eye-sore—nicknamed "Pepper's Manhattan" after its architect, K.H. Pepper—houses more than 100 shops, restaurants and cafés, a hotel, casino, thermal spa, two cinemas, and a central office of the Berlin Tourist Office, the Verkehrsamt. For a spec-tacular view of the city, take the elevator to the i-Punkt restau-rant and observation terrace on the top floor.

At its eastern end, the Ku'damm leads into another major Ber-lin shopping street, Tauentzianstrasse, where on the right you'll find the city's largest department store, the Kaufhaus
㉑ des Westens, universally known as **KaDeWe.** It's claimed that KaDeWe is the largest department store not only in Berlin but also in all Europe, although that boast is challenged by at least three London and Paris concerns. Try placing an outlandish or-der and waiting for a batted eyelid by the management, which assures customers it can provide anything from a rare aspidis-tra to a zebra. The top floor is unquestionably tops: a culinary cornucopia of display cases proferring, among other delicacies, more than 150 sausages, myriad variations of herring, and hun-dreds of salads. If all this sets you salivating, you can pull up a stool at one of the many counters and sample much of what you see displayed, accompanied by wine, champagne, and beer. It's a great place for lunch or even an early dinner (KaDeWe closes at 6:30 PM weekdays).

Across the road from KaDeWe you'll see the neoclassical outline of the beautifully restored turn-of-the-century subway station **Wittenbergplatz.** Ride the subway (U-1 line) one stop toward
㉒ Ruhleben to **Zoologischer Garten.** You're back roughly where you began the tour, but you're also at the gates of Berlin's ex-traordinary zoo. It's one of the world's oldest, founded in 1841, and it has the largest number of individual species of all the world's zoos. Less than 50 years ago, however, it had to start practically from zero. Only 91 animals survived the war; now there are more than 11,000. The public's favorite is Bao-Bao, a panda given to the people of Berlin by the Republic of China. But Bao-Bao isn't the only crowd pleaser, and scarcely a week goes by without the zoo announcing an attractive new addition to its animal population. *Entrances at Hardenbergpl. and Budapesterstr. Zoo admission: DM 8 adults, DM 4 children. Aquarium and zoo admission: DM 12.50 adults, DM 6 chil-dren. Open daily 9 AM–dusk.*

Tour 4: On and around Unter den Linden, Museumsinsel

Numbers in the margin correspond to points of interest on the Inner Berlin map.

㉓ **Unter den Linden** is repeatedly described as eastern Berlin's Champs-Élysées, but that does justice to neither street. The mile-long thoroughfare that runs east from the Brandenburger Tor into Karl-Lieb-Knecht-Strasse at Museumsinsel lacks the

Paris boulevard's grand scale and sweep, but it's lined for much of the way with imperial buildings that the French could well envy. Wartime bombing left great gaps that in the 1950s were filled in by hurriedly thrown-up blocks of buildings, and virtually all the original lime trees—the *Linden*—were either destroyed by bombs or chopped down for fuel. The replacement trees aren't mature yet, but they're a pretty sight in summer. The ugly blocks of indifferent shops are still there, but that scene is changing, too, as western entrepreneurs move in. So Unter den Linden is on the way toward recapturing its prewar appearance and charm. Don't hurry your stroll along its length; in fact, if you have time and energy, take one side of the street at a time. You'll be slowed constantly anyway by the demands for your attention made by the historic buildings from Berlin's Prussian past that stand like sentinels on either side and imperiously seek your gaze.

None of them, however, date from the beginnings of Under den Linden, which was originally a bridle path, widened by the Prince-Elector Friedrich Wilhelm in 1647 to accommodate the hunting parties he and other members of the nobility led out into the woodland that is now the Tiergarten. Grand homes arose along its length, and in the 18th century Friedrich II built an opera house, a stately library, a cathedral, and a palace for the crown prince. They are there today, some rebuilt after wartime devastation and some serving different purposes (the crown prince's palace is Berlin's renowned Humboldt University), but all contributing to a harmonious historical entity that's unique in Germany.

The first large building you'll encounter as you head east along the boulevard from Pariser Platz, in front of the Brandenburger Tor, is a monumental diplomatic "palace," the **Soviet Embassy,** now reduced—like all former embassies to East Germany—to the role of a consular mission. Behind the forbidding railings is one of the few Lenin busts you'll find these days in Berlin. One block up on the same side is eastern Berlin's newest and most expensive hotel, the Grand (with a tempting shopping arcade). Behind it you'll see the gables of the **Komische Oper,** home of the eponymous company, whose productions are known for being innovative. The **Alte Palais,** the former palace of the Emperor Wilhelm I, is next on the right, and flanking it in the middle of Unter den Linden is a striking bronze equestrian sculpture of **Friedrich II,** riding his favorite horse, Conde. The sculptor Rauch, who completed the work in 1851, decorated the plinth with reliefs of various German historical figures, mischievously positioning right under the horse's tail the heads of two outspoken critics of Friedrich II: Gotthold Lessing and Immanuel Kant. For years the sculpture was exiled to Potsdam, the ruler's favorite abode, but in 1980 the communist government apparently thought him sufficiently rehabilitated to reinstall him.

㉔ The lime-tree-framed square that recedes to the right, **Bebelplatz,** played a less happy role in German history: It was here, before the buildings that represented a high point in German culture, that Hitler's Nazi philistines burned the books of banned authors on May 11, 1933, an episode that has come to be known as the *Bücherverbrennung*. The square presents a much more cultivated face these days, flanked on one side by one of Berlin's main opera houses, the Deutsche

Staatsoper, and on the other by the delicate Baroque-style Prinzessinnenpalais (Princesses' Palace), a copy of the original from 1733. In the background sits the elegantly curved facade of the former royal library, the Alte Bibliothek, dubbed the **"Kommode"** (chest of drawers) by irreverent Berliners because of its shape. A brass plate on the outside wall recalls that Lenin did some of his early research here in 1895.

The Deutsche Staatsoper, first designed by Georg von Knobelsdorff, the architect of Friedrich II's beloved Sanssouci Palace, in 1741–43 in a combination of Rococo and Classical styles, was one of the world's first opera houses. It burned down in 1843, and Karl Ferdinand Langhans, son of Carl Gotthard Langhans, rebuilt it in the Neoclassical form you see today. It's a curiously charming building, monumental but modest beside the great structures that otherwise make up Unter den Linden. A visit to the Deutsche Staatsoper is a must even for the tone-deaf (*see* The Arts, below); tickets aren't difficult to get. *Unter den Linden 7. Box office: Open weekdays, noon–6.*

Time Out No princess lives there anymore, but you can spoil yourself royally in the gilded splendor of the **Operncafe,** an elegant café/restaurant on the ground floor of the Prinzessinenpalais. The cake display case is a spectacle to rival anything at the nearby opera house. For more substantial fare, try the **Schinkel Klause,** a tavern named after the architect Schinkel and housed in the **Palais Unter den Linden** (once the Kronprinzenpalais), on Überwallstrasse, which runs down the side of the Operncafe. The palace is now a government guest house, but the Schinkel Klause is open to all.

㉕ Just behind the Deutsche Staatsoper is **St. Hedwig's Cathedral,** a substantial, circular building that's similar to the Pantheon in Rome. Note the tiny street called Hinter der Katholische Kirche; it means "Behind the Catholic Church." When the cathedral was erected in 1747 it was the first Catholic church built in resolutely Protestant Berlin since the Reformation in the 16th century. Although Knobbelsdorff was the official architect of the church, it's thought that Friedrich II contributed substantially to its design.

㉖ On the other side of Unter den Linden you'll see a surprisingly modest Schinkel creation (his first building, in fact), the **Neue Wache,** built in the style of a Roman temple in 1816–18 as a guardhouse and given a new use after World War II as a war memorial. An eternal flame burns in the center of the small, pillared hall, and before it lie the tombs of the "unknown warrior" and an "unknown resistance fighter." Until the unification of Germany, helmeted and jack-booted East German soldiers stood guard there, and the changing of the guard was a top tourist attraction. The sight is no more—it was one of the first rituals of the East German communists to be discarded.

Just west of the Neue Wache is the palace complex of the renowned **Humboldt University.** It was built in 1748–68 as a palace for Friedrich II's brother Prince Heinrich, and in 1810 the von Humboldt brothers, Wilhelm and Alexander, founded a university within its walls. The names of the famous men of letters and science who either studied or taught here comprise an illustrious list, including Marx, Engels, Hegel, Einstein, and

Max Planck. Statues of Wilhelm and Alexander von Humboldt stand proudly before their university. On the other side of the Neue Wache, right at the end of Unter den Linden, is the former arsenal, the Zeughaus, 1695–1705. It was the first large building to grace the avenue. A masterpiece of early Baroque, it was used at the turn of the century as a hall of fame glorifying **㉗** Prusso-German militarism. Today, it's the **Deutsches Historisches Museum** (German History Museum), covering the period from 1789 to the present. Displays focus on a range of relics, including the hat Napoleon wore at the Battle of Waterloo. *Unter den Linden 2. Admission: DM 4 adults, DM 2 children. Open Thurs.–Tues. 10–6.*

Heading east you'll come to the **Karl-Liebknecht-Brücke** (formerly the Marx-Engels-Brücke), a charming bridge designed by Schinkel and punctuated by classical statues. The bridge leads into a large island, the northwestern part of which is **㉘** called **Museumsinsel** (Museum Island), on the site of one of Berlin's two original settlements, Cölln, dating back to 1237. Today, you'll find a complex of four remarkable museums here. *Admission: Varies from DM 1 to DM 8 for special exhibits (extra if you want to take photographs). Wed.–Sun. 10–6. Pergamonmuseum: Open daily 10–6. Check hours before visiting, as they can occasionally change.*

The **Altes Museum** (Old Museum; entrance Lustgarten) is an austere neoclassical building just north of Marx-Engels-Platz that features postwar East German art; its large etching and drawing collection, from the Old Masters to the present, is a treasure trove. The **Nationalgalerie** (National Gallery; entrance on Bodestrasse) houses an outstanding collection of 18th-, 19th-, and early-20th-century paintings and sculptures and often hosts special temporary exhibits. Works by Cézanne, Rodin, Degas, and one of Germany's most famous portrait artists, Max Liebermann, are part of the permanent exhibition.

Even if you aren't generally inclined toward the ancient world, make an exception for the **Pergamonmuseum** (entrance on Am Kupfergraben). It is not only the standout in this complex; it is one of Europe's greatest museums. The museum's name is derived from its principal and best-loved display, the Pergamon altar, a monumental Greek temple found in what's now Turkey and dating from 180 BC. Adorning it are finely carved figures of gods locked in battle against giants. As much as anything, perhaps, this vast structure illustrates the zeal of Germany's 19th-century archaeologists, who had it shipped piece by piece from a mountain top to Berlin. Equally impressive is the Babylonian Processional Way in the Asia Minor department. As you walk through the museum, you cannot help but wonder how they ever got away with dismantling and exporting these vast treasures.

Last in the complex is the **Bodemuseum** (entrance on Monbijoubrücke), with its superb Egyptian, Byzantine, and early Christian relics, sculpture collections, and coin gallery. The Sphinx of Hatshepsut, from around 1500 BC, is stunning, as are the Burial Cult Room and Papyrus Collection. There is also a representative collection of Italian Renaissance paintings.

Museum Island eventually will house all the state archaeological collections. For example, the Egyptian holdings currently at Charlottenburg (*see* Tour 7, below) will be united with the

Egyptian collection at the Bodemuseum, and the Far Eastern art at the Pergamonmuseum will move to Dahlem, which will concentrate on ethnological collections. The 19th-century **New Museum,** still in ruins from World War II bombings, will be rebuilt, and the Nationalgalerie will display only 19th-century paintings, including those now at the Neue Nationalgalerie at the Kulturforum (*see* Tour 2, above). The changes will be gradual and will take years to complete; visitors should contact the Berlin Tourist Office for the current status of these collections.

From the museum complex, follow the Spree Canal back to Unter den Linden and the enormous, impressive 19th-century **29** **Berlin Cathedral** (Berliner Dom). A small museum in it (entrance on Unter den Linden) records the postwar reconstruction of the building, which, at press time, had not yet been completed. If you climb the stairs, you can reach a balcony from which you can observe up close the vast nave and dome, both of which were boarded up at press time and being totally rebuilt. The impact of the sight leaves many a visitor speechless.

Continue west on Unter den Linden, turning right into Friedrichstrasse. The upper Friedrichstrasse is undergoing reconstruction. Among its landmarks are the tall **International Trade Center,** next to the Friedrichstrasse rail station, and, farther up, the **Friedrichstadtpalast,** featuring a nightclub, dancing, and occasional musical shows. Despite the rebuilding, the street still houses a number of small shops, bookstores, and neighborhood establishments. Just after crossing the Spree, turn left into Schiffbauerdamm to see the **Berliner Ensemble** (*see* The Arts, below), founded by Bertolt Brecht, which continues to be a showcase for his works. Rejoin Friedrichstrasse and walk up beyond the bend, where the street turns into the Chausseestrasse (or take the U-6 to Oranienburger Tor) to find **30** the **Brecht-Haus** and a library for Brecht scholars. *Chausseestr. 125. Admission: DM 2 adults, DM 1 children. Open Tues.–Fri. 9–3.*

Brecht is actually buried next door, along with his wife Helene Weigel and more than 100 other celebrated Berliners, in the **Dorotheenstädtischer Cemetery.** They include Hegel, Heinrich Mann, the neoclassical architects Schinkel and Schadow as well as the Berlin printer Litfass, the man who invented those stumpy cylindrical columns you'll find across Europe carrying advertisements and theater schedules.

Head back toward the center and turn left down Oranien- **31** burgerstrasse to the ruins of the massive city **synagogue,** now being restored. It's an exotic amalgam of styles, the whole faintly Middle Eastern, built between 1894 and 1905. It was largely ruined on the night of November 11, 1938, the infamous Kristalnacht (crystal night), when Nazi looters and soldiers rampaged across Germany and Austria, burning synagogues and smashing the few Jewish shops and homes left in the country. It was further ruined during the bombing of the city toward the end of the war. From here, take the subway from Oranienburger Tor back to the center of the city.

Tour 5: Kreuzberg, Schöneberg

Numbers in the margin correspond to points of interest on the Inner Berlin map.

519 M.P.H.

190 M.P.H.

75 M.P.H.

0 M.P.H.

WE LET YOU SEE EUROPE AT YOUR OWN PACE.

Regardless of your personal speed limits, Rail Europe offers everything to get you over, around and through anywhere you want in Europe. For more information, call your travel agent or **1-800-4-EURAIL.**

Rail Europe

MCI brings Europe and America closer together.

Call the U.S. for less with MCI CALL USA®.

It's easy and affordable to call home when you use MCI CALL USA!

- Less expensive than calling through hotel operators
- Available from over 65 countries and locations worldwide
- You're connected to English-speaking MCI® Operators
- Even call 800 numbers in the U.S.

Call the U.S. for less from these European locations.

Dial the toll-free access number for the country you're calling from. Give the U.S. MCI Operator the number you're calling and the method of payment: MCI Card, U.S. local phone company card, Telecom Canada Card or collect. Your call will be completed!

Austria	022-903-012	Hungary	00*800-01411	Poland	0*-01-04-800-222
Belgium	078-11-00-12	Ireland	1800-551-001	Portugal	05-017-1234
Czechoslovakia	00-42-000112	Italy	172-1022	San Marino	172-1022
Denmark	8001-0022	Liechtenstein	155-0222	Spain	900-99-0014
Finland	9800-102-80	Luxembourg	0800-0112	Sweden	020-795-922
France	19*-00-19	Monaco	19*-00-19	Switzerland	155-0222
Germany	0130-0012	Netherlands	06*-022-91-22	United Kingdom	0800-89-0222
Greece	00-800-1211	Norway	050-12912	Vatican City	172-1022

* Wait for 2nd dial tone. Collect calls not accepted on MCI CALL USA calls to 800 numbers

MCI®

Call **1-800-444-4444** in the U.S. to apply for your MCI Card® now!

Once a separate village until it was absorbed by Berlin in the 19th century, **Kreuzberg** is the largest Turkish town outside Turkey, a colorful area that immigrant workers from Anatolia and Istanbul have made their own. Racial tensions sometimes surface, but for the most part there's a live-and-let-live atmosphere in the lively streets of this precinct south of Checkpoint Charlie and north of Tempelhof airfield, and nowhere else in Berlin will the visitor receive a warmer welcome. The food is good, authentic, and cheap, and the company noisy and friendly. Especially in east Kreuzberg, restaurants and pubs jostle for space with basement discotheques and back-room delicatessens. Maybe it's not the place to stay, but you haven't seen Berlin until you've walked a street or two in Kreuzberg. Take the U-1 or U-8 line, alighting at **Kottbusser Tor.** The real heart of Kreuzberg life beats between Kottbusser Tor, Planufer, and Naunynstrasse. Walk east on Skalitzerstrasse, turn left into Mariannenstrasse, and you'll come to Muskauerstrasse, where you'll find one of Berlin's liveliest markets, the Eisenbahn-Markthalle. Visit it with a keen appetite and you won't leave disappointed or hungry. It's open daily from 7:30 AM.

The **Kreuzberg** is a hill—Berlin's highest—after which the district is named. Get there by taking the U-1 subway to Hallisches Tor and changing to the southbound U-6, toward Alt-Mariendorf. At the next stop, Mehringdamm, leave by the Kruezbergstrasse exit and you'll see the Kreuzberg on your left, crowned by an iron cross resembling a Gothic spire. Designed by Schinkel, the monument was erected in 1821 to commemorate the 1813–15 Wars of Liberation. The view from the top embraces the center of East Berlin to the north and Tempelhof airfield to the south. A vineyard on the sheltered southern slope of the Kreuzberg produces Germany's rarest wine, the Kreuzneroberger. It is produced in such small quantities that it is only served at official Berlin functions.

The district of **Schöneberg**—one of Berlin's oldest, and, like Kreuzberg, once a separate community—is bounded by Kreuzberg on the east, Wilmersdorf on the west, and the Tiergarten to the north. Although it has a colorful market, the radio and television station RIAS, a pleasant park named after the poet Kleist, a planetarium, and some good restaurants and watering holes, especially around Winterfeldtplatz, this middle-class residential area is chiefly of interest for its famous city hall, the **Rathaus Schöneberg** (Schöneberg Town Hall). If you're walking from the Kreuzberg, leave the park by the western exit on Monumentenstrasse and continue until you reach the intersection with Potsdamerstrasse on the right. Turn left into Hauptstrasse and continue south until you reach Dominicus-Strasse. Turn right here and take the first turning on your left, Elsas-Strasse. It will lead you straight to the building. From Nollendorfplatz, you can take the U-4 line to the Rathaus Schöneberg stop. Walk east along Volkspark, then turn left into Martin-Luther-Strasse. You'll see the city hall on the left.

Since the division of the two Berlins in 1948, the Rathaus Schöneberg has been home to the West Berlin Chamber of Deputies and their Senate. The Rathaus is of special interest to Americans, for it was here, on June 26, 1963, that John F. Kennedy made his memorable "Ich bin ein Berliner" speech just months before his assassination.

Completed in 1914, the Rathaus has a 237-foot-high tower from which a replica of the Liberty Bell is rung each day at noon. The bell was given by the American people as a symbol of their support for the West Berliners' struggle to preserve freedom. A document bears the signatures of 17 million Americans who pledged their solidarity with the people of West Berlin. *Rathaus Schöneberg Bell Tower. John-F.-Kennedy-Platz. Open Wed. and Sun. 10–4.*

Tour 6: Nikolaiviertel, Fischerinsel

Numbers in the margin correspond to points of interest on the Inner Berlin map.

The true heart of Berlin is a small patch of land, little more than 30 acres bordered on the east by the Spree River and with the city's oldest church, the Nikolaikirche, as its geographical and spiritual center. This is the **Nikolaiviertel,** the Nikolai quarter, a picturesque re-creation (or evocation) of old Berlin. It's just southwest of the Rotes Rathaus—cross Spandauerstrasse and you're there. By subway take U-2 from Alexanderplatz to Spittelmarkt and cross the Spree on Mühlendamm; the quarter is on the left. The area can be covered in an hour at the most, unless, of course, you linger in any of the more than 20 taverns, restaurants, and cafés that cram each of its four main alleys.

The **Nikolaikirche,** dedicated to a very important Berlin saint—Nicholas, patron of traders and fisherfolk—was built between 1230 and 1240 in solid, late-Romanesque style. Gothic refinements were added, and the twin towers weren't built until the 19th century. But wartime bombing destroyed all but the early foundation walls, rough-hewn stonework that forms the base of the rebuilt church you see today. The interior is almost entirely Gothic, but without the gloomy solemnity of so many churches of the period. Light streams through the high, arched windows, illuminating the gaily decorated interior and, incidentally, the exhibits about medieval Berlin in the side aisles and choir. *Admission: DM 1 adults, 50 pf children. Open Tues.–Fri. 9–5, weekends 9–6.*

In front of the church is an early representation in carved stone of the arms of Berlin, borne by a bear and enclosed by finely wrought iron. To one side you'll see the first of several replicas of historic old houses that crowd the area, the **Knoblauchhaus,** once the home of a wealthy silk merchant, Christian Knoblauch. The house now contains a museum tracing the family history (which is very much a history of Berlin) and a wine tavern, the Historische Weinstube. Head along Poststrasse in the direction of Mühlendamm and you'll find another interesting tavern on the corner. It's called Zur Rippe (The Rib), and if you look above the entrance you'll see why: There's a huge rib bone hanging there. The story goes that it's a giant's rib. At any rate, by all appearances it's certainly a real rib. Don't be tempted to stop for a drink there (the pub itself is disappointing, marred by a slot machine and laminated tables), but walk a few yards up Mühlendamm toward the Spree and then take your pick of a number of delightful restaurants and cafés spread out along the riverbank.

On the corner is Berlin's finest Rococo house, the **Ephraimpalais.** Friedrich II had it built in 1761–66 for his court jeweler, Veitel Ephraim. Ephraim was Jewish, and in 1935 the Nazis tore his beautiful house down, ostensibly to make way for road improvements. But in 1987 the house, actually a small palace, was rebuilt using pieces of the original facade that were found in West Berlin. Today it houses an art gallery (open Tues.–Fri. 9–5, weekends 10–6) and an excellent restaurant.

Time Out   If you haven't already stopped off at one of the cafés lining the Nikolaiviertel's riverbank, Spreeufer, round out your tour of the area by hunting out the **Zum Nussbaum** tavern, sitting snugly at the corner of Propststrasse and the alley called Am Nussbaum, right by the church. A replica, this was Berlin's oldest inn, and was serving its fine Berlin brew long before Friedrich II ascended the throne.

Head north to Rathausstrasse, then turn left. After crossing the Spree, walk left into Breitestrasse. The immediate area possesses an array of fine old buildings, some rebuilt, some actually moved to this location from elsewhere in Berlin. Continue on Breitestrasse, and after crossing Mühlendamm, you'll be
❸❻ in the **Fischerinsel** area, which retains some of its medieval character. It provides a refreshing change, too, from some of the heavy and uninspired postwar architecture.

Cross over the Gertraudenstrasse and wander up the south
❸❼ bank of the canal to the red-brick **Märkisches Museum,** the museum of city history. It includes a special section on the city's theatrical past and a fascinating collection of mechanical musical instruments. These are demonstrated on Sun. 11–noon, Wed. 3–4. Next door to the museum live the (live) bears, Berlin's symbol. *Am Köllnischen Park 5. Admission: DM 2 adults, DM 1 children. Open Wed.–Sun. 10–6.*

Tour 7: Charlottenburg

Numbers in the margin correspond to points of interest on the Inner Berlin map.

Before it was swallowed up by Greater Berlin in 1920, **Charlottenburg** was the wealthiest municipality in all of Prussia. Wealth poured into the area because of its royal associations, which began with the patronage of Prussia's King Friedrich I in 1701. He established a royal country residence in Schloss Lützenburg and then renamed the palace Charlottenburg, after his wife Sophie Charlotte. The area around the palace, built in 1695, grew into a small town, graced by the homes of palace officials, and it acquired the name of the palace. Friedrich was
❸❽ its first Lord Mayor. **Schloss Charlottenburg** and its gardens became the showpiece of the former West Berlin, rivalled now by the newly accessible architectural treasures of the eastern part of the city but still an imperative stop in any visitor's itinerary.

As additional buildings were annexed to the original palace— and Berlin grew—this sumptuous palace became the city residence for the Prussian rulers. It has on occasion been referred to as Berlin's very own Versailles. Indeed, some claim that it was Napoléon, when he invaded Berlin in 1806, who first made the comparison to the Sun King's spectacular château near Paris. The comparison hardly seems appropriate. Charlottenburg is on a smaller, more intimate scale than Versailles. Its proportions are restrained; the formal gardens are not nearly as vast.

Nor are you likely to encounter the kind of crowds that flock to Versailles. But you are sure to be suitably impressed.

A full day is not too much time to devote to Charlottenburg. In addition to the apartments of the Prussian nobility, there are the landscaped gardens to be visited, and several excellent museums set within and just outside the grounds.

Friedrich II—Frederick the Great—was captivated by Charlottenburg, and he made a number of additions, such as the dome and several wings in the Rococo style. In time the complex evolved into the massive royal domain you see today.

The palace was severely damaged during World War II but has been painstakingly restored. Many of the original furnishings and works of art survived the war and are on display.

Behind heavy iron gates, the Court of Honor—the courtyard in front of the palace—is dominated by a fine Baroque statue, the *Reiterstandbild des Grossen Kurfürsten* (the Equestrian Statue of the Great Elector). A 156-foot-high domed tower capped by a gilded statue of Fortune rises above the main entrance to the palace.

Inside, in the main building, the suites of Friedrich I and his wife, Sophie Charlotte, are furnished in the prevailing style of the era. Paintings include royal portraits by Antoine Pesne, a noted court painter of the 18th century. On the first floor you can visit the Oak Gallery, the early 18th-century Palace Chapel, and the suites of Frederick Wilhelm II and Frederick Wilhelm III, furnished in the Biedermeier style.

Visits to the royal apartments are by guided tour only. Tours are in German, but are worth taking even if you don't speak the language; they leave every hour on the hour from 9 to 4. Parks and gardens can be visited for free and offer a pleasant respite from sightseeing.

A gracious staircase leads up to the sumptuous State Dining Room and the 138-foot-long Golden Gallery. West of the staircase are the rooms of Frederick the Great, in which the king's extravagant collection of works by Watteau, Chardin, and Pesne are displayed. In one glass cupboard you'll see the coronation crown, stripped of its jewels by the king, who gave the most valuable gemstones to his wife. Also in the so-called New Wing is the National Gallery's collection of masterpieces from 19th-century German painters such as Caspar David Friedrich, the leading member of the German Romantic school. *Schloss Charlottenburg. Luisenpl., tel. 030/320–911. Admission (includes guided tour): DM 7. Open Tues.–Fri. 9–5, weekends 10–5.*

The park surrounding the palace was first laid out in 1697. Destroyed during the war, it has since been restored to its original Baroque design. An avenue of cypress trees leads to the lake.

There are several buildings in the park that deserve particular attention, among which are the Belvedere, a teahouse overlooking the lake and Spree River that now houses a collection of Berlin porcelain, and the Schinkel Pavilion behind the palace near the river. The pavilion, modeled on a villa in Naples where the king stayed in 1822, was designed in 1824–25 by Schinkel on an appropriately intimate scale. It houses paintings by Caspar David Friedrich and late-18th-century furniture. Also of interest in the park is the mausoleum, also by Schinkel, which contains the tombs of King Frederick Wilhelm II and Queen Louise.

Just to the south of the palace are four small, distinguished museums. The first, across from the palace, is the **Ägyptisches Museum** (Egyptian Museum). The building, once the east guardhouse and residence of the king's bodyguard, is now home to the famous portrait bust of the exquisite Queen Nefertiti. The 3,300-year old Egyptian queen is the centerpiece of a collection of works that spans Egypt's history from 4,000 BC and includes one of the best preserved mummies outside Cairo. *Schloss Str. 70, tel. 030/320–911. Admission: DM 4 adults, DM 2 children. Open Mon.–Thurs. 9–5, weekends 10–5.*

Opposite the Ägyptisches Museum in the former west guardhouse is the **Antikenmuseum** (Antique Museum). The collection comprises ceramics and bronzes as well as everyday utensils from ancient Greece and Rome and a number of Greek vases from the 6th to 4th century BC. Also on display is a collection of Scythian gold and silver ware and jewelry found in the Mediterranean basin. *Schloss Str. 1, tel. 030/320–911. Admission free. Open Mon.–Thurs. 9–5, weekends 10–5.*

Next door to the Antikenmuseum is the delightful **Bröhan-Museum,** which, with its collection of Jugendstil and Art Deco decorative arts in period settings, provides for some a welcome break from art of the ancients. The porcelain is particularly noteworthy. Special exhibitions are on display in an airy gallery two flights up. *Schloss Str. 1a, tel. 030/3214029. Admission: DM 4. Open Tues., Wed., Fri.–Sun. 10–6, Thurs. 10–9.*

The final museum, the **Museum für Vor- und Frügeschichte** (Museum of Pre- and Proto-history), is located in the western extension of the palace opposite Klausener Platz. The museum depicts the stages of the evolution of man from 1,000,000 BC to the Bronze Age. *Spandauer Damm, tel. 030/320–911. Admission free. Open Mon.–Thurs. 9–5, Sat.–Sun. 10–5.*

All the collections at Charlottenburg (except that at the Bröhan-Museum) will eventually be moving: the ancient art to Museumsinsel, the 19th-century paintings to the Kulturforum. The process will be gradual; contact the Berlin Tourist Office for the latest information on closings.

One of Charlottenburg's curiosities is a late-19th-century mansion on the upper part of Kurfürstendamm (no. 218), formerly the Chinese Embassy. The Chinese moved out in 1980, leaving behind a richly furnished house full of antique furniture, silk carpets, lamps, and exquisite ceramics. The house, with all its treasures, passed into private ownership and now includes a fine Chinese restaurant, perhaps the only one in Berlin with landmark status (*see* Dining, below), and a café and chocolate shop.

Outlying Sights and Attractions

Numbers in the margin correspond to points of interest on the Greater Berlin map.

Although the historic and cultural core of eastern Berlin is to be found along the central stretch of the Spree, amid the monumental architecture on and around Unter den Linden and in the picturesque alleys and corners of the Nikolai quarter, the center of everyday life is farther east, in the hilltop **Prenzlauer Berg** district. Here is where the typical eastern Berliner resides, in a tiny, poorly serviced apartment, or, if he is lucky or has good connections, a chic one. Here is where the average eastern Berlin worker has his favorite *Kneipe*, or neighborhood pub, and where the young and upwardly mobile flit from disco to basement dive. Factory worker and former communist executive rub shoulders on its drab streets or in its few well-restored boulevards.

To search for what makes this fascinating area tick, start from Alexanderplatz (bus 100 from Breitscheidplatz gets you there), walking along Karl-Liebknecht-Strasse, which becomes Prenzlauerallee. About halfway up the hill, turn left into Wörtherstrasse, then left again into Rykestrasse. Ahead of you **❶** you'll see the **Prenzlauer Berg** itself, a hilltop crowned by a 150-year-old brick water tower. On the way there, at the end of Rykestrasse, you'll find a synagogue that escaped the worst of the Nazi terror, a 100-year-old brick structure with fine tile decoration and a courtyard that offers a haven of peace from the bustle of the Prenzlauer Berg street scene.

The "Berg" is actually a small park, with steps leading up to the water tower. At its base you'll find a plaque commemorating a group of anti-Nazi activists who were killed here in 1933 by Hitler's stormtroopers. Leave the park by the opposite side and head north along Kollwitzstrasse, to **Käthe-Kollwitz-Platz,** named after one of Berlin's best-loved figures, the artist Käthe Kollwitz, whose images of the proletarian world around her are filled with genuine pathos. She lived nearby (her home was destroyed in an air raid) and died a few weeks before war's end. In the center of the small Parisian-style park that forms the square you'll find an utterly charming sculpture by the artist, *The Mother*, bulky but graceful and throbbing with character. To see her work, visit the Käthe Kollwitz Museum in western Berlin.

Time Out | If you're thirsty after climbing the Prenzlauer Berg, the ice cream café on Käthe-Kollwitz-Platz serves not only *Eis* but a good cup of coffee and a locally brewed beer. In summer, you can sit in the small garden in front of the café.

At the corner of Käthe-Kollwitz-Platz and Wörtherstrasse begins one of eastern Berlin's most extraordinary streets, **Husemannstrasse,** which alone is a highlight of any visit to this part of the city. The stately houses on Husemannstrasse were built toward the end of the 19th century using, for the first time anywhere in Berlin, factory-produced stucco facades. In the postwar years of neglect and municipal penury, Husemannstrasse went the way of the rest of East Berlin. But in 1986 East Germany's communist rulers ordered it to be returned to its former glory, to the pastel-colored harmony you see today. But don't walk too far down Husemannstrasse—the money for its restoration ran out and only half the street was completed.

That completed half, however, is magnificent, a breath of fresh air after the uniform drabness of its surroundings, with elegant dark-green, wrought-iron balconies adding a whiff of Paris. A comparison with a film set isn't out of place, either, for if

Greater Berlin

KEY

Rail Lines

Subway Lines

AE American Express Office

0   500 yards
0   500 meters

FRIEDRICHS-HAIN

Penzlauer Berg 1

PRENZLAUER BERG

NEUKÖLLN

TEMPEL-HOF

KREUZ-BERG

INNER BERLIN

TIERGARTEN

FORMER LOCATION OF BERLIN WALL

STADTRING GOERDELER

CHARLOTTEN-BURG

Zitadelle 5

WILMERS-DORF

Grunewald 3

ZEHLEN-DORF

Dahlem Museum Complex 2

Grosser Wannsee 4

Havel

Bersarin Str.
Dimitroff Str.
Frankfurter Allee
Warschauer Str.
Prenzlauer Allee
Karl-Marx-Str.
Unter Den Linden
Friedrich Str.
Sonnen Allee
Karl Marx Str.
Buschkrug Str.
Oranien Str.
Skalitzer Str.
Hermann Str.
Urban Str.
Silberstein Str.
Grade Str.
Columbia Damm
Gneisenau Str.
Marien Dorfer Damm
Germania Str.
Tempelhofer Damm
Teltie Str.
Arnulf Str.
Str. Des 17 Juni
Invaliden Str.
Moabit Alt
Bismarck Str.
March Str.
Beusse Str.
Duden Str.
Yorck Str.
Potsdamer Str.
Sachsen Damm
Grunewald Str.
Haupt Str.
Grazer Damm
Rhein Str.
Stieglitzer Damm
Bundes Allee
Letzenburger Allee
Wiesbadener Str.
Kant Str.
Kurfürstendamm
Kaiser Damm
Spandauer Damm
Reichs Str.
Hohenzollern Damm
Königin-Luise Str.
Clay Allee
Koenigs Allee
Eichenschloss
Berliner Str.
U.D.
Charlottenburger
Heerstrasse
Teufelsee Chaussee
Verbindungschaussee
AVUS
Argentinische Allee
Fischer hütten Str.
Huhten Weg
Fischer hütten Str.
Spanische Allee
Nonnendamm
Juliusturm
Ruhlebener Str.
Seegefelder Str.
Brunsbüteler Damm
Magistrats W. Heerstrasse
Weinmeisterhorn
Potsdammer Chaussee
Gatower Str.
Havelchaussee
Kladower Damm
N

you peep into the backyards of Husemannstrasse you'll see the peeling parts that the painters and restorers didn't reach.

The street contains two offbeat museums: the **Friseurmuseum,** a hair-dressing museum claiming to be the only one of its kind in the world, and the **Museum Berliner Arbeiterleben um 1900** (Museum of Berlin Workers' Life Around 1900). In the Friseurmuseum (Husemannstrasse 8) you step into another, more leisurely era, when even the back-street bureaucrats of Berlin popped into the barber's shop for their morning shave. Here you'll find re-created Jugendstil barber shops, with instruments that once belonged to Kaiser Wilhelm's royal barber, and a very early example of the safety razor that changed the shaving scene so radically. Lovingly mounted snippets from the hair of Iron Chancellor Bismarck and (so it's claimed) Goethe are among the museum's many curiosities. *Husemann-str. 8. Admission free. Open Mon.–Wed. 10–5. Guided tours: Mon., Tues. 10, 12, 1, and 5.*

The Museum Berliner Arbeiterleben um 1900 is two houses up, and gives a fascinating picture of Berlin working-class life around the turn of the century. *Husemannstr. 12. Admission: DM 2 adults, DM 1 children. Open Tues.–Thurs., Sat. 10–6, Fri. 10–3.*

Husemannstrasse is also full of small shops and boutiques of a quality seldom seen in eastern Berlin. Smokers should make for no. 4, a beautifully preserved tobacco shop whose dark-paneled interior is redolent with the aroma of fine cigars and rare tobaccos. On the other side of the street, at no. 11, the Raritäts Galerie is packed with small antiques and objets d'art. On the corner, a good Berlin beer is served at the Budike bar, and in the evenings, the Jugendstil-decorated Cafe-Stube attracts a stylish eastern Berlin crowd.

Return to Käthe-Kollwitz-Platz and follow Kollwitzstrasse down the hill to where it joins with Schönhauserallee, the district's main street. Return a short distance along Schönhauserallee and at no. 23 you'll find the Prenzlauer Berg's **Jewish Cemetery,** where the portraitist Max Liebermann and the opera composer Giacomo Meyerbeer are buried. Turn back now toward the city center and on the way you'll pass one of Berlin's most charming memorials, a surprisingly humorous one in such drab surroundings. The sculptured group portrays Alois Senefelder, pioneer of lithography, sternly watching two urchins scribbling his name on the base of his statue. The pair have written his name in reverse, and one of them is holding a piece of chalk, a witty reference to Senefelder's discovery that figures and outlines written with chalk on a certain kind of slate absorbed color, creating a form of printing surface. At the bottom of Schönhauserallee you'll cross into Rosa-Luxemburg-Strasse, which leads back to Alexanderplatz.

Time Out Stop in at the **Theaterklause** (Rosa-Luxemburg-Strasse 39), opposite the famous eastern Berlin theater, the Volksbühne. It's a typical eastern Berlin dining room, with few flourishes, but the food is wholesome and cheap (the Steak Strindberg costs DM 10), and in the evenings you might be sharing a table with one of the Volksbühne cast.

Eastern Berlin has its Museumsinsel; western Berlin's version is Dahlem, a complex of outstanding museums in the neighbor-

hood of the same name (take the U-2 subway from Wittenbergplatz toward Krumme Lanke and alight at Dahlem-Dorf
station). You emerge into a leafy district that seems more like a
sleepy village. Walk south on Fabeckstrasse and enter the
2 **Dahlem Museum Complex** to your right at either Arnimallee
23–27 or Lansstrasse 8.

The complex consists of eight museums, all but one under one
gigantic roof. The greatest of these are the **Gemäldegalerie**
(Picture Gallery), the **Kupferstichkabinett** (Drawings and
Prints Collection), the **Museum fur Völkerkunde** (Ethnographic Museum), and the **Skulpturengalerie** (Sculpture Gallery). By
1997, the displays at Dahlem will be devoted exclusively to ethnographic art, with the Gemäldegalerie and Skulpturengalerie
collections moving to the Kulturform (*see* Tour 2, above) and
the Islamic collection shifting to Museumsinsel (*see* Tour 4,
above). The changes will be gradual, with individual galleries
closing. Contact the Berlin Tourist Office for the latest status
of each museum.

Begin your tour with the **Gemäldegalerie.** One of Germany's
finest picture galleries, it houses a broad selection of European
paintings from the 13th to 18th century. Rembrandt devotees
will be particularly pleased to find the world's second largest
Rembrandt collection located on the second floor.

Several rooms on the first floor are reserved for paintings by
German masters, among them, Dürer, Cranach, and Holbein.
An adjoining gallery houses the works of the Italian masters—
Botticelli, Titian, Giotto, Filippo Lippi, and Raphael—and another gallery on the first floor is devoted to paintings by Dutch
masters of the 15th and 16th centuries: van Eyck, Bosch, Brue-
ghel, van Dyck, and van der Weyden.

Flemish and Dutch paintings from the 17th century are displayed on the floor above. In the Rembrandt section, where
there are 21 paintings by the master, you can see "The Man
with the Golden Helmet," a painting formerly attributed to
Rembrandt that has since proved by radioactive testing to have
been the work of another artist of the same era. *Arnimallee 23–
27, tel. 030/83011. Admission: DM 4 adults, DM 2 children.
Open Tues.–Fri. 9–5, weekends 10–5.*

The **Kupferstichkabinett** (Drawings and Prints Collection),
which includes European woodcuts and engravings from the
15th to 18th century, several pen-and-ink drawings by Dürer,
150 drawings by Rembrandt, and a photographic archive is
closed until summer 1993, when it will reopen in a new building
at the Kulturforum.

The **Museum für Völkerkunde** (Ethnographic Museum) is internationally famous for its arts and artifacts from Africa, Asia,
the South Seas, and ancient America. American visitors home-
sick for a taste of their own history should look out for the
North American Indian wigwams and the feather cape that
once belonged to Hawaii's 18th-century King Kamehameha I.
Also of interest is the display of native huts from New Guinea
and New Zealand. *Entrance: Lansstr. 8, tel. 030/83011. Open
Tues.–Fri. 9–5, weekends 10–5. Admission free.*

The **Skulpturengalerie** (Sculpture Gallery) houses Byzantine
and European sculpture from the 3rd to 18th century. Included
in its collection is Donatello's *Madonna and Child*, sculpted in

1422. *Entrance: Arnimallee 23–27. Admission free. Open Tues.–Fri. 9–5, weekends 10–5.*

Beyond the tour of monuments, museums, and other aspects relating to the Wall and the divided city, no visit to Berlin would be complete without seeing the vast world of lakes and greenery along its western extremities. In no other city has such an expanse of uninterrupted natural surroundings been preserved within city limits.

Along the city's fringe are some 60 lakes, connected by rivers, streams, and canals, in a verdant setting of meadows, woods, and forests. Excursion steamers ply the water wonderland of the Wannsee and Havel. (*See* Guided Tours, above, for details.) You can tramp for hours through the green belt of the Grunewald. On weekends in spring and fall and daily in summer the Berliners are out in force, swimming, sailing their boats, tramping through the woods, riding horseback. To the north, close to the line of the old barbed-wire political boundary, there are still a few working farms. Time and progress seem to have passed right by the rustic village of Lubars.

❸ Grunewald is the playground of the western half of the city, an expanse of woodland and lakes in which you could spend a week's holiday without doubling your tracks. A weekend is all most Berliners can manage, however, and on fine-weather Saturdays and Sundays in both winter and summer the area is invaded by walkers, joggers, cyclists, sunbathers, and swim-**❹** mers. The area's largest lake, the **Grosser Wannsee**—actually an arm of the Havel River—has Berlin's biggest bathing beach, a sandy shore as wide and long as many along the Mediterranean. There are several smaller lakes tucked away in remote corners of the Grunewald. Amazingly, most of them are within yards of bustling Berlin streets and highways. The whole area is bisected by Germany's first motor-racing track, the Avus, which is now the main highway between downtown Berlin and Potsdam. The 9-km (5.5-mile) stretch was opened in 1921, and in 1937 racing star Bernd Rosemeyer established a world record of 276.3 kph (166 mph) on it. The highway is still used as a racing track for twice-yearly meets; some cynics say it never has lost its racetrack status with motoring Berliners. So if you drive to Grunewald and the Wannsee, beware. Otherwise, travel there on the S-1 or S-3 S-bahn lines.

The Wannsee and the Havel River are crisscrossed by excursion boats, and you'll find one landing pier on the bridge near the Grunewald S-bahn station. The bridge marks the boundary between the Grosser Wannsee and the much smaller **Kleiner Wannsee**, a narrow stretch of water lined by luxurious villas. On the northern bank you can visit the grave of the tragic German poet Heinrich von Kleist, at the spot where he killed himself in November 1811 in a suicide pact with his lover Henriette Vogel.

About a mile through the woods (follow the signs) lies the lovely **Pfaueninsel** (Peacock Island), idyllically set in a wide arm of the Havel. The island gets its name from the peacocks that the Prussian King Friedrich Wilhelm II released there after taking over the property in 1793, and there are still scores of them living wild in the undergrowth. Before the king fell under the spell of the island, the Berlin alchemist Johann Künkel von Löwenstein had tried to make gold in a secret workshop there, and although all his efforts failed, he did manage to produce a beautiful ruby-colored glass. Examples of his invention can be seen in the extravagant folly of a castle King Friedrich Wilhelm II built on the southern tip of the island for his mistress, Countess Lichtenau. She never lived there, however, for shortly after the castle was completed the king died. The castle itself has long outlived both, a gleaming white replica of what its original owner described as a "ruined Roman country mansion," sitting uncomfortably in the lush green vegetation like something from a Hollywood film set. *Admission: DM 3 adults, DM 1.50 children. Open daily Apr.–Sept. 9–5, Oct. 9–4.*

Time Out In the woods on the mainland opposite the castle (there's a frequent, cheap ferry service to and from the Pfaueninsel) is an entrancing country restaurant, a historic survivor from an earlier, leisured age: the **Blockhaus Nikolskoe,** built in Russian dacha style in 1819 by King Friedrich Wilhelm III for his daughter Charlotte and her husband, Czar Nicholas, and subsequently used by the Czar's coachmen and ostlers. It's an ideal spot for lunch or afternoon tea, with a lovely view of the water. The wine list, by the way, is excellent.

Other points of interest on the banks of the Havel and the Wannsee include the Kaiser-Wilhelm memorial tower, better known as the **Grunewaldturm,** built in red-brick Märkish style in 1897–98 in memory of Kaiser Wilhelm I. You can enjoy a fine view of the area from the observation platform 450 feet up, beneath the tower's turret.

Of all Berlin's many bridges none grabs the imagination as completely as the **Glienicker Brücke** over the Havel River between Wannsee and the Jungfernsee. Until November 1989, the fortified border between East and West Berlin ran across the center of the bridge, which became the established point for exchanging espionage agents. Many a Western spy came in from the cold across the Glienicker Brücke. Today the historic cast-iron bridge is a main traffic route between downtown Berlin and Potsdam. Above the bridge rises one of Berlin's most beautiful parks, the **Volkspark Klein-Glienicke,** with its elegant little palace, the **Schloss Klein-Glienicke** (Konigstr., tel. 030/805–3041; not open to the public). The palace was built on the orders of the Prussian Prince Carl, who asked the famous Schinkel and other Berlin architects and builders to create for him a Berlin version of the kind of country house he had admired on a tour of Italy. Schinkel's influence is everywhere to be found in the palace's harmonious mixture of Neoclassical and Romantic styles.

Schinkel went on to exercise his fantasy in the park itself, building pavilions at two vantage points and calling them Kleine Neugierde and Grosse Neugierde—Little Curiosity and Big Curiosity. Although the industrialization of nearby Potsdam has somewhat marred the vista, one can still enjoy a magnificent panorama of the Havel, Wannsee, and beyond.

Time Out King Friedrich Wilhelm IV married a Bavarian princess in 1823 and built a country house for her in the style of her homeland on the edge of the park, beside a tranquil pool called the Moorlake. Later it became a hunting lodge favored by the Hohenzollern rulers, and today it's a charming restaurant, the **Wirtshaus Moorlake.** In summer, you can dine and drink outside, in a pretty garden beside the lake. In winter, the oak-beamed interior encloses you in a warm welcome (*see* Dining, below).

North of this area is **Spandau,** best known, of course, for the prison that held, among other convicted Nazi War criminals, Rudolf Hess. Hitler's deputy remained there until his death, which occurred under mysterious circumstances. Hess was Spandau's last prisoner, and the jail has been torn down (it was located at Wilhelmstrasse 23), although the story of Hess still hangs over this otherwise quite bourgeois district of Berlin. Residents wince when they hear Spandau described as a district of Berlin, and you'll hear locals talk about "going up to the city" whenever they set off for a shopping trip downtown. When the foundation stone of the Spandau city hall was laid in 1911, a plea was made to the Kaiser to "protect us from Great Berlin," and although Berlin's rapid growth engulfed Spandau in 1920, there's still a strong spirit of municipal independence in its attractive streets.

Symbolic of Spandau's aggressive local patriotism is its unusual castle, the sturdy **Zitadelle** (reached by the U-7 line to the Zitadelle station), built by the city's princely rulers in 1560–94 in the Gothic style. You can set back the clock to those early times in the vaulted restaurant within the Zitadelle's massive tower, the Juliusturm, an earlier structure from the 12th century, where "medieval" banquets are served nightly (*see* Historische Gaststätte auf der Zitadelle in Dining, below). The tower once held the Imperial War Treasure, from 1874–1919: some 120 million gold marks, most of which was paid to France after Germany's defeat in World War I.

Spandau stands at the confluence of Berlin's two rivers, the Spree and the Havel, and it's a center for Berlin water sports enthusiasts. There are very pleasant walks along the riverbanks, and Spandau's old town center, Altstadt, beckons with boutiques, small shops, restaurants, and cafés.

Berlin for Free

Street entertainers are a fixture in every German city scene, of course, but the best seem to congregate in Berlin. They liven up **Breitscheidplatz,** parts of the **Ku'damm,** and **Tauenzianstrasse.** It's free entertainment, but a mark or two thrown into an upturned hat or open violin case is always appreciated.

Classical music fans can enjoy free **organ recitals** at most Berlin churches; check the calendar of events outside every church entrance or phone 030/319–00180 for concert schedules. Organ recitals are given most Saturdays at 4:30 at eastern Berlin's Marienkirche, on the edge of Alexanderplatz. Berlin's radio and television stations RIAS (tel. 030/85030) and SFB (tel. 030/303–11123) sometimes issue free tickets to **concert rehearsals** throughout the city.

What to See and Do with Children

Top of the list of children's attractions in Berlin is, of course, the **Zoologischer Garten,** one of the world's best zoos. The reunification of Berlin means the city now has two zoos. Eastern Berlin's **Tierpark Berlin,** at Am Tierpark 125 (U-5 to Tierpark station) is much smaller than the more famous zoo in the west but, as the Germans say, *"Klein aber fein"* (small but fine). *Admission: DM 5 adults, DM 2 children. Open Mon.–Sat. 9 AM–dusk.*

All Berlin parks have **playgrounds** and **adventure areas;** the best in western Berlin are in the Freizeitpark Tegel, Volkspark Rehberge, Volkspark Hasenheide, and, in eastern Berlin, Treptower Park.

On a wet day, try the **Museum für Verkehr und Technik** in Kreuzberg. The history of mechanized transport is traced in fascinating detail, and among the examples of power sources is a fully operational solar-energy installation. *Trebbinerstr. 9. Admission: DM 3.50 adults, DM 1.50 children. Open Tues.– Fri. 9–5:30, weekends 10–6. U-bahn: Gleisdreieck or Möckernbrücke.*

Another museum that can't fail to please youngsters is the **Hundemuseum** in eastern Berlin's Blankenburg, where dogs and everything canine are the exclusive theme. *Alt Blankenburg 33. Admission: DM 2 adults, DM 1 children. Open Tues., Thurs., Sat. 3–6, Sun. 11–5. S-bahn: Blankenburg.*

The **Panorama** cinema in the center of western Berlin shows a half-hour film about Berlin, with a 360-degree screen and six-channel sound. *Budapesterstrasse 38. Show times every hour 11 AM–10 PM. Admission: DM 10 adults, DM 8 children.*

Star-struck children can take their pick from two excellent planetariums. The **Planetarium am Insulaner** in Schöneberg has lectures only. *Münsterdamm 90. Lectures: 7 PM and 9 PM Tues. and Thurs.–Sat. at 9 PM, and Sun. at 3, 4, 6, and 9 PM. Admission: DM 5 adults, DM 3 children. S-bahn: Priesterweg.*

In eastern Berlin, there's the **Zeiss-Grossplanetarium** in Ernst-Thälmann-Park. *Prenzlauerallee 80. Admission: DM 4 adults, DM 2 children. Open Wed.–Sun. 1–8 PM. S-bahn: Prenzlaurerallee.*

Berlin has the world's first teddy bear museum, the **Teddy-Museum,** at Kurfürstendamm-Karree, admittedly as much an attraction for adult antiques collectors as for children. *Kurfürstendamm 206. Open Wed.–Mon. 3–10.*

Children will love the collection of dollhouses and antique toys on display at the **Museum für Deutsche Volkskunde,** part of the Dahlem Museum Complex (Dahlem-Dorf U-bahn station). They might not want to be reminded of school, but the **Schulmuseum,** Wallstrasse 32, gives an eye-opening and often amusing insight into classroom life of earlier centuries.

Off the Beaten Track

While **trams** are still an essential part of the transport system in eastern Berlin, only one line still exists in the western part of the city. It runs between Nollendorfplatz and Potsdamerstrasse, and for DM 1 (at press time, the price of a single ticket) you can join the locals and ride a piece of history.

Western Berliners and tourists rarely venture to eastern Berlin's **Müggelsee,** the largest lake in that part of the city. It's not really off-the-beaten-track territory, particularly at weekends, but here you'll be able to observe the eastern Berliner at play.

Berlin's *Hinterhöfe*—the backyards of city apartment blocks—
are where the real life of this amazing city is to be found. So say
those in the know, including the cultural tour operators Kultur-
Kontor (Savignyplatz 9–10, tel. 030/310–888), which organizes
"Hinterhöfe" tours.

Sightseeing Checklist

Points of interest discussed in Exploring, above, are indicated.

Museums **Brecht-Haus** (*see* Tour 4, Exploring, above). Bertold Brecht's
former home is now a museum devoted to the life and work of
the great playwright of the proletariat. *Chausseestr. 125, tel.
030/282–3417. Admission: DM 2 adults, DM 1 children. Open
Tues.–Fri. 9–3. U-bahn: Oranienburger Tor.*

Dahlem Museum Complex (*see* Outlying Sights, above). The
complex consists of the Gemaldegalerie, Skulpturengalerie,
Kupferstichkabinett, Museum für Indische Kunst, Museum für
Islamische Kunst, Museum für Ostasiatische Kunst, and Museum fur Völkerkunde. *Entrances: Lansstr. 8 and Arnimallee
23–27, tel. 030/83011. Admission: DM 4 adults, DM 2 children.
Mon.–Thurs. 9–5, weekends 10–5. U-bahn: Dahlem-Dort.*

Haus am Checkpoint Charlie, (*see* Tour 1, Exploring, above).
This museum examines the history of the Berlin Wall and documents the most daring escapes over (and under) it. *Friedrichstr. 44, tel. 030/251–1031. Admission: DM 7.50 adults, DM
4 children. Open daily 9 AM–10 PM. U-bahn: Kochstrasse.*

Kunstgewerbemuseum, (*see* Tour 2, Exploring, above). This
museum surveys arts and crafts from medieval times to the
present. *Tiergartenstr. 6, tel. 030/266–2629. Admission: DM 4
adults, DM 2 children. Open Tues.–Fri. 9–5, weekends 10–5.
Buses 341, 129, 148, 284, 187. U-bahn: Potsdamerplatz.*

Märkisches Museum (*see* Tour 6, Exploring, above). Eastern
Berlin's cultural-historical museum contains exhibits on the
prehistory of the Berlin area, Berlin's history from 1307–1848,
and the development of Berlin art, handicrafts, and theater.
*Am Kollnischen Park 5, tel. 030/270–0514. Admission: DM 2
adults, DM 1 children. Open Wed.–Sun. 10–6. U-bahn:
Märkisches Museum.*

Deutsches Historisches Museum (*see* Tour 4, Exploring, above).
This museum of German history has in the past emphasized
revolutionary movements of the 19th and 20th centuries. All
the galleries on the GDR have been closed down, but plans are
brewing to replace them with a new exhibition, which will be
written and displayed according to Western, democratic think-
ing. This will not take place, however, until 1996. *Unter den
Linden 2, tel. 030/200–941. Admission: DM 4 adults, children
DM 2. Open Thurs.–Tues. 10–6. U-bahn: Französischestr.*

Museum fur Naturkunde. Eastern Berlin's outstanding natural
history museum is part of Humboldt University. *Invalidenstr.
43, tel. 030/289–72540. Admission: DM 3 adults, 1.50 children.
Open daily Tues.–Sun. 9:30–5. U-bahn: Oranienburger Tor.*

Museumsinsel (*see* Tour 4, Exploring, above). Eastern Berlin's
major museum complex, on a Spree River island, consists of the
Altes Museum, Bodemuseum, Nationalgalerie, and Pergamonmuseum. *Bodestr. 1–3, tel. 030/220–0381. Admission: varies*

from free to DM 8 for special exhibits. Open Wed.–Sun. 10–6. Pergamonmuseum: daily 10–6. U-bahn: Friedrichstr.

Musikinstrumenten-Museum (*see* Tour 2, Exploring, above). This historical collection of musical instruments run by the State Institute for Musical Research includes an original Wurlitzer organ, which is demonstrated every Saturday at noon. *Tiergartenstr. 1, tel. 030/254–810. Admission free. Open Tues.–Fri. 9–5, weekends 10–5. Buses 129, 142, 148, 248, 341.*

Neue Nationalgalerie (*see* Tour 2, Exploring, above). Art of the 19th and 20th centuries is on display. *Potsdamerstr. 50, tel. 030/266–2662. Admission: DM 4 adults, DM 2 children. Open Tues.–Fri. 9–5, weekends 10–5. Buses 341, 129, 148, 284.*

Schinkelmuseum (*see* Tour 1, Exploring, above). Housed in the Friedrichswerdersche Kirche by Schinkel, the museum is devoted to the work of the Neoclassical architect. *Werderstr., tel. 030/208–1323. Admission: DM 1 adults, 50 pf children. Open Wed.–Sun. 10–6. U-bahn: Spittelmarkt.*

Schloss Charlottenburg Museums (*see* Tour 7, Exploring, above). These consist of the Ägyptisches Museum (Schloss Str. 70, tel. 030/320–911), Antikenmuseum and Schatzkammer (Schloss Str. 1, tel. 030/320–911), Galerie der Romantik der Nationalgalerie (New Wing, Schloss Charlottenburg, tel. 030/320–911), and Museum für Vor- und Früngeschichte (Langhansbau, Schloss Charlottenburg, tel. 030/320–911). *Admission free. Tues.–Fri. 9–5, weekends 10–5. U-bahn: Sophie-Charlotte-Platz.*

Historic Buildings and Homes

Alter und Neuer Marstall (*see* Tour 1, Exploring, above). The former royal stables now house eastern Berlin's art academy (and special exhibitions) and a state library, respectively. *U-bahn: Stadtmitte.*

Altes Palais (*see* Tour 4, Exploring, above). The palace, built in Neoclassical style in 1834–37, is now part of Humboldt University. *U-bahn: Französischestr.*

Deutsche Staatsbibliothek (*see* Tour 4, Exploring, above). The former royal library is now part of Humboldt University. *U-bahn: Französischestr.*

Deutsche Staatsoper (*see* Tour 4, Exploring, above). The home of the premier opera company of eastern Berlin, it is one of the finest creations of the royal architect Georg Wenzeslaus von Knobelsdorff, built in 1741–43. *U-bahn: Französischestr.*

Hamburger Bahnhof. Berlin's oldest railway station, built in 1845–47, is now a railway and transport museum. *Invalidenstrasse 51. Admission free. Tues.–Sun. 9–5. U-bahn: Hamburgerstr.*

Humboldt Universitat (*see* Tour 4, Exploring, above). Eastern Berlin's university was originally a palace built for the brother of Frederick the Great and converted to its present use by the Humboldt brothers in 1809. *S-bahn: Unter den Linden.*

Kongresshalle (*see* Tour 2, Exploring, above). America's contribution to the 1957 International Building exhibition, Interbau, is often called "The Oyster" because of its bizarre form. *U-bahn: Bellevue.*

Martin-Gropius-Bau. The former arts and crafts museum was designed in 1822 by Martin Gropius, an uncle of Bauhaus pioneer Walter Gropius. The historic building now contains art galleries that show special art exhibitions. *Stresemannstr. 110, tel. 030/2548600. Admission varies with exhibitions. Open Tues.–Sun. 10–10. U-bahn: Kochstr.*

Neue Wache (*see* Tour 4, Exploring, above). Built as a Neoclassical sentry post by Schinkel, it is now a memorial to the victims of fascism and militarism. *S-bahn: Unter den Linden.*

Rathaus Schöneberg (*see* Outlying Sights, above). The city hall of the suburb of Schöneberg is the site of John F. Kennedy's famous "Ich bin ein Berliner" speech, and a copy of the Liberty Bell, a gift from the American people, hangs in the tower. *U-bahn: Rathaus Schöneberg.*

Reichstag (*see* Tour 2, Exploring, above). Berlin's century-old parliament building will now return to its former use as the home of the German Bundestag. *S-bahn: Unter den Linden.*

Ribbeckhaus (*see* Tour 1, Exploring, above). Berlin's only Renaissance house is now the home of city offices. *U-bahn: Französischestr.*

Rotes Rathaus (*see* Tour 1, Exploring, above). Eastern Berlin's city hall is called red not because of the communists who once met there but for the bricks with which it was built. *U-bahn: Stadtmitte.*

Schauspielhaus (*see* Tour 1, Exploring, above). Schinkel's greatest work in Berlin, the theater now serves as a concert hall. *U-bahn: Französischestr.*

Schloss Bellevue (*see* Tour 2, above). The Berlin residence of the German president, the palace is surrounded by grounds that contain the English Gardens, a favorite park among Berliners. *S-bahn: Bellevue.*

Schloss Britz. This 18th-century Prussian nobleman's home in the Neukölln district was converted to its present form in the late 19th century and is maintained as a museum of the *Gründerzeit* (German Empire) style. Its park is also a living example of Gründerzeit garden design. *Alt-Britz 73, tel. 030/606–6051. Admission (guided tour only): DM 2 adults, DM 1 children. Open Wed. 2–6. U-bahn: Parchimer Allee.*

Schloss Charlottenburg (*see* Tour 7, Exploring, above). Berlin's only remaining Hohenzollern palace was built for Queen Sophie Charlotte in 1695 and subsequently expanded by Friedrich II, among others. *U-bahn: Sophie-Charlotte-Platz.*

Schloss Friedrichsfelde. One of East Berlin's few surviving Baroque mansions, it was built in 1695 and extended in Neoclassical style in the early 18th century. Chamber music concerts are regularly held here. *Am Tierpark 125, tel. 030/510–0111. Admission by guided tour only: Tues.–Sun. 11, 1, 3. U-bahn and S-bahn: Friedrichsfelde.*

Schloss Niederschönhausen. This beautiful small palace, built in 1664 as a country residence for the Countess von Dohna, was extended in 1704 and for more than 50 years was the home of Friedrich II's despised wife, Elisabeth Christine. Only the park is open to visitors. *Ossietzkystr., Pankow. S-bahn: Pankow.*

Schloss Pfaueninsel (*see* Outlying Sights, above), a romantic castle on an island in the Havel built by King Friedrich Wilhelm II for his mistress. *S-bahn: Grunewald.*

Jagdschloss Grunewald. This former hunting lodge (really a large country house) deep in the Grunewald woods is a survivor from the Renaissance and now contains a small but select collection of German and Flemish paintings from the 15th–19th centuries and an exhibition of hunting weapons. *Am Grunewald See, Zehlendorf, tel. 030/813–3597. Admission: DM 2 adults, DM 1 children. Open Tues.–Fri. 10–2, weekends 11–4. S-bahn: Zehlendorf.*

Zitadelle Spandau (*see* Outlying Sights, above) is Spandau's stout fort, which houses a museum and restaurant. *U-bahn: Zitadelle.*

Architecture **Brandenburger Tor** (*see* Tour 2, Exploring, above). This is probably Berlin's most famous monument and symbol, a triumphal arch built by Carl Langhans in 1788–91. *S-bahn: Unter den Linden.*

Radio and Television Towers. Here's one respect where western Berlin lags far behind the east: its radio and television tower, the Funkturm (Messedamm/Masuremallee), only 500 feet high. It's a dwarf compared with eastern Berlin's Fernsehturm on Alexanderplatz, which is more than double the height. All that said, the western tower is older, having been built in 1924–26.

Churches and Temples **Berliner Dom** (*see* Tour 4, Exploring, above). Berlin's cathedral, built in 1893–1905 in Italian High Renaissance style, is in the process of reconstruction. The crypt contains many Hohenzollern royal family tombs. *U-bahn: Friedrichstr.*

Deutscher Dom (*see* Tour 1, Exploring, above). Berlin's "German Cathedral," built in 1701–08, is a component of the harmonious Gendarmenmarkt. It is currently closed for restoration. *U-bahn: Französischerstr.*

Dorfkirche Buckow. Berlin has around 50 medieval village churches and this one, built in the mid-13th century, is one of the finest. You'll find it in the Buckow district. *Marienselderchaussee 66. U-bahn: Johannisthalerchaussee.*

Französischer Dom (*see* Tour 1, Exploring, above). Berlin's "French Cathedral," on the Gendarmenmarkt, contains a Huguenot museum and, in the tower, a good restaurant with a marvelous view of the square from a tiny terrace. *U-bahn: Französischerstr.*

Marienkirche (*see* Tour 1, Exploring, above). This north German Gothic church built on Romanesque remains is famous for its Gothic *Dance of Death* fresco. *U-bahn: Französischerstr.*

Nikolaikirche (*see* Tour 6, Exploring, above). Reputedly Berlin's oldest church, it's the center of the picturesque Nikolaiviertel. *U-bahn: Stadtmitte.*

St. Hedwig's Cathedral (*see* Tour 4, Exploring, above). The cathedral of the Berlin diocese, the church on Bebelplatz was designed in the 18th century along the lines of the Pantheon in Rome. Rebuilt after the war, it has a totally modern interior. Organ recitals are given every Wednesday at 3 PM. *U-bahn: Französischerstr.*

Sophienkirche. Named after Queen Sophie Luise, this 18th-century church is the only one in Berlin with a Baroque tower. *Grosse Hamburger Strasse. U-bahn: Hamburger Strasse.*

Statues and Monuments

Grunewaldturm (*see* Outlying Sights, above). This observation tower is deep in the Grunewald forest. *S-bahn: Grunewald.*

Friedrich II equestrian statue (*see* Tour 4, Exploring, above). This fine sculpture of Prussia's greatest king can be found in the middle of Unter den Linden opposite Humboldt University. *S-bahn: Unter den Linden.*

Kaiser-Wilhelm-Gedächtniskirche (*see* Tour 3, Exploring, above). The late-19th-century church dedicated to Germany's last emperor is now, in its ruined state, a war memorial. *U-bahn: Kurfürstendamm.*

Kreuzberg Monument (*see* Tour 5, Exploring, above). This Gothic monument of iron was designed by Schinkel to honor the Prussian soldiers who died fighting Napoléon. *U-bahn: Mehringdamm.*

Neptunbrunnen. Berlin isn't a city of fountains, but this graceful group of figures was one of the world's biggest when built in 1888–91. It faces the Rotes Rathaus. *U-bahn and S-bahn: Alexanderpl.*

Plötzensee Memorial. The buildings where more than 2,500 dissidents were executed by the Nazis are a chilling reminder of the city's dark past. *Hüttigpfad 13, tel. 030/344–32226. Admission free. Open daily 8–6. U-bahn: Putlitzstr.*

Siegessäule (*see* Tour 2, Exploring, above). Berlin's victory column was erected in 1873 in front of the Reichstag but moved to its present site by the Nazis. *S-bahn: Tiergarten.*

Parks and Gardens

Botanischer Garten. This botanical garden in Dahlem is one of the world's leading botanical gardens, with the world's highest tropical-house. Laid out in 1899–1910, the gardens and hot houses have more than 18,000 different plant species. *Königin-Luise-Strasse 6–8, tel. 030/830–060. Admission: DM 2.50 adults, DM 1.20 children. Open daily 9–dusk. U-bahn: Dahlem-Dorf.*

Pfaueninsel (*see* Outlying Sights, above). An idyllic Havel River island bought by King Friedrich Wilhelm II in 1793. *S-bahn: Grunewald.*

Tiergarten (*see* Tour 2, Exploring, above). The name means "zoological garden," but Berlin's zoo takes up only a corner of this large, central park that contains or borders on some of the city's most famous landmarks. *U-bahn and S-bahn: Tiergarten.*

Volkspark Klein-Glienicke (*see* Outlying Sights, above). The park was laid out in 1824–60 on the banks of the Havel, and contain pavilions and a palace by Schinkel. *S-bahn: Wannsee.*

Zoos

Zoologischer Garten (*see* Tour 3, Exploring, above). Berlin's oldest and largest zoo is in the center of western Berlin. *U-bahn and S-bahn: Zoologischer Garten.*

Tierpark Berlin. Eastern Berlin's zoo is much smaller than western Berlin's Zoologischer Garten, but the setting, within the grounds of the Schloss Friedrichsfelde, couldn't be better.

Am Tierpark 125, tel. 030/512–3143. Admission: DM 5 adults, DM 2 children. Open Mon.–Sat. 9 AM–dusk. U-bahn: Tierpark.

Other Places of Interest

Berlin Wall (*see* Tour 1, Exploring, above). A bit of the Wall has been kept for posterity on Mühlenstrasse, between the Jannowitz and Überbaum bridges. Artists from all over the world have been busy painting on the 1.3-km (.8-mi)-long remnant, dubbed the East Side Gallery, contributing to a work on the theme of peace and human rights. *S-bahn: Friedrichshain.*

Breitscheidplatz (*see* Tour 3, Exploring, above). Western Berlin's true center, this square bordered by Europa Center and the Kaiser-Wilhelm-Gedächtniskirche is where the city hums 24 hours a day. *U-bahn: Kurfürstendamm.*

Glienecker Brücke (*see* Outlying Sights, above). The cast-iron bridge on the former southwest border between East and West Berlin is where spies were traditionally exchanged. *S-bahn: Wannsee, then bus 116.*

Husemannstrasse (*see* Outlying Sights, above). This is one of eastern Berlin's showpiece streets, but its restoration is only facade-deep. *U-bahn and S-bahn: Alexanderpl.*

Olympiastadion. Site of the 1936 Olympic Games and the accompanying Nazi pageantry, it is still used, for sports and musical events. Even by today's standards, it is immense. *Charlottenburg, tel. 030/304–06746. Admission (for visiting only): DM 1 adults, 50 pf children. Open daily 7–dusk. U-bahn: Olympia-Stadion.*

Shopping

Berlin is still a divided city when it comes to shopping, with the western part of the city still far ahead in the size, scope, and quality of its stores and the merchandise they offer. However, this situation is changing rapidly. Clothes are *the* thing to buy in western Berlin, which claims to be Germany's leading fashion center. Prices are generally lower than in cities like Munich and Hamburg. Berlin's recent history, from the fall of the Wall to the reunification celebrations, is emblazoned on virtually every T-shirt you'll find in the shops around Breitscheidplatz. Nobody wants to leave Berlin without a piece of the Wall, and you'll have no difficulty finding prepacked, painted pieces of it, complete with guarantees of authenticity. But the guarantees are worth no more than the paper they're printed on, for how do you test the authenticity of a piece of concrete? So if you buy what's claimed to be a piece of the Wall, swallow your skepticism.

Stores usually open at 9 AM and close at 6 PM (1 or 1:30 PM on Saturday), although some smaller shops open earlier and close for lunch. On Thursday the larger stores stay open until 8:30 PM or later, and on the first Saturday of every month most shops stay open until 4 PM.

Shopping Districts

Western Berlin has one of Germany's most famous shopping streets, the Kurfürstendamm, universally known as the **Ku'damm**, but the best buys are to be found in side streets leading off this glittering boulevard, especially between **Breitscheidplatz** and **Olivaerplatz**. The multistory **Europa Center** on Breitscheidplatz has more than 100 boutiques, stores, cafés, and restaurants, but this is no place to bargain-hunt. Less expensive options can be found on two streets leading into the square, **Budapesterstrasse** and **Tauenzianstrasse.** At the end of Tauenzianstrasse (about three minutes' walk from Breit-scheidplatz) is Berlin's biggest department store, the **Kaufhaus des Westens** (known popularly as the **KaDeWe**), which boasts that it stocks everything possible on its six floors.

For trendier and more elegant clothing, try the boutiques lining the Kurfürstendamm, from Meinekstrasse to Olivaerplatz. Here you'll find designer boutiques from Sonia Rykel, Yves St. Laurent, and Cartier, as well as fine porcelain stores and the best of the German automobile showrooms.

For budget shopping and the kind of wares you won't find at home, try **Kantstrasse, Wilmersdorferstrasse,** or **Karl-Marx-Strasse** in Neukölln, **Schloss Strasse** in Steglitz, **Turmstrasse** in Moabit, **Berlinerstrasse,** and the **Tegel-Center** in Reinickendorf. More adventurous souls might venture out to **Spandau** and explore the Altstadt.

In eastern Berlin, **Unter den Linden** and **Friedrichstrasse** are being restored to the premier position they once held among the glittering shopping boulevards of Berlin, but in 1992 they still had some way to go before being able to compete with the Ku'damm. Alexanderplatz now includes branches of the German department stores Herties and Kaufhof. Some of eastern Berlin's luxury hotels—the Palast and the Grand, for example—have Western-style shopping malls.

Department Stores Berlin has Europe's largest department store, the Kaufhaus des Westens, or **KaDeWe**, a grand-scale emporium in modern guise at Wittenbergplatz. Be sure to visit the sixth floor, which is entirely devoted to food and drink; only Harrods in London can boast anything comparable. The Ku'damm has several department stores, the largest of which is **Wertheim.** Although it's not as attractive as KaDeWe, it nonetheless offers a large selection of fine merchandise. Department stores in eastern Berlin, such as **Kaufhof** (formerly Centrum), on the north side of Alexanderplatz, have been upgraded to match western standards. You can still find good buys in such eastern German specialties as wooden toys and ceramics.

Gift Ideas Fine **porcelain** is still produced at the former Royal Prussian Porcelain Factory, now called **Staatliche Porzellan Manufactur,** or KPM. This delicate, handmade, hand-painted china is sold at KPM's store at Kurfürstendamm 26A (tel. 030/881–1802), but it may be more fun to visit the factory salesroom at Wegelystrasse 1. It also sells seconds at reduced prices. If you long to have the Egyptian Museum's Queen Nefertiti on your mantelpiece at home, try the **Gipsformerei der Staatlichen Museen Preussicher Kulturbesitz** (Sophie-Charlotte-Str. 17, tel. 030/321–7011, open weekdays 9–4). It sells plaster casts of this and other treasures from the city's museums. Take home a regiment of **tin figures,** painted or to paint yourself, from the **Berliner Zinnfigurenkabinett** (Knesebeckstr. 88).

Street Markets Every Berlin district has its market (usually twice a week), but the best are both to be found in **Schöneberg:** in front of the Schöneberg city hall (Tuesday and Friday 8–1) and at Winterfeldtplatz (Wednesday and Saturday 8–1). You'll find everything here, from fresh fruit and vegetables to new and secondhand clothing. The **Türkenmarkt** (Turkish market) on Neukölln's Maybachufer (Tuesday and Friday noon–6:30) is the nearest thing to an oriental bazaar this side of the German border, and it's become a top tourist attraction. The **Ackerhalle** on the corner of Invalidenstrasse and Ackerstrasse in Berlin's Mitte district is the city's only surviving 19th-century covered market; take your camera.

Antiques and Flea Markets
Apart from the Strasse des 17 Juni market (*see* Crafts, below), other leading sources of antiques and secondhand goods can be found in **Kreuzberg** (the Krempelmarkt, on the corner of Reichpietschufer and Linkstrasse, Saturday and Sunday 8–3:30), **Wilmersdorf** (Fehrbellinerplatz, Sunday 7–4), and **Schöneberg** (the Flohmarkt in a part of the disused Nollendorfplatz U-bahn station, daily except Tuesday 11–7. The stalls are located in 16 old subway cars, and on Sunday mornings the Nolles Salonorchester livens things up still further with jazz and swing). In eastern Berlin, there's the **Trödelmarkt** at Arkonaplatz (near the Rosenthaler Platz subway station, Saturday 9–4).

Crafts
On Saturday and Sunday from 10 to 5, the colorful and lively antiques and handicrafts fair on a stretch of Strasse des 17 Juni (east of Ernst-Reuter-Platz) swings into action. Much of what's on offer is kitsch, although some fine workmanship and imaginative artistry can be found among the stalls. Farther along is a secondhand and antiques section. Homemade curries and chili are offered at the food stands that dot the area, and in winter mulled wine is ladled out to chilled shoppers.

Food
In addition to neighborhood markets and the food floor at KaDeWe, Berlin's other major food markets are the **Arminius-Markthalle**, Arminiusstrasse 2, and the **Eisenbahn-Markthalle**, Eisenbahnstrasse 43–44. They're both open Monday–Friday 8–6 and Saturday 8–1. They're great sources for a quick, inexpensive lunch.

Specialty Stores
Antiques
Not far from Wittenbergplatz is **Keithstrasse,** a street given over to antiques stores. There are also several small antiques stores in the converted subway cars of the **Nollendorfplatz Flohmarkt.** Eisenacherstrasse, Fuggerstrasse, Kalckreuthstrasse, Motzstrasse, and Nollendorfstrasse—all close to Nollendorfplatz—have many antiques stores of varying quality. Another good street for antiques is **Suarezstrasse,** between Kantstrasse and Bismarckstrasse. The venerable auction house **Christie's** recently opened an outpost at Fasanenstrasse 72 (tel. 030/882–7778), just off the Ku'damm.

Klewer, at Viktoria-Luise-Platz 12a, Schöneberg, features fine antique German furniture and paintings; German Jugendstil and European Art Deco are the specialties at **Bleibtreu Antiques,** Bleibtreustrasse 5a, Charlottenburg. The antique glass and jewelry at **Lee,** Kurfürstendamm 32, are exceptional.

In eastern Berlin, antiques are sold in the **Metropol** and **Palast hotels,** in the **Nikolai quarter,** and in the restored **Husemannstrasse.** Some private stores along the stretch of **Friedrichstrasse** north of the Spree Bridge offer old books and prints. **Southeby's** auction house has set up shop at the Palais am Festungsgraben on Unter den Linden (tel. 030/304–6369).

Books
Düwal, Schlüterstr. 17, Charlottenburg, and **Koch,** Kurfürstendamm 216, both offer a very wide range of antique books, old maps, and prints.

International Press
The leading hotels stock American and British newpapers. Other outlets include **KaDeWe** and the souvenir shops at

Joachimstrasse 1 (next to the Bahnhof Zoo) and Kurfürsten-damm 206–209.

Jewelry Fine hand-crafted jewelry can be found at **Wurzbarcher** (Ku'damm 36). **Axel Selatzek** (Ku'damm 45) also offers a good selection, but with a twist: He'll custom design body jewelry for men and women. Eastern Berlin's **Galerie Skarabäus** (Frankfurter Allee 80) and **Galerie "re"** (Finowstr. 2) offer good values.

Men's Clothing **Mientus** (Wilmersdorferstr. 73), a large, exclusive men's store, caters to expensive tastes, as does **Brand** (Ku'damm 184). They offer both conventional/businesswear as well as sporty and modern looks, and carry many top designer labels; Brand, how-ever, serves more conservative tastes. For men's shoes, try **Budapester Schuhe** (Ku'damm 199). **Norbert's** (Bleibtreu-strasse 24, between the Ku'damm and Leitzenburgerstr.) also stocks the leading designer labels. Slightly less expensive and exclusive but still up there is **Erdmann** (in the Europa Center facing Tauenzienstr). At the other end of the scale, nothing in the **Kleidermarkt** (Bergmannstr. 102) is more expensive than DM 40 (there are women's fashions, too).

Women's Clothing Berlin fashion designers claim to lead the field in Germany. Whether that's true or not, Berlin's fashion boutiques are sec-ond to none. Among the best are **News of Fashion** (Kurfürsten-damm 56–57) and **Rival** (Nürnbergerstr. 14). For German designer wear, try **Zenker** (Ku'damm 45). It's not cheap, but the styling is classic. If you're looking for international labels, drop by **E. Braun & Co.** (Ku'damm 43) or **Kramberg** (Ku'damm 56), and then go next door to **Granny's Step**, where you'll find eveningwear styled along the lines of bygone times. For mod-ern, Berlin-designed chic, check out **Filato** (Nürenbergstr. 24A). If you're feeling daring, browse through the extraordi-nary lingerie store **Nouvelle** (Bleibtreustr. 24). Elegant '20s in-timate-wear made of fine, old-fashioned materials is its specialty. For German folk-inspired outfits, try **Pupi's Loden** (Schlüterstr. 54 and Ansbacherstr. 30a).

Sports and Fitness

Bicycling There are bike paths throughout the downtown area and the rest of the city. *See* Getting Around, above, for details of rent-ing bikes.

Golf Berlin's leading club is the **Golf- und Landclub Wannsee** (Stölpchenweg, Wannsee, tel. 030/805–5075).

Jogging The **Tiergarten** is the best place for jogging in the downtown area. Run its length and back and you'll cover 5 miles. Joggers can also take advantage of the grounds of **Charlottenburg** cas-tle, 2 miles around. For longer runs, anything up to 20 miles, make for **Grunewald.**

Riding Horses are rented out by the **Reitschule Onkel Toms Hütte** (Onkel-Tom-Str. 172, tel. 030/813–2081). Children's ponies are stabled at **Ponyhof Lange** (Buckower Chaussee 82, Marienfelde, tel. 030/721–6008) and the **Ponyhof Wittenau** (Wittenauerstr. 80, tel. 030/402–8535).

Sailing and Windsurfing Boats and boards of all kinds are rented by **Jürgen Schöne** (tel. 030/381–5037) and **Scharfe Lanke** (tel. 030/361–5066).

Swimming The **Wannsee** and **Plötzensee** both have beaches; they get crowded during summer weekends, however. There are pools throughout the city; there's bound to be at least one near where you're staying. For full listings, ask at the tourist office. The most impressive pool is the **Olympia-Schwimmstadion** at Olympischer Platz (U-bahn: Olympiastadion). The **Blub Padeparadis** lido (Buschkrugallee 64, tel. 030/606–6060) has indoor and outdoor pools, hot tubs, and a solarium (U-Bahn: Grenzallee).

Tennis and Squash There are tennis courts and squash centers throughout the city; ask your hotel to direct you to the nearest. **Tennis & Squash City** (Brandenburgischestr. 31, Wilmersdorf, tel. 030/879–097) has seven tennis courts and 11 squash courts. You can even step off the Ku'damm and onto a tennis court, at **"Tennisplätze am Ku'damm"** (Cicerostr. 55A, tel. 030/896– 630).

Dining

Dining in Berlin can mean sophisticated nouvelle specialties in upscale restaurants with linen tablecloths and hand-painted porcelain plates, or hearty local specialties in atmospheric and inexpensive inns: The range is as vast as the city. Specialties include *Eisbein mit Sauerkraut*, knuckle of pork with pickled cabbage; *Rouladen*, rolled stuffed beef; *Spanferkel*, suckling pig; *Berliner Sülze*, potted meat in aspic; *Schlachteplatte*, mixed grill; *Hackepeter*, ground beef; and *Kartoffelpuffer*, fried potato cakes. *Bockwurst* is a chubby frankfurter that's served in a variety of ways and sold in restaurants and at sausage stands all over the city. *Schlesisches Himmerlreich* is roast goose or pork served with potato dumplings in rich gravy. *Königsberger Klopse* consists of meatballs with a herring and capers sauce—it tastes much better than it sounds.

Eastern Germany's former ties to the Eastern Bloc persist in restaurants featuring the national cuisine of those other one-time socialist states, although such exotica as Japanese, Chinese, Indonesian, and French food are slowly appearing. Wines and spirits imported from those other countries can be quite good; try Hungarian, Yugoslav, and Bulgarian wines (the whites are lighter), and Polish and Russian vodkas. But like everything else, their prices are no longer cheap.

Highly recommended restaurants are indicated by a star ★.

Western Berlin

Very Expensive (over DM 100) ★ **Bamberger Reiter.** One of the city's leading restaurants, this is presided over by Tirolean chef Franz Raneburger. He relies on fresh market produce for his *Neue Deutsche Küche* (German nouvelle cuisine), so the menu changes daily. Fresh flowers set off this attractive oak-beamed restaurant. *Regensburgerstr. 7, tel. 030/244–282. Reservations essential. Jacket and tie required. DC, V. Closed lunch, Sun., Mon., and Aug. 1–20.*

Frühsammer's Restaurant an der Rehwiese. Here you can watch chef Peter Frühsammer at work in his open kitchen. His choice of daily menu is never remiss; the salmon is always a treat. The restaurant is in the annex of a turn-of-the-century villa in the Zehlendorf district (U-bahn to Krumme Lanke and then bus No. 53 to Rehweise). *Matterhornstr. 101, tel. 030/803–2720. Reservations essential. Jacket and tie required. MC, V.*

Berlin Dining

Alt-Berliner
Weissbierstube, **23**
Alt-Cöllner
Schankstuben, **24**
Alt-Luxembourg, **5**
Alt-Nürnberg, **15**
Bamberger Reiter, **17**
Berlin Esprit, **28**
Blockhaus
Nikolskoe, **8**

Conti Fischstuben, **16**
Eierschale, **14**
Ermeler-Haus, **31**
Französischer Hof, **22**
Frühsammer's
Restaurant an der
Rehwiese, **7**
Ganymed, **20**
Grand Slam, **6**
Hardtke, **13**

Hecker's Deele, **11**
Historische Gaststätte
auf der Zitadelle, **4**
Ho Lin Wah, **10**
Karagiosi, **2**
Mundart
Restaurant, **18**
Ponte Vecchio, **3**
Raabe Diele, **30**
Ratskeller, **27**
Schwalbennest, **25**

Thürnagel, **19**
Trio, **1**
Wibb's, **12**
Wirtshaus
Moorlake, **9**
Zur Goldenen
Gans, **21**
Zur Letzen
Instanz, **29**
Zur Rippe, **26**

Paulstr.

Lüneburgstr.

Moltkestr.

20

Unter den Linden

Str. des 17 Juni

Entlastungsstr.

Tiergarten

21

Otto Grotewohlstr.

Friedrichstr.

AE

Gendarmen-
markt

22

Marx-Engels
Pl.

Karl-
Liebknecht-Str.

Rathausstr.

28

25

27

26   Stralauerstr.

29

Tiergarten   Str.

Potsdamer
Pl.

Leipzigerstr.

24

Wallstr.

31   **30**

FORMER LOCATION OF BERLIN WALL

Wilhelmstr.

Friedrichstr.

Oranienstr.

Ritterstr.

H. Heinestr.

Lützowstr.

Spree

Potsdamerstr.

Schönebergerstr.

Möckernstr.

Lindenstr.

23

Bülowstr.

Gitschinerstr.

Prinzenstr.

Potsdamerstr.

Yorckstr.

Möckernstr.

Yorckstr.

Urban - str.

Baerwaldstr.

Gneisenaustr.

19

N

Kreuzbergstr.

Mehringdamm

SCHÖNEBERG

Monumentenstr.

**Viktoria
Park**

Kolonnenstr.

Dudenstr.

18

Columbiadamm

**Volkspark
Hasenheide**

Ebersstr.

Westarngenle

Monumentenstr.

KEY

AE   American Express
Office

i   Tourist Information

0   750 yards

0   750 meters

Closed lunch, Sun., and 3 weeks during the school summer holidays.

Grand Slam. Overlooking a lake and nestled among the trees on the property of the exclusive Rot-Weiss tennis club in Grunewald, this restaurant is German fine-dining at its best, with excellent service and no pretentiousness. Four-course lunch menus and six-course dinner menus are available for DM 149. Try the salmon and caviar appetizer and the marinated duck breast with a tinge of quince. *Gottfried von Cramm-weg 47–55, tel. 030/825–3810. Reservations essential. Jacket and tie recommended. AE, DC, MC, V. Closed Sun. and Mon.*

Expensive (DM 75–DM 100)
★
Alt-Luxembourg. There are only nine tables at this popular restaurant in the Charlottenburg district, with attentive service enhancing the intimate setting. Chef Kurt Wannebacher produces a divine lobster lasagna. *Windscheidstr. 14, tel. 030/323–8730. Reservations essential. Jacket and tie required. DC, V. Closed Sun., Mon., 3 weeks in Jan., and 3 weeks during June and July.*

Moderate (DM 50–DM 75)
Alt-Nürnberg. Step into the tavernlike interior and you could be in Füssen or Garmisch in Bavaria; the waitresses even wear dirndls. The Bavarian colors of blue and white are everywhere, and that region's culinary delights, like *Schweinshaxe* (knuckle of pork), dominate the menu. If you prefer to eat Prussian-style, order calves' liver *Berliner Art. Europa-Center, tel. 030/261–4397. Reservations advised. Dress: informal. AE, DC, MC, V.*

★
Conti Fischstuben. This is the best fish restaurant in Berlin. Watery light from the fish tank in the center of the dining room reflects from the dark-paneled walls to create a sophisticated and different atmosphere. The restaurant is located in the Hotel Ambassador. *Bayreutherstrasse 43, tel. 030/219–02362. Reservations essential. Jacket and tie required. AE, DC, MC, V. Closed lunch and Sun.*

Hecker's Deele. Antique church pews complement the oak-beamed interior of this restaurant that specializes in Westphalian dishes. The *Westfälische Schlachtplatte* (a selection of meats) will set you up for a whole day's sightseeing—the Ku'damm is right outside. *Grolmannstr. 35, tel. 030/88901. Reservations advised. Dress: informal. AE, DC, MC, V.*

Historische Gaststätte auf der Zitadelle. Here you'll dine like a medieval noble, served a multicourse menu by Prussian wenches and serenaded by a minstrel group. In winter, a roaring fire helps light and warm the vaulted restaurant, which is part of Spandau's historic Zitadelle. Its medieval banquets are popular, so make sure to reserve your spot at one of the heavy oak antique tables. *Am Juliusturm, Spandau, tel. 030/334–2106. Reservations advised. Dress: informal. AE, DC, MC, V.*

Ho Lin Wah. Until 1980 this was the Chinese Embassy in Berlin, and much of the restaurant's decor was retained after the Chinese moved out. China's loss was Berlin's gain: This is one of the city's best Chinese restaurants, family-run and with first-class (mostly Cantonese) cuisine and attentive service. *Kurfürstendamm 218, tel. 030/882–3271. Reservations advised. Dress: informal. AE, DC, MC, V.*

Mundart Restaurant. Five chefs work the kitchen of this popular restaurant in the Kreuzberg district. You can't go wrong with the fish soup or any of the daily specials. *Muskauerstr. 33–34, tel. 030/612–2061. Dress: informal. Reservations advised. No credit cards. Closed lunch, Mon., and Tues.*

★ **Ponte Vecchio.** Delicious Tuscan-style Italian food is served here in a handsome, light-wood dining room. Ask the friendly waiters for their recommendations—the food is excellent and simply presented. Try the delicate *Vitello tonnato*, veal with a tuna sauce. *Spielhagenstr. 3, tel. 030/342–1999. Reservations essential. Jacket and tie required. DC. Closed lunch (except Sun.), Tues., and 4 weeks in summer.*

Trio. This little gem is tucked away on Klausenerplatz, in the shadow of the Schloss Charlottenberg. There are only eight or 10 tables, but the management does not rush you; you can enjoy your meal at leisure, no matter how long it takes. The menu changes almost daily, and chef Siegfried Stier often decides only late in the afternoon what he will serve, depending on what he finds at the local markets. The cuisine is neue Deutsche küche, with an accent on light rather than stodgy food. A typical meal starts with calves' liver with tiny green lentils and is followed by baby sole cooked in Riesling with *waldemeister* (a German herb) and a rabbit dish served with miniature fresh vegetables. Leave room for one of the creative desserts, such as vanilla cream with warm raspberries. *14 Klausenerpl., tel. 030/321–7782. Reservations advised. Dress: casual but neat. No credit cards. Dinner only. Closed Wed. and Thurs.*

Wibb's. Gabi, Martin and Christian Wibbke (the "Wibb" family) run this smart corner restaurant with friendly efficiency and exemplary kitchen skills. Competition in Uhlandstrasse is keen, with restaurants dueling for pavement space, but Wibb's stands out. Fresh-cut flowers on the tables and well-chosen prints on the walls give a splash of color to the slightly formal surroundings. The menu is relatively small but packed with good things, particularly the imaginative fish dishes. *Uhlandstr. 142, tel. 030/861–5310. Reservations advised. Dress: informal. AE, MC, V.*

Wirtshaus Moorlake. You need a car to reach this enchanting lakeside country-style restaurant, deep in the Grunewald, but the excursion is well worth it. Built in 1840 as a royal hunting lodge, it became an established stagecoach stop on the Berlin-Potsdam run. Now it's a popular destination for weekending Berliners, so go on a weekday; reserve a table upstairs under the exposed beams. Despite the Bavarian character of the surroundings, the menu is mostly Berlin fare. Try the *Königsberger Klopse. An der Moorlake, tel. 030/805–5809. Reservations advised. Dress: informal. AE, DC, MC, V. Closed Tues. and winter evenings.*

Inexpensive (under DM 50) **Alt-Berliner Wiessbierstube.** A visit to the Berlin Museum must include a stop at the museum's pub-style restaurant. There's a buffet packed with Berlin specialties, and you can take in live jazz here on Saturday and Sunday mornings. *Berlin Museum, Lindenstr. 14, tel. 030/251–0121. No reservations. Dress: informal. No credit cards. Closed Mon.*

Blockhaus Nikolskoe. Prussian King Wilhelm III built this Russian-style wooden lodge for his daughter Charlotte, wife of Russian Czar Nicholas I. Located south of the city on Glienecker Park, it offers open-air riverside dining in the summer. Game dishes are prominently featured. *Nikolskoer Weg, tel. 030/805–2914. Reservations advised. Dress: informal. AE, DC, MC, V.*

Eierschale. Berlin is famous for its breakfast cafés, and this is one of the best—and the best-located, on the corner of central Rankestrasse and the Ku'damm. It serves breakfast at all hours, but really gets going in the evenings, when jazz groups perform in a neighboring room. The lunch and supper menus feature filling Berlin fare, but if Mexican-style spareribs are on offer, they're especially to be recommended. Sunday morning is *Frühschoppen* time, when live jazz accompanies the buffet brunch; great fun and an opportunity to witness the highlight of a Berliner's weekend. *Rankestrasse 1, tel. 030/882–5305. Reservations advised. Dress: informal. MC.*

★ **Hardtke.** This is about the most authentic old Berlin restaurant in the city. The decor is simple, with paneled walls and wood floor. The food is similarly traditional and hearty. It's a great place to try *Eisbein.* Wash it down with a large stein of beer. *Meinekestr. 27, tel. 030/881–9827. Reservations advised. Dress: informal. No credit cards.*

Karagiosi. A short walk from the Charlottenburg palace, this simply furnished, friendly Greek restaurant is just the place to round out a day's sightseeing. The decor is minimal, but the food is so authentic you could be in Athens, and if you're in luck there'll be live music the night you call. *Klausenerpl. 4, tel. 030/ 798–2379. No reservations. Dress: informal. V.*

Thürnagel. At this vegetarian restaurant in the Kreuzberg district, it's not only healthy to eat, but fun. The seitan in sherry sauce or the tempeh curry are good enough to convert a seasoned carnivore. *Gneisenaustr. 57, tel. 030/691–4800. Reservations advised. No credit cards. Dinner only.*

Eastern Berlin

Prices in eastern Berlin have risen rapidly to approximately the same level as in the western part of the city. Our categories, therefore, correspond with those in the Western Berlin dining section.

Expensive
(DM 75–DM 100)
★ **Ermeler-Haus.** The Rococo grandeur of this wine restaurant located in a series of upstairs rooms reflects the elegance of the restored patrician home—which dates from the mid-16th century—in which it's housed. The atmosphere is subdued and formal, the wines are imported, and the service and German cuisine are excellent. There's dancing every Saturday evening. *Märkisches Ufer 10–12, tel. 030/275–5103. Reservations advised. Jacket and tie required. AE, DC, MC, V.*

★ **Schwalbennest.** On the edge of the Nikolai quarter, overlooking the Marx-Engels-Forum, this is a fairly new establishment, yet it is already known for its outstanding food and service. The choice is wide for main dishes and wines. The grilled selections are excellent, but note that the flambéed dishes cost extra, although no additional price is indicated on the menu. *Am Marstall (upstairs), Rathausstr. at Marx-Engels-Forum, tel. 030/212–6919. Reservations essential. Dress: informal at lunch, jacket and tie required at dinner. No credit cards.*

Zur Goldenen Gans. Regional specialties are featured here, particularly game and venison dishes prepared Thüringer Forest style. *Friedrichstr. 158–164, in the Grand Hotel, tel. 030/ 20920. Reservations advised. Dress: informal. AE, DC, MC, V.*

Moderate
(DM 50–DM 75)
★ **Berlin Esprit.** For authentic Berlin specialties you'll probably do no better; the atmosphere is also thoroughly relaxing. *Alexanderpl., in the Hotel Stadt Berlin, tel. 030/2190. Reservations advised. Dress: informal. AE, DC, MC, V.*

Französischer Hof. Not for the infirm or those who are afraid of heights, this restaurant is tucked away below the cupola of the Französicher Dom, the church that sits in classical splendor on one side of the beautiful Gendarmenmarkt. The restaurant, which runs a circular course around the base of the cupola, is approached by a long, winding staircase—fine for working up an appetite but certainly not recommended for the faint-hearted. The reward at the top of the stairs is a table in one of Berlin's most original and attractive restaurants. The menu is as short as the stairway is long, but there's an impressive wine list. *Französischer Dom, Gendarmenmarkt, tel. 030/229–3969. Reservations strongly advised (the frustration of being turned away after that climb could spoil anyone's day). No credit cards.*

Ratskeller. This is actually two restaurants in one, composed of a wine and a beer cellar, each highly popular, and each with great atmosphere (entrances at opposite corners of the building). Menus are somewhat limited, but include good solid Berlin fare. The brick-walled beer cellar is guaranteed to be packed during main dining hours, at which time reservations sometimes get ignored; Berliners simply line up to get in. The wine cellar is less crowded, in part because it is slightly more expensive. Among the menu selections are Hungarian goulash soup, chicken, and steaks. *Rathausstr. 15–18 (in the basement of the Rotes Rathaus, or Red Town Hall), tel. 030/212–4464 and 030/212–5301. Reservations advised. Dress: informal. No credit cards.*

Inexpensive (under DM 50)
★ **Alt-Cöllner Schankstuben.** Four tiny restaurants are contained within this charming, historic Berlin house. The section to the side of the canal on the Kleine Gertraudenstrasse, where there are tables set outside, serves as a café. The menu is relatively limited, but quality, like the service, is good. *Friederichsgracht 50, tel. 030/212–5972. No reservations. Dress: informal. No credit cards.*

★ **Raabe Diele.** The location of this restaurant is the basement of the 16th-century Ermeler-Haus (*see* above). It was largely rebuilt in 1969, meaning that the pine-paneled cellar is new—with canned music—and offers considerably less elegance and atmosphere than the handsome rooms upstairs. On the other hand, the prices are far lower and the menu consists of good Berlin-style cuisine. The service down here is just as attentive as it is upstairs. *Märkisches Ufer 10–12, in Ermeler-Haus, tel. 030/279–4036. Dress: informal. Reservations advised, particularly at night. AE, DC, MC, V.*

★ **Zur Letzen Instanz.** Unquestionably Berlin's oldest restaurant, established in 1525, this place is imbued with an old-world charm rarely found these days in the modern city. The choice of food is, as usual, limited, but it is prepared in the genuine Berlin tradition and is truly hearty—you'll find beer in the cooking as well as in your mug. *Waisenstr. 14–16 (U-bahn Klosterstr.), tel. 030/212–5528. Reservations essential. Dress: informal. No credit cards.*

Zur Rippe. This famous eating place near Alexanderplatz serves wholesome food in an intimate setting with oak paneling and ceramic tiles. Specialties include the Märkische cheese platter and herring casserole. *Poststr. 17, tel. 030/217–3235. Reservations not necessary. No credit cards.*

Lodging

Berlin lost all of its grand old luxury hotels in the bombing during World War II; though some were rebuilt, many of the best hotels today are modern. While they lack little in service and comfort, you may find some short on atmosphere. For first-class or luxury accommodations, eastern Berlin is easily as good as western, for the East German government, eager for hard currency, built several elegant hotels—the Grand, Palast, Dom (now called Hilton International), and Metropol—which are up to the very best international standards and place in the very top price category. If you're seeking something more moderate, the better choice may be western Berlin, where there are large numbers of good-value pensions and small hotels, many of them in older buildings with some character. In eastern Berlin, however, the hostels run by the Evangelical church offer outstanding value for your money.

There are no longer any restrictions on who can stay where in the former East Berlin, as there were in the past. In western Berlin, business conventions year-round and the influx of summer tourists mean that you should make reservations well in advance. If you arrive without reservations, consult the board at Tegel Airport that shows hotels with vacancies, or go to the tourist office at the airport. The main tourist office in the Europa Center can also help with reservations (*see* Important Addresses and Numbers, above).

Highly recommended hotels are indicated by a star ★.

Category	Cost*
Very Expensive	over DM 250
Expensive	DM 180–DM 250
Moderate	DM 120–DM 180
Inexpensive	under DM 120

*for two people in a double room, including tax and service

Western Berlin

Very Expensive
★

Bristol Hotel Kempinski. Destroyed in the war, rebuilt in 1952, and renovated in 1980, the "Kempi" is a renowned Berlin classic. Located on the Ku'damm in the heart of the city, it has the best shopping at its doorstep plus some fine boutiques of its own within. Rooms and suites are luxuriously decorated, English-style, and with all amenities. *Ku'damm 27, tel. 030/884–340. 334 rooms with bath. Facilities: 3 restaurants, indoor pool, sauna, solarium, masseur, hairdresser, limousine service. AE, DC, MC, V.*

Grand Hotel Esplanade. Opened in 1988, the Grand Hotel Esplanade exudes luxury. Uncompromisingly modern architecture, chicly styled rooms, and works of art by some of Berlin's most acclaimed artists are its outstanding visual aspects. Then there are the superb facilities and impeccable service. The enormous grand suite comes complete with sauna, whirlpool, and a grand piano for DM 1,200 per night. *Lützowufer 15, tel. 030/261–011. 369 rooms, 33 suites. Facilities: 2 restaurants, pub, poolside bar, pool, sauna, whirlpool, steam bath, solari-*

um, masseur, hairdresser, boutique, medical station, library.
AE, DC, MC, V.

Hotel Berlin. The hotel that bears Berlin's name is actually part
of a prominent Scandinavian group, hence the birch-tree
bright and light look, modern but furnished in enduring, un-
derstated good taste. The location is handy for both the
Ku'damm and Unter den Linden. *Lützowplatz 17, tel. 030/*
26050. 490 rooms and 21 suites with bath. Facilities: sauna, so-
larium, beauty center, boutiques, restaurant, beer tavern, pi-
ano bar. AE, DC, MC, V.

★ **Inter-Continental Berlin.** The top-billed "Diplomaten Suite" is
in a class of its own: It's as large as a suburban house and furnished in exotic Oriental style. Other rooms and suites may not
be so opulently furnished but still show individuality and taste.
The lobby is worth a visit even if you're not staying here. It's
one-fourth the size of a football field and lavishly decorated;
stop by for afternoon tea and pastries. *Budapesterstr. 2, tel.*
030/26020. 600 rooms with bath. Facilities: 3 restaurants, in-
door pool, sauna, boutiques, Pan Am check-in service. AE,
DC, MC, V.

Steigenberger Berlin. The Steigenberger group's exemplary
Berlin hotel is centrally situated, only a few steps from the
Ku'damm and Breidscheidplatz, but remarkably quiet. Small
touches that lift the hotel above the usual run of chain estab-
lishments include a nightly weather forecast dropped on your
bedside table to help you plan for the next day. *Los-Angeles-*
Platz 1, tel. 030/21080. 389 rooms and 11 suites, all with bath.
Facilities: pool and poolside bar, sauna, solarium, massage
room, 2 restaurants, cocktail bar, café, tavern. AE, DC, MC,
V.

Expensive **Hotel Hamburg.** The Ring group's Berlin establishment offers all the expected comfort and facilities in a quiet location
handy for both parts of Berlin. If you book well in advance,
you can take advantage of a two-night package for little more
than the price of one night's stay, with a city tour, a welcome
drink, complimentary breakfast, a dinner, and opera or theater tickets all thrown in. *Landgrafenstr. 4, tel. 030/269-161.*
240 rooms with bath. Facilities: restaurant, bar. AE, DC, MC,
V.

★ **Landhaus Schlachtensee.** Opened in 1987, this former villa
(built in 1905) is now a cozy bed-and-breakfast hotel. The
Landhaus Schlachtensee offers personal and efficient service,
well-equipped rooms, and a quiet location in the Zehlendorf district. The nearby Schlachtensee and Krumme Lanke lakes
beckon you to swim, boat, or walk along their shores.
Bogotastr. 9, tel. 030/816-0060. 19 rooms with bath. Facilities:
breakfast buffet. AE, DC, MC, V.

Schweizerhof Berlin. A newly completed program of refurbishing has not taken away the rustic look in this centrally located
hotel; the extras, like room video players and mini-bars, are
up-to-the-minute. Ask for a room in the west wing, where
rooms are larger. Standards are high throughout. The indoor
pool is the largest hotel pool in Berlin. *Budapesterstr. 21-31,*
tel. 030/26960. 430 rooms with bath. Facilities: sauna, solar-
ium, pool, fitness room, hairdresser, beauty salon. AE, DC,
MC, V.

★ **Seehof.** This handsome lakeside hotel is close to the Berlin fairgrounds and within easy reach of downtown. Most rooms overlook Lietzensee lake; ask for a balcony room on the second floor.

Berlin Lodging

Quedlinburgerstr.

Schloss-garten

R.-Wagner-pl.

Otto-Suhr-Allee

Schlossstr.

Kaiser-Friedrich-Str.

Suarezstr.

Kantstr.

Gervinusstr.

Kurfürstendamm

Westfälischestr.

Seesenerstr.

Stadtring

Kaiserdamm

Bismarckstr.

Ernst-Reuter-Pl.

Cauerstr.

Marchstr.

Dovestr.

Levetzowstr.

Spree

Altonaerstr.

Bachstr.

Grosser Stern

Str. des 17 Juni

Hardenbergstr.

Wilmersdorferstr.

Kantstr.

Leibnizstr.

Olivaer Pl.

Brandenburgische Str.

Konstanzer Str.

Kurfürstendamm

Düsseldorfer Str.

Hohenzollern-Damm

Uhlandstr.

Berlinerstr.

Lietzenburgerstr.

Spichern

Nachodstr.

Bundesallee

Budapesterstr.

Zoologischer Garten

Nürnbgrstr.

Kleiststr.

Kurfürstenstr.

Motzstr.

Hohenstaufenstr.

Grunewaldstr.

Berlinerstr.

Badenschestr.

WILMERSDORF

Volkspark

Mecklenburgstr.

Hauptstr.

River

Hofjäger und Klingelhöferstr.

KEY

AE American Express Office

i Tourist Information

The large indoor pool overlooks the lake, too, and has access to a bar. Dine in the Au Lac restaurant, with its frescoed ceilings and Gobelin tapestries; it specializes in French cuisine and serves a fine six-course gourmet menu. *Lietzensee-Ufer 11, tel. 030/320–020. 77 rooms with bath. Facilities: restaurant, terrace with outdoor bar, indoor pool, sauna, solarium. AE, DC, MC, V.*

Moderate
★
Casino Hotel. What was once a barracks has been skillfully converted into an appealing hotel with large, comfortable rooms, all tastefully furnished and well-equipped—the Prussian soldiers never had it so good! You'll detect the Bavarian owner's influence in the south German cuisine at the restaurant. The Casino is in the Charlottenburg district. *Königen-Elisabeth-Str. 47a, tel. 030/303–090. 24 rooms with bath. Facilities: restaurant, beer garden. AE, DC, MC, V.*

Riehmers Hofgarten. A few minutes' walk from the Kreuzberg hill in the heart of the colorful Kreuzberg district and close to Tempelhof airport, the Riehmers Hofgarten is a small hotel housed in a late-19th-century building. The high-ceiling rooms are comfortable, with crisp linens and firm beds. *Yorckstr. 83, tel. 030/781–011. 21 rooms with bath. AE, DC, MC, V.*

Inexpensive
Atrium Hotel. This little privately run hotel is located within reasonable reach of downtown. The modest rooms are comfortably furnished and clean, the staff efficient and helpful. The only drawback is that there's no restaurant. *Motzstr. 87, tel. 030/244–057. 22 rooms with bath. MC.*

Econtel. This family-oriented hotel is within walking distance of Charlottenburg Palace. Rooms have a homey feel and are spotlessly clean. *Sommeringstr. 24, tel. 030/344–001. 205 rooms with bath. Facilities: snack bar. MC.*

Herbst. This plain and simple bed-and-breakfast pension is in the Spandau district, where Hitler's mysterious deputy Rudolph Hess spent more than 40 years in jail. There are good connections to downtown by S-Bahn. *Moritzstr. 21, tel. 030/333–4032. 22 rooms with bath. AE, DC.*

★
Ravenna. A small, friendly hotel in the Steglitz district, Ravenna is near the Botanical Garden and Dahlem museums. All the rooms are well-equipped. Suite 111B is a bargain: It includes a large living room and kitchen for only DM 200. *Grunewaldstr. 8–9, tel. 030/792–8031. 45 rooms with bath. AE, DC, MC, V.*

Savigny. A hotel in central Berlin doesn't come any cheaper: A double room costs just DM 110, and that includes breakfast. The rooms are sparsely furnished, and there are no private bathrooms. But the service is friendly, and you're just 500 yards from the Ku'damm. *Brandenbürgischestr. 21, tel. 030/881–3001. 50 rooms, none with bath. Facilities: bar. No credit cards.*

Eastern Berlin

Very Expensive
Grand Hotel. Eastern Berlin's most expensive hotel lives up to its name; opened in 1987, this hotel is grand in every sense of the word. From the moment you step into the air-conditioned atrium lobby, you'll wonder how this example of capitalism at its most elegant ever fitted into a socialist society. From there on in, all is couched in luxury, and really, you could be in any modern, commodious hotel in the world. *Friedrichstr. 158–164, corner Behrenstr., tel. 030/23270. 315 rooms and 35 suites, all with bath. Facilities: 4 restaurants, winter garden,*

Bierstube (beer room), bars, concert café, casino, pool, sauna,
squash courts, shopping arcade, hairdresser, theater ticket of-
fice, car and yacht rental. AE, DC, MC, V.

Hilton International. Berlin's newest hotel opened in 1991 as
the Dom Hotel, and was soon taken over by Hilton. It overlooks
the historic Gendarmenmarkt, with the German and French
cathedrals and the Neoclassical Schauspielhaus. Near Checkpoint Charlie, the location is central to the whole city. All the
right touches are here, from heated bathtubs to special rooms
for handicapped travelers, nonsmokers, and businesswomen.
Mohrenstr. 30, tel. 030/23826. 366 rooms. Facilities: 3 restau-
rants, cafeteria, pub, wine cellar, bar, discotheque, indoor
pool, sauna, solarium, fitness room, bowling, garage. AE,
DC, MC, V.

★ **Metropol.** This is the choice of businesspeople, not just for its
excellent location across from the Friedrichstrasse train station and the International Trade Center; the service is outstanding. The best rooms are on the front side, facing north.
All rooms are well-equipped (but note that only public areas are
air-conditioned); the hotel's antiques gallery is small but interesting, and the nightclub is an unusually good one, while the
restaurants are only fair (except in price!); the exception is the
hotel grill-restaurant off the lobby, which is about the best in
eastern Berlin. *Friedrichstr. 150–153, tel. 030/203–070. 300*
rooms with bath. Facilities: 3 restaurants, nightclub, bars, ga-
rage, pool, sauna, fitness room, solarium, antiques gallery,
shopping mall, car, horse-drawn carriage, and yacht rental
available. AE, DC, MC, V.

★ **Palast.** This is a favorite with tour groups because of its proximity to eastern Berlin's Museum Island—and because it's another of the city's mega-facility hotels. The best rooms overlook
the Spree River; those on the Alexanderplatz side can be noisy.
The shopping mall includes a travel agency, an antiques gallery, and eastern Berlin's central ticket agency. The restaurants are recommended. *Karl-Liebknecht-Str. 5, tel. 030/*
23828. 583 rooms with bath. Facilities: 6 restaurants, 4 bars,
garage, Bierstube, nightclub, pool, sauna, fitness room, solar-
ium, bowling, travel office, theater ticket office, antiques gal-
lery, shopping mall, car and yacht rental. AE, DC, MC, V.

Expensive **Berolina.** If being a little way from the city's main tourist attractions is no deterrent, this is a pleasant place to stay near
Alexanderplatz. Its roof-garden restaurant (Restaurant Krö-
gel, on the 11th floor) will give you a fine view out over Berlin.
Karl-Marx-Allee 31, tel. 030/210–9541. 344 rooms with bath.
Facilities: 3 restaurants, roof garden, souvenir shop, café, bar,
sauna, garage. AE, DC, MC, V.

Forum Hotel Berlin. With its 40 stories, the Forum Hotel Berlin at the top end of Alexanderplatz competes with the nearby
Fernsehturm for the title of premier downtown landmark. The
roof dining room features good food and service and stunning
views (reservations are essential). As the city's largest hotel, it
is understandably less personal. The bar on the 37th floor
claims to be the highest in Europe and is open until 5 AM.
Alexanderpl., tel. 030/23890. 997 rooms with bath or shower.
Facilities: 4 restaurants (including roof dining room), 3 bars,
garage, shopping, beer garden, Bierstube, sauna. AE, DC,
MC, V.

Hotel Müggelsee. Berlin's biggest and some say most beautiful
lake is just beyond your balcony in this establishment, which

was once a favorite among East Germany's communist leaders. The hotel even has its own yacht for the use of its guests. *Am Grossen Müggelsee, tel. 030/660-20. 166 rooms with bath. Facilities: Boutiques, tennis court, 2 restaurants, bar, nightclub. AE, DC, MC, V.*

★ **Unter den Linden.** The international quality of the gigantic, newer hotels may be missing here, but the location couldn't be better. The restaurant is known for the best food on Unter den Linden. *Unter den Linden 14, corner Friedrichstr., tel. 030/ 238110. 307 rooms with bath or shower. Facilities: restaurant. AE, DC, MC, V.*

Moderate **Charlottenhof.** This popular hotel-pension, ideally located on the beautiful Gendarmenmarkt, was taken over by a large western group in 1991. Happily, room prices have stayed moderate and the homey, friendly nature of the original establishment has remained unscathed. With this, the Charlottenhof has moved into the ranks of eastern Berlin's most recommendable hotels. *Charlottenstr. 52, tel. 030/392-8426. 86 rooms with bath. Facilities: restaurant, bar. AE, DC, MC, V.*

Hotel Krone. Opened in 1991, the Krone is part of the Hilton Hotel complex, sharing Hilton's excellent location on the beautiful Gendarmenmarkt, but not its high prices. The facilities offered by the Krone are correspondingly fewer, but rooms are comfortable and adequately furnished. There's no restaurant, but most of eastern Berlin's better eating haunts are within a 10-minute walk. *Gendarmenmarkt, tel. 030/23820. 148 rooms with bath. Facilities: restaurant, bar. AE, DC, MC, V.*

Newa. This older hotel, popular because of its affordability, is just a 10-minute streetcar-ride away from the downtown area. Rooms in the back are quieter. At press time, the hotel was undergoing major renovations, scheduled to be completed by September 1993; call ahead to check on its status. *Invalidenstr. 115, tel. 030/282-5461. 57 rooms, most with bath. No credit cards.*

Inexpensive **Hospiz am Bahnhof Friedrichstrasse.** This Evangelical church-
★ run hostel, both because of price and a convenient location, gets booked up months in advance. It is enormously popular with families, so the public areas are not always particularly restful. The restaurant is cheap and usually busy. Not all rooms have their own bathrooms. *Albrechstr. 8, tel. 030/282-5396. 110 rooms, most with bath. Facilities: restaurant. No credit cards.*

Hospiz Augustrasse. Comfortable rooms and friendly staff make this very low-priced hotel—also run by the Evangelical church—appealing. It is roughly a 10-minute streetcar ride into downtown Berlin. Breakfast is the only meal served here. *Augustr. 82, tel. 030/282-5321. 70 rooms, some with bath. No credit cards.*

The Arts and Nightlife

The Arts

Today's Berlin has a tough task living up to the reputation it gained from the film *Cabaret*, but if nightlife is a little toned down since the '30s, the arts still flourish. In addition to the many hotels that book seats, there are several ticket agencies, including **Theaterkasse Sasse** (Ku'damm 24, tel. 030/882-7360),

Theater-kasse Centrum (Mienekestr. 25, tel. 030/882–7611), and **Wildbad-Kiosk,** (Rankestr. 1, tel. 030/881–4507). Most of the big stores (KaDeWe, Hertie, Wertheim, and Karstadt, for example) also have ticket agencies, while in eastern Berlin tickets can be obtained from the tourist office in Alexanderplatz, and at ticket offices in the Palast and Grand hotels. Detailed information about what's going on in Berlin can be found in *Berlin Programm*, a monthly guide to Berlin arts (DM 2.50), and the magazines *Tip* and *Zitty*, which appear every two weeks and provide full arts listings.

Theater Theater in Berlin is outstanding, but performances are usually in German. The exceptions are operettas and the (nonliterary) cabarets. Of the city's more than 50 theaters, the most renowned for both its modern and classical productions is the **Schaubühne am Lehniner Platz.** Also important are the **Schiller-Theater** (Bismarckstr. 110, tel. 030/319–5236), which has an excellent workshop—the **Werkstatt,** specializing in experimental and avant-garde theater; **the Schlosspark-Theater** (Schlossstr. 48, tel. 030/793–1515); **the Renaissance-Theater** (Hardenbergstr. 6, tel. 030/312–4202); the **Freie Volksbühne** (Schaperstr. 24, tel. 030/881–3742). For *Boulevard* plays (fashionable social comedies), there is the **Komödie** (Kurfürstendamm 206, tel. 030/882–7893), and at the same address the **Theater am Kurfürstendamm** (tel. 030/882–3789), and the **Hansa Theater** (Alt Moabit 48, tel. 030/391–4460). Among the smaller, more experimental theaters is the **Tribune** (Otto-Suhr-Allee 18–20, tel. 030/341–2600), a youthful enterprise.

Eastern Berlin's leading theaters include: the **Berliner Ensemble** (Bertolt–Brecht–Pl., tel. 030/282–3160), dedicated to Brecht and works of other international playwrights; **Deutches Theater** (Schumannstr. 13–14, tel. 030/287–1225), for outstanding classical and contemporary German drama; **Friedrichstadtpalais** (Friedrichstr. 107, tel. 030/283–6474), a glossy showcase for variety revues and historic old Berlin theater pieces; **Kammerspiele** (Schumannstr. 13–14, tel. 030/287–1226), a studio theater attached to the Deutsches Theater; **Maxim-Gorki-Theater** (Am Festungsgraben, tel. 030/208–2783), featuring plays by local authors and some contemporary humor; and **Volksbühne** (Rosa-Luxemburg-Pl., tel. 030/282–8978), featuring classical and contemporary drama.

Berlin's savage and debunking idiom is particularly suited to social and political satire, a long tradition in cabaret theaters here. The **Stachelschweine** (Europa-Center, tel. 030/261–4795) and **Die Wühlmäuse** (1/30 Nümbergerstr. 33, tel. 030/213–7047) carry on that tradition with biting wit and style; eastern Berlin's equivalent is **Distel** (Friedrichstr. 100, tel. 030/200–4704). For children's theater, try **Klecks** (Schinkestr. 8/9, tel. 030/693–7731). **Puppentheater** (Greifswalderstr. 81–84, tel. 030/436–1343), eastern Berlin's puppet theater, is nominally for children but can be good entertainment for adults as well.

Concerts Berlin is the home of one of the world's leading orchestras, the **Berliner Philharmonisches Orchester** (Berlin Philharmonic—*see* Philharmonic, below) in addition to a number of other major symphony orchestras and orchestral ensembles. The **Berlin Festival Weeks,** held annually from August to October, combine a wide range of concerts, operas, ballet, theater, and art exhibitions. For information and reservations, write **Festspiele GmbH** (Kartenbüro, Budapesterstr. 50, 1000 Berlin 30).

Concert halls in Berlin include:

Grosser Sendesaal des SFB (Haus des Rundfunks, Masurenallee 8–14, tel. 030/303–11123). Part of the Sender Freies Berlin, one of Berlin's broadcasting stations, the Grosser Sendesaal is the home of the Radio Symphonic Orchestra.

Konzertsaal der Hochschule der Künste (Hardenbergstr. 33, tel. 030/318–52374). The concert hall of the Academy of Fine Arts is Berlin's second biggest—also known as the "symphony garage."

Philharmonie (Matthaikircherstr. 1, tel. 030/254–880 or 030/261–4383). The Berlin Philharmonic is based here. Tickets have to be reserved and purchased at the box office; telephone bookings are not accepted.

Schauspielhaus (Gendarmenmarkt, tel. 030/209–02267). This beautifully restored hall is a prime venue for concerts in eastern Berlin.

Waldbühne (Am Glockenturm, close to the Olympic Stadium). Modeled along the lines of an ancient Roman theater, this open-air site accommodates nearly 20,000 people. Tickets are available through ticket agencies.

Opera, Ballet, and Musicals The **Deutsche Oper Berlin** (Bismarckstr. 35, tel. 030/341–0249) is one of Germany's leading opera houses and presents outstanding productions year-round. The ballet also performs here. Tickets for both are expensive and sell out quickly. At the **Neuköllner Oper** (Karl-Marx-Str. 131–133, tel. 030/687–6061) you'll find showy, fun performances of long-forgotten operas and humorous musical productions. The skillfully restored **Theater des Westens** (Kantstr. 12, tel. 030/319–03193) is the ideal setting for comic operas and musicals like *West Side Story*, *A Chorus Line*, and *Cabaret*. Experimental ballet and modern dance are presented at the **Tanzfabrik** in Kreuzberg (Möckernstr. 66, tel. 030/786–5861).

Eastern Berlin's main sites for opera, operettas, and dance are the **Deutsche Staatsoper** (Unter den Linden 7, tel. 030/200–4762), the **Komische Oper** (Behrenstr. 55–57, tel. 030/229–2555), and the **Metropol Theater** (Friedrichstr. 101, tel. 030/208–2715).

Film Berlin has around 90 movie theaters, showing about 100 movies a day. International and German movies are shown in the big theaters around the Ku'damm; the "Off-Ku-damm" theaters show less commercial movies. For (un-dubbed) movies in English, go to the **Odeon** (Hauptstr. 116, tel. 030/781–5667), **Kurbel** (Gniesebrechtstr. 4, tel. 030/8835325), or the **Arsenal** (Welserstr. 25, tel. 030/246–848). Films from eastern Germany's state archives are shown Tuesday and Friday at 5:30 and 8 at **Filmtheater Babylon** (Rosa-Luxemburg-Str. 30, tel. 030/212–5076).

In February, Berlin hosts the **Internationale Filmfestspiele**, an internationally famous film festival, conferring "Golden Bear" awards on the best films, directors, and actors. The organizers, under pressure from an increasingly popular film festival that takes place in Munich every June, are considering moving the two-week event to summer. Call tel. 030/254–890 for information.

Nightlife

Berlin's nightlife has always been notorious. There are scads of places in western Berlin to seek your nighttime entertainment, and the quality ranges widely from tacky to spectacular. Eastern Berlin's nightlife has not been on a par with the western sector, although that is changing. Dinner-dancing is generally offered at the international-style hotels; some also have night-clubs.

All Berlin tour operators offer **Night Club Tours** (around DM 100, including entrance fees to up to three shows, free drinks, and, in some cases, supper). Most places in western Berlin stay open late; some have all-night liquor licenses.

Clubs   **Chez Nous** (Marburgerstr. 14, tel. 030/213–1810) lives up to Berlin's reputation as the drag-show center of Germany. Empire-style plush is the backdrop for two nightly shows (reservations recommended).

You'll find three more conventional stage shows at **Dollywood** (Kurfürstenstr. 114, tel. 030/248–950) each night, plus a disco. **La Vie en Rose** (Europa-Centre, tel. 030/323–6006) is a revue theater with spectacular light shows that also showcases international stars (book ahead). If the strip show at the **New Eden** (Ku'damm 71, tel. 030/323–5849) doesn't grab you, maybe the dance music will (two bands nightly). The **New York Bar** (Olivaer Pl. 16, tel. 030/883–6258) is a mellow drinking haven compared to its rowdier neighbors. Despite Mississippi-inspired decor, the **Riverboat** (Hohenzollerndamm 177, tel. 030/878–476) has great Berlin atmosphere. You have a choice at **Zeleste** (Marburgerstr. 2, tel. 030/213–4302): Sit back and listen to jazz or dance the night away in its disco.

Jazz Clubs   Berlin's lively music scene is dominated by jazz and rock. For jazz enthusiasts, *the* events of the year are the summer's **Jazz in the Garden** festival and the international autumn **Jazz Fest Berlin.** For information call the **Berlin Tourist Information Center** (Europa-Center, tel. 030/262–6031).

Traditionally, the best **live jazz** can be found at:
Eierschale (Podbielskiallee 50, tel. 030/832–7097). A variety of jazz groups appear here at the "Egg Shell," daily from 8:30 PM, admission free.
Flöz (Nassauischestr. 36A, tel. 030/861–1000). The sizzling jazz at this club is sometimes incorporated into theater presentations.
Kunstlerhaus Bethanien (Mariannenpl. 2, tel. 030/614–8010). Jazz and 'Free Music' concerts are held at this big venue.
Quartier Latin (Potsdamerstr. 96, tel. 030/2629016). The Quartier Latin is one of the leaders in Berlin's jazz scene. Jazz and rock are both presented.

Discos   **Blue Note** (Courbierestr. 13, tel. 030/247–248). For an escape from the usual disco sounds, try the Blue Note; you'll find a tasty mixture of jazz, bebop, and Latin American rhythms. Open until 6 AM.
Dschungel (Nürnbergerstr. 53, tel. 030/246–698). A funky disco, "Jungle," is a current "in" spot. Dance until you drop, or at least until 4 AM. Closed Tuesday.
Hafenbar (Chauseestr. 20). This is a popular eastern Berlin disco decorated in '50s style. Closed Wednesdays.
Metropol (Nollendorfpl. 5, tel. 030/216–2787). Berlin's largest

disco, which stages occasional concerts, is a hot spot for the younger tourist. The black dance floor upstairs is the scene for a magnificent light and laser show. The DM 10 cover includes your first drink.

Kneipen Berlin has roughly 5,000 bars and pubs; this includes the dives, too. All come under the heading of *Kneipen*—the place round the corner where you stop in for a beer, a snack, a conversation, and sometimes, to dance.

Bogen 597 (Savignypl., S-bahn passage). Sound effects are provided by the S-bahn—you'll hear and feel the trains passing on the tracks overhead. This is a cozy place that serves a fine selection of wines in addition to the inevitable beer.

Ku'dorf (Joachimstaler-Str. 15). The Ku'dorf makes it easy to go from one Kneipe to another—there are 18 located under one roof here, underground, just off the Ku'damm. Open Monday–Saturday from 8 PM.

Leydicke (Mansteinstr. 4). This historic spot is a must for out-of-towners. The proprietors operate their own distillery and have a superb selection of wines and liqueurs; definitely the right atmosphere in which to enjoy a few glasses.

Zur Nolle (Nollendorfpl.). You can sit in an old subway car in this converted (above-ground) subway station and enjoy live Dixieland music. Berlin specialties are served from the buffet. Check it out on a Sunday morning as you stroll around the local flea market.

Sperlingsgasse (Lietzenburgerstr. 82–84). Look for the replica of the Brandenburg Gate on the sidewalk. It'll point you in the direction of the 13 different Kneipen here. All open at 7 PM.

Wilhelm Hoeck (Wilmersdorferstr. 149). Berlin's oldest Kneipe is also its most beautiful. Its superb interior dates back to 1892—all original. Frequented by a colorful cross section of the public, this is a place that's definitely worth a visit.

Wirthaus Wuppke (Schlüterstr. 21). Come here if you're seeking a mellower, quieter atmosphere. It gets as crowded as the others, but it's not so hectic. The food is good and inexpensive.

Yorckschlösschen (Yorckstr. 15). In the summer you can sit in the garden and enjoy a beer and a snack or a hearty meal. If you're lucky, there may be live music.

Zwiebelfisch (Savignypl. 7). Literally translated as the "onion fish," this Kneipe has become the meeting place of literary Bohemians of all ages. It has a good atmosphere for getting to know people. The beer is good, the menu small.

Casinos Western Berlin's leading casino is in the Europa Center. It has 10 roulette tables and three blackjack tables, and is open 3 AM–3 PM. Eastern Berlin's poshest casino is at the Grand Hotel.

4 Excursions from Berlin

Including Potsdam, Magdeburg, and Frankfurt an der Oder

Potsdam

Important Addresses and Numbers

Tourist Information The tourist office is **Potsdam-Information** (Friedrich-Ebert-Strasse 5, Potsdam 1561; tel. 0331/21100, 0331/329217, and 0331/329220). It's open Monday–Friday 9–8, weekends 9–6. Rooms in private homes (but not hotel rooms) can be reserved through Potsdam-Information, either at a special counter open until 6, or by telephoning 0331/23385 or 0331/21100, fax 0331/23012.

Emergencies **Police:** tel. 0331/110. **Ambulance:** tel. 0331/410 or 0331/412–581. **Medical emergencies:** Poliklinik, Turkstrasse, tel. 0331/410. **Doctor and dentist:** 0331/410. **Late-night pharmacies:** Zentralapotheke, Heinrich-Rau-Allee 40, tel. 0331/24069. When this pharmacy is closed, a sign is posted on its door identifying the nearest late-night pharmacy.

Getting There

Potsdam is virtually a suburb of Berlin, some 20 kilometers (12 miles) southwest of the city center and a half-hour journey by car, train, or bus. City traffic is heavy, however, and a train journey is recommended, even though there are no direct trains. Perhaps the most effortless way to visit Potsdam and its attractions is to book a tour with one of the big Berlin operators (*see* Guided Tours, below).

By Car From Berlin center (Strasse des 17 Juni) take the Potsdamerstrasse south until it becomes Route 1 and then follow the signs to Potsdam.

By Train Take the S-bahn, either the S-5 or the S-1 line, to Wannsee. Change there for the short rail trip (the trains leave only hourly) to Potsdam West (for Schloss Sanssouci and Schloss Charlottenhof), and Wildpark (for Neues Palais) stations. You also can take bus 113 from Wannsee to the Bassanplatz bus station. From there you can take bus 695 to Sanssouci park, or you can walk down Brandenburgerstrasse to Platz der Nationen and on to the Green Gate, the main entrance to Sanssouci park.

By Bus There is regular bus service from the bus station at the Funkturm, Messedamm 8 (reached by U-1 to Kaiserdamm).

By Boat Boats leave hourly 10–6 from Wannsee landing.

Guided Tours from Berlin

Severin & Kühn offers a whole-day tour for DM 89 (including lunch). **Berliner Bären Stadtrundfahrt** conducts an afternoon tour that includes tea in its DM 65 price. Berolina and Bus-Verkehr-Berlin also offer tours of Potsdam from Berlin. (*See* Guided Tours in Essential Information, above.)

Exploring Potsdam

Germany's most famous king, Friedrich II—Frederick the Great—spent more time at his summer residence in Potsdam than at the official court in Berlin, and it's no wonder. Frederick was an aesthetic ruler, and he clearly fell for the sheer beau-

Berlin Excursions

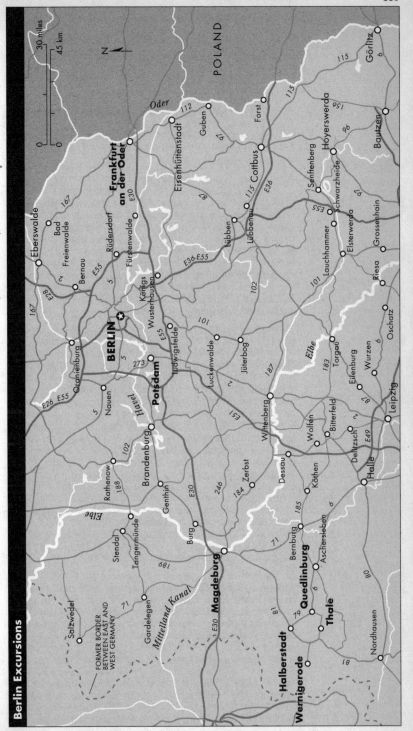

ty of a sleepy township lost among the hills, meadows, and lakes of this rural corner of mighty Prussia. Frederick's father, Friedrich Wilhelm I, had established the Prussian court at Potsdam, but the royal castle didn't match the demanding tastes of his son and heir, who built a summer palace of his own amid green lawns above the Havel River. He called it "Sanssouci," meaning "without a care" in the French language he cultivated in his own private circle and within the court. Designed by Georg Wenzeslaus von Knobelsdorff, Sanssouci became one of Germany's greatest tourist attractions (5 million visitors a year file through the palace and grounds). In 1993, Potsdam celebrates its 1,000th birthday, so if you plan to visit this year book well in advance.

As you walk through Potsdam's own **Brandenburger Tor** (a victory arch built 25 years after Sanssouci) and on past the Grünes Gitter, the main entrance, at Platz der Nationen, you see the Hohenzollern palace complex, contained in a beautifully landscaped park. One of the most important European royal residences of its time, it is today largely re-created. Just weeks before the end of World War II, Potsdam was razed by British bombing, and the battle for Berlin finished it off. The East Germans did a magnificent restoration job. There is no charge to enter the grounds. It's recommended that you purchase the excellent map of the park sold at the Grünes Gitter; it's easy to get lost in this huge complex without it.

The vine-covered terraces on which **Sanssouci** stands are actually an artificial hill, rising in majestic steps from a side stream of the Havel. Executed according to Frederick's impeccable, French-influenced taste, the palace is extravagantly Rococo, with scarcely a patch of wall left unadorned. Strangely, Frederick occupied only five rooms; of these, his bedroom, study, and circular library (beautifully paneled with cedar wood) can be visited. Five rooms were kept for guests, one exclusively reserved for the French writer and philosopher Voltaire. Johann Sebastian Bach was also a welcome visitor; he and Frederick, a competent musician, performed together in the palace music chamber, considered one of Germany's finest Rococo interiors. To the west of the palace are the **Neue Kammern** (New Chambers), 1747, which housed guests of the king's family; originally it functioned as a greenhouse until it was remodeled in 1771–74. Just east of Sanssouci palace is the **Picture Gallery** (1755–1763), which still displays Frederick's collection of 17th-century Italian, Flemish, and Dutch paintings, including Cavaggio's *Doubting Thomas*. Frederick opened the gallery to the public, creating the first museum of its kind in Germany.

At the end of the long, straight avenue that runs through Sanssouci Park you'll see a much larger and grander palace, the **Neues Palais** (New Palace). Frederick loosened the pursestrings in building this palace after the Seven Years War (1756–63), and it's said he wanted to demonstrate to his subjects that the state coffers hadn't been depleted too severely by the long conflict. Frederick rarely stayed here, however, preferring the relative coziness of Sanssouci. Still, the Neues Palais has much of interest, including an indoor grotto hall, a Jules Verne-like extravaganza of walls and columns set with shells, coral, and other aquatic decoration. There's a fascinating collection of musical instruments, which includes a 900-year-old portable organ; the Upper Gallery, which contains paintings by 17th-century Italian masters; and a recently restored bijou court theater in which performances are still given throughout the year by Potsdam's Hans Otto Theater.

After Frederick died in 1786 (he is buried on the terrace of Sanssouci palace), the ambitious Sanssouci building program ground to a halt and the park fell into neglect. It was 50 years before another Prussian king, Frederick William III, restored Sanssouci's earlier glory. He engaged the great Berlin architect Karl Friedrich Schinkel to build a small palace for the crown prince. The result is the **Schloss Charlottenhof,** set in its own grounds in the southern part of the Sanssouci park. Schinkel gave it a classical, almost Roman appearance, and he let his imagination loose in the interior, too—decorating one of the rooms as a Roman tent, with its walls and ceiling draped in striped canvas.

Just north of the Schloss Charlottenhof, on the path back to Sanssouci, you'll find two other later additions to the park: Friedrich Wilhelm II's **Römische Bäder** (Roman Baths), 1836, and a **tea-house** built in 1757 in the Chinese style, which was all the rage at the time. Between the Neues Palais and the Sanssouci is the **Orangerie** (completed in 1860), which, with two massive towers (one of which is open, providing a splendid view) linked by a colonnade, evokes an Italian Renaissance palace. Today it houses 47 copies of paintings by Raphael. Elsewhere in the park, a delicious layercake **"mosque"** disguises pump works that operated the fountains in the Sanssouci park; the minaret concealed the chimney. The Italianate **Friedenskirche** (Peace Church, 1845–48) houses a 12th-century Byzantine mosaic taken from an island near Venice. The **Belvedere,** an 18th-century tower near the **Drachenhaus** (*see* Time Out, below), was scheduled to be restored by the end of 1992, and should provide stupendous vistas of the entire complex.

Time Out   Halfway up the park's Drachenberg hill, above the Orangery, stands the curious **Drachenhaus** (Dragon House), modeled in 1770 after the Pagoda at London's Kew Gardens and named for the gargoyles ornamenting the roof corners. When built, it served as the residence of the palace vintner; it now houses a popular café.

Another corner of Potsdam—about five minutes by car from Sanssouci—is equally exotic. Resembling a rambling, half-timbered country manor house, the **Schloss Cecilienhof** was built for Crown Prince Wilhelm in 1913 in a newly laid out stretch of park bordering the Heiliger See, called the New Garden. It was here that the allied leaders Truman, Atlee, and Stalin hammered out the fate of postwar Germany, at the 1945 Potsdam Conference. You can see the round table where they held their meetings; in fact, you can stay the night under the roof where they gathered to make history, for the Cecilienhof is today a very comfortable hotel (*see* Lodging, below). Also in the New Garden is the substantial two-story **Marmorpalais** (Marble Palace), completed in 1792, using gray-white Silesian marble to ornament the red brickwork. Formerly housing a military museum, it is closed for restoration until 2000. *Information Center, Sanssouci: tel. 0331/22051. Open April–Oct., daily 9–4:30. Schloss Sanssouci admission (guided tours only): DM 6 adults, DM 3 children. Open April–mid-Oct., daily 9–5; mid-*

Oct.–Jan. 9–3; Feb. and March, daily 9–4; closed first and third Mon. of month. Neue Kammern admission (guided tours only): DM 3 adults, DM 2 children. Open Sat.–Thurs. 9–noon and 12:30–4. Picture Gallery admission: DM 3 adults, DM 1.50 children. Open mid-May–mid-Oct., daily 9–5, closed fourth Wed. of month. Neues Palais admission with tour: DM 6 adults, DM 3 children. Open April–mid-Oct., daily 9–5; mid-Oct.–Jan., daily 9–3; Feb. and March, daily 9–4; closed second and fourth Mon. of month. Schloss Charlottenhof admission (guided tours only): DM 3 adults, DM 2 children. Open mid-May–mid-Oct., daily 9–5; closed fourth Mon. of month. Römische Bäder admission free. Open mid-May–mid-Oct., daily 9–5; closed third Mon. of month. Chinese tea-house admission: DM 1. Open mid-May–mid-Oct., daily 9–5; closed one Mon. a month. Orangerie admission (additional charge for special exhibitions): DM 3 adults, DM 1.50 children. Open mid-May–mid-Oct., daily 9–5; closed fourth Thurs. of month. Mosque admission: DM 3. Open mid-May–mid-Oct., daily 9–5; closed fourth Mon. in month. Schloss Cecilienhof admission (nonguests): DM 3, DM 1.50 children. Open daily 9–4:15, closed second and fourth Mon. of month.

Don't leave Potsdam without looking over the town itself, which still retains the imperial character lent to it by the many years it served as royal residence and garrison quarters. The central market square, the **Alter Markt,** sums it all up: the stately, domed **Nikolaikirche** (1724), a square Baroque church with classical columns; an **Egyptian obelisk** erected by Schloss Sanssouci architect Georg von Knobelsdorff; and the officious facade of the former city hall (1755), now the Haus Marchiwitza, with a gilded figure of Atlas atop the tower. Wander around some of the adjacent streets, particularly Wilhelm-Külz-Strasse, to admire the handsome restored burghers' houses.

Three blocks north of the Alter Markt is the **Holländisches Viertel,** built by Friedrich Wilhelm I in 1732 to induce Dutch artisans to settle in a city that needed migrant labor to support its rapid growth. (Few Dutch came, and the gabled, hip-roofed brick houses were used mostly to house staff.) The Dutch government has promised to finance some of the cost of repairing the damage done by more than four decades of Communist administration.

Dining

Am Stadttor. A five-minute walk from the Schloss Sanssouci and located on Potsdam's main shopping street, the Stadttor is the ideal spot for lunch. The menu isn't exactly imperial Prussian, but the dishes are filling and inexpensive. The soups are particularly wholesome, and the Berlin-style liver is as good as any you'll find in the city. The place is popular, so it's advisable to book a table. *Brandenburgerstrasse 1–3, tel. 0331/21729. Reservations advised. Dress: informal. No credit cards. Inexpensive.*

Lodging

Schloss Cecilienhof. This Tudor country-style mansion is where Truman, Atlee, and Stalin drew up the 1945 Potsdam Agreement. It's here that Truman received the news of the first successful atom bomb test (July 16, 1945). Given the fateful events that took place here, the hotel rooms are somewhat mundane, although comfortable and adequately equipped. The Schloss is set in its own parkland bordering the Jungfernsee and is a pleasant stroll from Sanssouci and the city center. *Neuer Garten, tel. 0331/231–4144, fax 0331/22498. 42 rooms with bath or shower. Facilities: sauna, masseur, restaurant. AE, D, MC, V. Moderate.*

Magdeburg

Magdeburg's great Gothic cathedral—Germany's oldest and, some say, the country's finest—is worth the trip from Berlin. Much of the city was rebuilt after the 1945 bombing in the dull utilitarian style favored by the Communists, but there are nevertheless corners of the old town where Magdeburg's 1,200-year history still lingers. Apart from the cathedral, the monastery church of Unser Lieben Frauen contains much of interest. Both are a few strides from the Elbe River, where some fine walks open up through the wooded Kulturpark.

Important Addresses and Numbers

Tourist Information The tourist office is **Information-Magdeburg** (Alter Markt 9, Postfach 266, Magdeburg 3010; tel. 0391/31667). It's open Monday–Friday 10–6, Saturday 8–11. The tourist office can make reservations for accommodations; call 0391/35362.

Emergencies **Police:** tel. 0391/4370. **Ambulance:** tel. 0391/115. **Doctors, dentists, and late-night pharmacies:** tel. 0391/51176. **Medical emergencies:** Poliklinik Mitte, Tränsberg 21–23m, tel. 0391/51176.

Getting There

By Car Magdeburg is located just off the E–8 motorway, the old transit road connecting Berlin and Hannover. It's 150 kilometers (90 miles) west of Berlin, a 90-minute drive as long as the motorway is clear. (In summer and at weekends, when the E–8 gets crowded, the two-hour train ride from Berlin might be preferable.) To get to the town center follow the signs for Magdeburg-Stadtmitte.

By Train Trains leave approximately every two hours from Bahnhof Zoo in Berlin; the trip takes about two hours.

By Bus Buses leave from the Funkturm bus station in Berlin.

Guided Tours

There are no guided tours of Magdeburg originating in Berlin.

Exploring Magdeburg

If you arrive in Magdeburg by train or bus, head east from the main railway station (the bus depot is beside it) for two blocks to the city center, the **Alter Markt,** which is dominated from the west side by the 17th-century **Rathaus** (City Hall), one of Magdeburg's few remaining Baroque buildings. In front of its arcaded facade is a 1966 bronze copy of Germany's oldest equestrian statue, the **Magdeburger Reiter,** completed by an unknown master around 1240. The sandstone original is now in the nearby **Kulturhistorisches Museum,** where you can also see the simple invention with which the 17th-century scientist Otto von Güricke proved the extraordinary power created by a vacuum. The device consisted of just two iron cups; von Güricke sealed them together by pumping out the air—and then attached the hollow sphere to two teams of eight cart-horses, which were urged to pull the cups apart. The vacuum proved stronger. *Otto-von Güricke-Strasse 68–73. Admission: DM 3 adults, children DM 1.50. Open Tues.–Sun. 10–6.*

Head down Breiter Weg; to your left you'll see the mighty twin towers of Magdeburg's Gothic **Dom** (cathedral) of saints Maurice and Catherine rearing up above the rooftops. Opposite the post office on Breiter Weg turn left into Domplatz, and there is the soaring west front of the cathedral before you. The awesome structure was begun in 1209, making it the oldest Gothic church in Germany; it was completed in 1520. The founder of the Holy Roman Empire, Otto I, lies buried beneath the choir, his tomb overshadowed by graceful columns of Ravenna marble. Study the representations of famous Christian martyrs on the walls of the nave; you'll find them all standing determinedly on the heads of their persecutors (that's Nero under the heel of St. Paul). A more recent memorial is Expressionist artist Ernst Barlach's sculptured group warning of the horrors of war. It was removed by the Nazis in 1933, but it's back with all its original force. *Open Mon.–Sat. 10–noon and 2–4; Sun. 2–4. Guided tours: Mon.–Sat. 10 and 2, Sun 11:15 and 2.*

Just north of Domplatz and on the way back to the city center is Magdeburg's second great attraction, the Romanesque monastery church and cloisters of **Unser Lieben Frauen.** The church, built in the years 1064–1230, now serves as a concert hall and an art gallery. Gothic sculptures share space with modern east German works in sober surroundings that encourage meditation and reflection—there's also a café for more mundane requirements. *Regierungsstr. 4–6, tel. 0391/33741 (concert information). Open Tues.–Sun. 10–6.*

Dining

Haus des Handwerks. The large, echoing restaurant has the atmosphere of an East European railway station buffet, but the food is substantial and reasonably priced. The cordon bleu steak is always good. It's not central, but is well worth the 10-minute journey (number 10 tram). *Garaisstr. 10, tel. 0391/51422. Reservations advised. Dress: informal. No credit cards. Moderate.*

Stadt Prag. The "City of Prague" restaurant has a menu that reads like a culinary tour of the former Hapsburg empire, from chicken Viennese style to Bohemian dumplings by way of Hungarian goulash. *Wilhelm-Pieck-Allee 10, tel. 0391/51162. Reservations advised. Dress: informal. No credit cards. Moderate.*

Lodging

Hotel International. Magdeburg's leading hotel is typically East German postwar modern, but it has all the necessary facilities and comforts and is centrally located. Rooms are functional and uninspired in their decoration; if you're looking for space and above-average comfort, then reserve a suite apartment

(DM 300 or more). *Otto-von-Güricke-Strasse 2, tel. 0391/3840. 331 rooms and 9 suites with bath or shower. Facilities: sauna, garage, 3 restaurants, café, bar, nightclub. AE, DC, MC, V. Expensive.*

Grüner Baum. This is one of the few hotels in eastern Germany to have remained in private hands throughout the years of Communist state control. At press time, there were plans to give it a long-overdue renovation, so call beforehand to check on the availability of rooms. The rooms are large, and it's to be hoped they'll stay that way after refurbishing, which will give each room a private bathroom. *Wilhelm-Pieck-Allee 40, tel. 0391/30862. 40 rooms, none with bath (bathrooms are on each floor). No credit cards. Inexpensive.*

Excursions from Magdeburg

Magdeburg is an ideal center from which to explore the Elbe River countryside between the Harz Mountains and the Brandenburg plains. The Reisebüro (tourist office), near the main railway station (Wilhelm-Pieck-Allee 14), offers bus tours of the region. Ships of the eastern German shipping line Weisse Flotte (tel. 0391/31907) embark from Magdeburg on day trips and longer cruises on the Elbe.

Luxury cruises from Magdeburg to Bad Schandau (south of Dresden) and Vanov (near Prague, Czechoslovakia) are operated by the KD German Rhine Line, with ports of call including Wittenberg, Meissen, and Dresden. For information contact the company in the United States (tel. 914/948–3600 or 415/392–8817) or in Köln (tel. 0221/20880).

Southwest of Magdeburg is a group of historic old towns easily reached by train or car. From Magdeburg, Route 81 goes 53 kilometers (33 miles) to **Halberstadt,** the gateway to the Harz mountain area to the south. One of the key commercial and religious centers of the Middle Ages, about 85% of Halberstadt was destroyed in April 1945. Rebuilding has left some remarkable contrasts: Half-timbered 17th-century houses stand alongside stark modern blocks. Dominating the town, the twin-towered cathedral is one of the most noteworthy examples of German Gothic, completed in 1491 after 252 years of construction. Inside, note the tapestries and sculptures, the stained-glass windows, and the numerous ancient burial tombs.

Time Out

Just south of Halberstadt, the **Jagdschloss Spiegelberger,** a Baroque hunting lodge dating to 1782, now houses a pleasant country restaurant. In the basement is the "great wine cask," a huge wooden barrel constructed in 1594 and holding 132,760 liters (35,080 gallons) of wine.

Heading south on Route 81, look for the turnoff to the right about 9 kilometers (5½ miles), marked for Wernigerode, which is another 14 kilometers (9 miles) along. **Wernigerode** is a colorful small city of half-timbered houses from the Middle Ages, watched over by the castle atop the nearby Agnesberg hill. The castle was last rebuilt in 1862–85, but parts date from the 1670s and even earlier. Today the Feudalism Museum occupies 37 of its rooms. *Open Tues.–Sun. 9–5.*

The 1899 vintage **Harzquerbahn,** a fascinating narrow-gauge railway line mostly using steam power, starts from Wernigerode on its 3-hour, 60-kilometer (37½-mile) run through the northern Harz mountain area to Nordhausen.

From Wernigerode, a scenic drive winds south about 10 kilometers (6 miles) to Elbingerode, then west about 15 kilometers (9 miles) to Blankenburg. Just south of the town, a road cuts east 8 kilometers (5 miles) to **Thale,** site of the renowned **Hexentanzplatz** (Witches' Dancing Place). This rock plateau, with an elevation of 454 meters (1,475 feet), can be reached year-round by a four-minute cable-car ride from the Hubertusbrücke in Bodetal. From the top, there's a splendid view out over the neighboring countryside.

Fifteen kilometers (9 miles) beyond Thale is **Quedlinburg,** known for its picturesque half-timbered houses and detailed carved wood ornamentation. Wander around the town to enjoy the medieval houses, taking special note of the two-story **Rathaus** (City Hall), completed in 1615, its ornate stone front entry dramatically punctuating the Renaissance facade. From 966 to 1802, the castle atop the **Schlossberg** hill was the official residence of the Abbess of Quedlinburg Abbey; adjacent is the 12th-century Romanesque St. Servatius abbey church. The castle today houses a museum of local history.

Return to Berlin via Route 6 to Bernburg and then Route 71/E49 north to Magdeburg, where you can pick up the E30.

Frankfurt an der Oder

Poland is so near Berlin that a day trip to the border is no problem. If you want to go farther a visa is necessary, but at least you can stand on the banks of the famous Oder River, which now marks the eastern limits of united Germany, and look across to a Poland that is learning again to coexist with a central European colossus as neighbor. But where on the border? Frankfurt an der Oder is the obvious choice. Here you have an opportunity now missing in Berlin—to feel the chill of visiting the frontier of the old East and West and observe firsthand the new European order at work.

Important Addresses and Numbers

Tourist Information   The tourist information office is **Information-Frankfurt/Oder** (Karl-Marx-Strasse 8a, tel. 0335/22249 or 0335/325–216). It's open Monday–Friday 7 AM–4 PM, closed weekends.

Emergencies   **Police:** 0335/3790. **Ambulance, doctor, and dentist:** 0335/23514. **Medical emergencies:** Poliklinik, Am Keispark, tel. 0335/311–215. **Late-night pharmacies:** Bahnhofsapotheke, Dresdnerstrasse 5 (in main railway station), tel. 0335/23294.

Getting There

By Car   Frankfurt an der Oder is 90 kilometers (55 miles) east of Berlin, about an hour's drive. Head east on eastern Berlin's Leninallee, joining the E–55 ring-autobahn and heading south until the Frankfurt/Oder turnoff. Exit at Frankfurt-Stadtmitte.

By Train   Trains depart every two hours from eastern Berlin's Hauptbahnhof.

By Bus   There's infrequent bus service from eastern Berlin's Hauptbahnhof.

Exploring Frankfurt an der Oder

Ninety percent of the historic center of Frankfurt an der Oder was destroyed in May 1945, not by Allied bombing but in a devastating fire that broke out after Germany's capitulation. The fire was sparked by a confrontation between remaining units of the Nazi "Werwolf" resistance and Polish forces from across the Oder River. The flames spread rapidly because the conquered city had no fire brigade. Up until then, 80% of the city had survived the war undamaged; the clash between Werwolf fanatics and the Poles left it in smoldering ruins. Today, the strong undercurrent of anti-Polish feeling in Frankfurt an der Oder is palpable, and local police are kept busy smoothing over quarrels between the locals and Poles from across the river, for nowhere is the newly united Germany so close to the East European community with which it now has to live.

Poland virtually overlooks the center of the city, which sits in its faded Prussian glory on the banks of the Oder. The oldest building here is also the most imposing: the **City Hall,** on Marktplatz, 100 yards west of the Oder. First mentioned in official records in 1348, the building has a 17th-century Baroque facade that now looks out over the hustle and bustle of central Frankfurt. Behind the City Hall, on the banks of the Oder, you'll find another elegant, finely restored Baroque structure, the world's only museum devoted to one of Germany's greatest writers, Heinrich von Kleist (1777–1811). Kleist's birthplace in Frankfurt an der Oder was among the buildings consumed by fire in 1945, but the house containing the **Kleist Gedenk-und Forschungsstätte** does date from the year of the dramatist's birth. Kleist lived only 34 years—he shot himself in a suicide pact with his lover by the Wannsee near Potsdam in 1811—but his contribution to German literature was monumental. His works—notably the famous history play *Das Käthchen von Heilbronn* (source of one of Carl Orff's greatest compositions) and the comedy *Der Zerbrochene Krug* (premiered by Goethe in Weimar in 1808)—avoid all attempts at categorization. The original manuscripts of both those plays are to be seen in the museum, which traces Kleist's life and work with exemplary clarity and care. *Fährstr. 7, tel. 0335/24520. Open Tues.–Fri. 10–12 and 2–4, Sat.–Sun. 2–5.*

Dining and Lodging

Stadt Frankfurt. Frankfurt an der Oder is off the tourist track, so its leading hotel falls short of many of the expected facilities and comforts. Rooms are small, but the restaurant can be recommended, particularly its fresh-made *Gemüsetopf* (vegetable stew). *Karl-Marx-Str. 193, tel. 0335/389723. 186 rooms and 4 suites with bath or shower. Facilities: 2 restaurants, bar. AE, DC, MC, V. Moderate.*

5 Saxony and Thuringia

Including Leipzig, Dresden, and Weimar

To those familiar with eastern Germany—the former German Democratic Republic—the name may still conjure up images of dour landscapes and grim industrial cities. This image cannot be changed overnight, even since the collapse of the communist government. It will take years before the polluted, dying forests in the south can rejuvenate, and the ancient soot-stained factories are replaced. The deteriorating public housing projects of the '50s and '60s cannot be razed any more than the acrid smell of brown coal smoke can be eliminated overnight. But the small towns of eastern Germany—in regions once known as Prussia, Saxony, Thuringia—will tell much more about an older Germany than the frenetic lifestyles of Frankfurt, Hamburg, Stuttgart, or Köln. The communist influence—hard-line as it was—here never penetrated as deeply as did the American impact on West Germany. East Germany clung to its German heritage, proudly preserving connections with such national heroes as Luther, Goethe, Schiller, Bach, Handel, Hungarian-born Liszt, and Wagner. And although bombing raids in World War II devastated most of its cities, the East Germans, over the years, carried out an extensive program of restoring and rebuilding the historic neighborhoods. Meissen porcelain, Frederick the Great's palace at Potsdam, the astounding collections of the Pergamon and Bode museums in Berlin, and those in the Zwinger in Dresden will now be incorporated in the total national heritage.

Traditional tourist sights aside, eastern Germany is also worth visiting precisely because it *is* in transition, poised at a remarkable moment in history. In the wake of ebullient newspaper headlines and photographs of wild parties amidst the rubble of the Berlin Wall, it's all too easy to simplify what's going on in the former GDR as a quest for western-style democracy. The initiative for unification came as much from the west as it did from the east, and former East Germans have not been altogether happy with the consequences. Though they enjoyed the highest standard of living of all the Eastern Bloc countries, a number of eastern Germans still see their western compatriots as the "haves," and themselves as the "have-nots."

These people, bound politically and economically to the Soviet Union for 45 years, are still uncomfortable with their newly acquired freedoms and responsibilities. For most of those years, despite being communism's "Western front," the GDR was isolated from Western ideas, and many now resent the less savory elements of Western society imposed on what was an orderly, if unexciting, way of life. Time has not stood still east of the former border, but it has taken much less of a toll than it has in the West; the rampant commercial overdevelopment that has blighted much of Germany's western landscape is virtually unknown in the eastern part of the country. As one former East Berliner noted following her first visit to the western sector of the city, "The lights are brighter, so you can see the trash more readily."

The main differences for travelers are the absence of a border, no need to change currencies, and—regrettably—higher prices. But the most important change is that visitors now have complete freedom to go wherever they want, to choose their own hotels, and to wander off the "transit corridors" and explore eastern Germany at will.

Essential Information

At press time, the former German Democratic Republic—the "new federal states," or "eastern Germany"—was still in a state of flux, particularly in those areas most likely to affect visitors. The transportation and communications systems of the two halves of a country so long divided have to be completely integrated, and that will take time. Former state-run hotels are passing into private ownership and hundreds of others are being built to accommodate the surge of tourists and business travelers who followed the fall of the Berlin Wall and the opening of the frontiers.

The upheaval reaches down to the smallest concerns of everyday life, with prices rising to match those in western Germany. Travelers who remember East Germany as a low-budget paradise will be disappointed to find an area nearly as expensive as western Germany and where the cost of comfortable lodgings has gone through the roof. As this process of price adjustment is still under way, it is difficult to accurately predict costs. Museums and art galleries, for instance, were still converting their old admission charges into the new Deutschemark currency. Telephone exchanges in eastern Germany were also being expanded to accommodate the sudden surge in calls from the former West, and numbers were being altered at a frustrating rate. It's still a hopelessly difficult task to call eastern Germany from western Germany. One tip: If you are calling long-distance, ask the international operator to book an *Eilgespräch* (urgent call). It costs double, but the wait is less than halved.

We have given addresses, telephone numbers, and other logistical details based on the best available information, but remember that changes are taking place at a furious pace in everything from postal codes to street and even city names. We strongly recommend that you contact the German National Tourist Office (*see* Chapter 1) or your travel agent for the most up-to-date information.

Important Addresses and Numbers

Tourist Information *See* Important Addresses and Numbers in Chapter 3 for tourist offices in Berlin. For tourist information for individual cities, contact:

Chemnitz: Strasse der Nationen 3, tel. 0371/62051.
Dessau: Friedrich-Naumann-Str. 12, tel. 0340/4661.
Dresden: Box 201, Pragerstr. 10/11, tel. 0351/495–5025.
Eisenach: Bahnhofstr. 3–5, tel. 03691/4895.
Erfurt: Bahnhofstr. 37, tel. 0361/26267.
Freiberg: Weingasse 9.
Gera: Dr.-Rudolf Breitscheid-Str. 1, tel. 0365/26432.
Halle: Salzgrafenstrasse 3, tel. 0345/23340.
Leipzig: Sachsenplatz 1, tel. 0341/79590.
Meissen: Willy-Anker-Strasse 32, tel. 03521/4470.
Weimar: Box 647, Marktstr. 4, tel. 03643/2173.

Embassies With the reunification of Germany the embassies of the United States and the United Kingdom in eastern Berlin have been downgraded to the rank of consulates or missions. The **Canadian Embassy** in Bonn (Friedrich-Wilhelmstrasse 18, tel. 0228/231061) is responsible for eastern Germany. The **United States'**

office in eastern Berlin is at Neustädtische Kirchstr. 4–5, tel. 030/220–2741; the **United Kingdom**'s mission is at Unter den Linden 32–34, tel. 030/220–2431.

Travel Agencies **American Express:** Hotel Bellevue, Köpckestr., **Dresden**, 15, tel. 0351/56620; Europäisches Reisebüro, Katherinenstrasse, **Leipzig**, tel. 0341/79210.

Car Rental

Cars can be rented at all major hotels and at airports. Rental cars can be driven into neighboring countries, including Poland and Czechoslovakia. Rental charges correspond with those in western Germany. All the major international car rental firms are now represented throughout eastern Germany, but don't expect quite the same range of choice in models and reserve well in advance. All major Western credit cards are accepted.

Avis: Karl-Marx-Strasse 264, tel. 030/685–2093, and Schönefeld airport, tel. 0351/672–2441, **Eastern Berlin;** Dresden airport, tel. 0341/583–141, **Dresden;** Leipzig airport, tel. 0341/391–1132, **Leipzig.**

Hertz: Behrens-Str. 23 (opposite Grand Hotel), tel. 030/672–2607, and Herzbergstr, 40-43, tel. 030/255–96164, **Eastern Berlin;** Köpckestr. 15 (in Hotel Bellevue), tel. 0351/584–169, Tiergartenstr. 94, tel. 0351/232–8218, and Dresden airport, tel. 0351/588–348, **Dresden;** Platz der Republik 2 (in Hotel Astoria), tel. 0341/722–470, and Leipzig airport, tel. 0341/243–3026, **Leipzig.**

InterRent-Europcar: Rosa-Luxemburg-Str. 2, tel. 030/246–3209, Siegfriedstr. 49–60, Lichtenberg, tel. 030/558–9825, and Schönefeld airport, tel. 030/672–2606, **Eastern Berlin;** Liebstadterstr. 5, tel. 0351/232–3399, and Dresden airport, tel. 0351/232–3399, **Dresden;** Johannisplatz 14, tel. 0341/718–9300, and Leipzig airport, 0341/243–028, **Leipzig.**

Sixt-Budget: Friedrichstrasse 150–153, tel. 030/203–07293, and Schönefeld airport, tel. 030/672–2608, **Eastern Berlin;** An der Frauenkirche 5 (in Hotel Dresdner Hof), tel. 0351/484–1696, Pragerstr. (in Hotel Newa) tel. 0351/496–7112, **Dresden;** Gerberstr 15 (in Hotel Merkur), tel. 0341/799–1149, and Leipzig airport, tel. 0341/3017, **Leipzig.**

Arriving and Departing by Plane

Berlin's **Tegel** airport is only 6 kilometers (4 miles) from downtown; eastern Berlin's **Schönefeld** airport lies about 24 kilometers (15 miles) outside the downtown area. **Dresden Airport** (tel. 0351/589–141) lies about 10 kilometers (6 miles) north of the city. Leipzig's **Schkeuditz** airport is 12 kilometers (8 miles) northwest of the city.

Arriving and Departing by Car and Train

By Car Expressways connect Berlin with Dresden and Leipzig.

By Train International trains stop at Friedrichstrasse or Ostbahnhof stations in eastern Berlin; from there, there is direct service to Dresden, Leipzig, and most towns covered below. Meissen requires a bus connection from the rail line.

Getting Around

By Car Nearly 1,000 miles of autobahn and 7,000 miles of secondary roads crisscross eastern Germany. Traffic regulations are strictly enforced, from parking rules to speed limits (130 kph/82 mph on autobahns, 80 kph/50 mph on main roads, and 50 kph/30 mph in towns). The eastern German police have been known to levy fines for the slightest offense, and drinking and driving is particularly forbidden. If not otherwise indicated, cars coming from the right have the right-of-way. On heavily traveled north–south routes, you can avoid some of the trucking by keeping to the roads that run parallel to the autobahn, if you don't feel pressed for time.

Gasoline is available at either **Minol** or **Intertank** filling stations, although increasingly now you'll also find the familiar signs of gasoline brands you know. Diesel fuel may not be available at all stations, and unleaded fuel is sold only on expressways and in main towns. On back roads, filling stations may be scarce, so be careful not to let fuel reserves get too low.

By Train East Germany has three types of trains—Express, the fastest, shown as "IEx" or "Ex" in timetables; fast, shown as "D"; and regular/local services indicated with an "E." The Euro-City and InterCity services of the German Federal Railways, the Bundesbahn, are being progressively incorporated into the east German system. The fast categories have varying supplementary fares; local trains do not. Most long- and medium-distance trains have both first- and second-class cars and many have either dining or buffet cars, although these may be joined to the train only from and to specific destinations. First- and second-class sleeping cars and couchettes are available. As rail travel is popular and space is limited, trains are usually full and reservations—make them either via the Reisebüro der DDR or at any major train station—are recommended.

Railway buffs are increasingly welcome, particularly around the narrow-gauge lines in the mountainous south.

By Boat "White Fleets" of inland boats, including paddle sidewheelers, ply the Elbe River with their starting point at Dresden, going downstream and on into Czechoslovakia.

The **KD German Rhine Line** is now operating two luxury cruises in both directions on the Elbe River from May to October: a five-day voyage from Bad Schandau (south of Dresden) to Magdeburg, and a seven-day journey from Bad Schandau to Hamburg. Ports of call include Dresden, Meissen, and Wittenberg. From April to October, cruises run between Bad Schandau and Vanov, Czechoslovakia, near Prague, and between Magdeburg and Vanov. The cruises, aboard new modern power vessels, are in great demand, so reservations should be made several months in advance. For details of the cruises, contact the company in the United States at 170 Hamilton Avenue, White Plains, New York 10601–1788, tel. 914/948–3600, and at 323 Geary Street, San Francisco, California 94102–1860, tel. 415/392–8817; in Germany contact Köln-Düsseldorfer Deutsche Rheinschiffahrt AG, Frankenwerft 15, 5000–Köln 1, tel. 0221/20880.

By Bus Long-distance bus services link Frankfurt with Dresden and Leipzig. Within Saxony and Thuringia, most areas are accessible by bus, but service is infrequent, and mainly serves to connect with rail lines. Check schedules carefully.

Guided Tours

Information on travel and tours to and around eastern Germany is available from most travel agents, but those who specialized in this region before the change in regimes probably will still give you better assistance, particularly during the transition period. Leading agents include:

Berolina Travel (20 Conduit St., London W1R 9TD, tel. 0371/629–1664).
Koch (157 E. 86 St., New York, NY 10028, tel. 212/369–3800).
Love Tours (15315 Magnolia Blvd., Suite 110, Sherman Oaks, CA 91403, tel. 800/501–6868).
Maupintour (Box 807, Lawrence, KS 60044, tel. 800/255–4266).
Orbis (342 Madison Ave., Suite 1512, New York, NY 10173, tel. 212/867–5011).
Pecum Tours (2002 Colfax Ave., Minneapolis, MN 55405, tel. 612/871–8171).
Travcoa (2350 SE Bristol, Santa Ana, CA 92707, tel. 800/992–2003).

Exploring Saxony and Thuringia

Highlights for First-time Visitors

Thomaskirche and Nikolaikirche, Leipzig
Buchenwald
Zwinger palace, Dresden
Schiller and Goethe houses, Weimar
Erfurt
Wartburg castle, Eisenach

Dessau to Leipzig

Numbers in the margin correspond to points of interest on the Eastern Germany map.

The southern districts of Germany—Thuringia and Saxony—represent the old Germany of medieval times, and as you travel these regions, you'll see ample evidence of the grandeur of the past, although much has been rebuilt to replace war damage. Alas, you'll also see the ongoing (and just as devastating) damage of a modern industrial society: landscape scarred by coalpits around Leipzig, chemical pollution in the air around Bitterfeld and Wolfen north of Leipzig, and to the southeast thousands of acres of woodland destroyed by that pollution. South of Dresden, as the Elbe river leaves its broad valley, it passes through a region of dramatic narrow channels confined by stone mountains, almost like a miniature Grand Canyon. To the south, the *Erzgebirge*, or ore mountains, form a natural boundary with Czechoslovakia.

Leaving Berlin, go south on the E-51, marked for Leipzig. About 120 kilometers (75 miles) from Berlin, you'll pass
❶ Dessau, a name known to every student of modern architecture.

Eastern Germany

DENMARK

Baltic Sea

Rügen

Barth
Bergen

Warnemünde
Bad Doberan
Ribnitz-
Damgarten
Stralsund
Greifswald

Wismar
Rostock
MECKLENBURG-
WEST POMERANIA
Anklam

Schwerin
Güstrow
Teterow
Neubrandenburg

Neustadt-
Glewe
Waren
Neustrelitz

Ludwigslust
Pritzwalk

POLAND

FORMER BORDER
BETWEEN EAST AND
WEST GERMANY
Perleberg
Wittenberge
Neuruppin

Salzwedel

Stendal
Oranienburg

Oebisfelde
Brandenburg
Potsdam
Berlin
BERLIN
Frankfurt
an der Oder

Magdeburg

SAXONY-
ANHALT
Lübben

Halberstadt
Bernburg
Dessau
BRANDENBURG
Cottbus

Wernigerode
Quedlinburg
Bitterfeld

Thale
Halle
Leipzig

Nordhausen
Meissen
Dresden
Görlitz

Mühlhausen
SAXONY

Erfurt
Weimar
Gera

Eisenach
THURINGIA
Freiberg
Chemnitz

Saalfeld
Zwickau

Meiningen
Suhl
Plauen

CZECHOSLOVAKIA

N

0   50 miles
0   75 km

Here the architect Walter Gropius in 1925–26 set up his Bauhaus school of design, probably the most widespread influence on 20th-century architecture and decorative arts. Gropius's concept was to simplify design to allow mechanized construction; 316 villas in the Törten section of the city were built in the '20s using his ideas and methods. Stop to view the refurbished Bauhaus building; this was the fountainhead of ideas that has determined the appearance of cities such as New York and Chicago. Still used as an architecture school, the building can be visited Monday–Friday 10–5, and exhibits are also open Saturday–Sunday 10–12:30, 2–5.

For a contrast to the no-nonsense Bauhaus architecture, look at Dessau's older buildings, including St. George's church, built in 1712 in Dutch Baroque style, or the 18th-century late-Baroque **Schloss Mosigkau,** 9 kilometers (5½ miles) southwest of Dessau, now a museum.

Try to visit the exquisite mid-18th-century country palace in late afternoon or early evening, when the setting sun lends a warm glow to the biscuit-colored facades of the three wings. Prince Leopold of Anhalt-Dessau commissioned the palace built for his favorite daughter, Anna Wilhelmine. She lived alone at the palace, for she never married, and when she died she left the property to an order of nuns. They immediately tore up the formal grounds to make an English-style park, and after a post-World War II attempt to restore the original Baroque appearance, money and enthusiasm ran out. The palace itself, however, was always well maintained, and the present custodians are so concerned about its preservation that you'll be asked to put on felt slippers on your tour of its rooms. Only about one-quarter of the rooms can be visited, but they include one of Germany's very few Baroque picture galleries. Its stucco ceiling is a marvel of Rococo decoration, a swirling composition of pastel-colored motifs. *Tel. 0340/831–139. Admission: DM 2 adults, DM 1 children. Open May–Oct. daily 9–6, Nov.–Apr., by appointment only.*

② The autobahn E51 branches left and right 40 kilometers (25 miles) south of Dessau: left to Leipzig, right to **Halle.** The temptation is to turn left and ignore Halle, particularly if you're in a hurry. The 1,000-year-old city, built on the salt trade, is one of eastern Germany's worst examples of communist urban planning, with a hastily built residential area whose name Halle-Neustadt has been shortened cynically by the locals to "Hanoi." But if you have the time, Halle is worth a visit, if only to view its fine central market place, the **Markt,** its northern side bristling with five distinctive, sharp-steepled towers. Four of them (two connected by a catwalk bridge) belong to the late-Gothic **Marienkirche** (St. Mary's Church), completed in 1529, where Martin Luther preached and George Frideric Handel learned to play the organ. Handel was born in Halle, in 1685, and you'll find several memorials to the great composer in and around the city. The house where he was born, the **Händelhaus,** is a few steps away from the Markt, at Grosse Nikolaistrasse 5–6. It's now a Handel museum. *Admission: DM 2 adults, DM 1 children. Open Tues., Wed., and Fri.–Sun. 9:30–5:30; Thurs. 9:30–7.*

The fifth tower on the Markt is the celebrated Roter Turm (Red Tower), built between 1418 and 1506 as an expression of the city's power and wealth; it houses a bell carillon. The tower looks a bit incongruous against the backdrop of modern Halle, like an elaborate sandcastle stranded by the tide. Between the Roter Turm and Marienkirche is the **Marktschlösschen,** a late Renaissance structure now serving as a gallery. On the northwest edge of the old town is a much more traditional expression of Halle's early might (which vanished with the Thirty Years' War), the **Moritzburg,** a castle built in the late-15th century by the Archbishop of Magdeburg after he had claimed the city for his archdiocese. The castle is a typical late-Gothic fortress, with a sturdy round tower at each of its four corners and a dry moat. There's a cloisterlike peace in the central courtyard today, quite a contrast to the years when one army of occupation followed another with bloody regularity. In prewar years, the castle contained a leading gallery of German Expressionist paintings, which were ripped from the walls by the Nazis and condemned as "degenerate." Some of the works so disdained by the Nazis are back in place, together with some outstanding late-19th and early 20th-century art. You'll find Rodin's famous sculpture *The Kiss* here. *Staatliche Galerie Moritzburg, Friedemann-Bach-Platz 5. Admission: DM 2 adults, DM 1 children. Open Wed.–Sun. 10–1 and 2–6, Tues. 2–9.*

Some 200 yards southeast of the Moritzburg is Halle's cathedral, the **Dom,** an early Gothic church whose nave and side aisles are of equal height. The nearby former Episcopal residence, the 16th-century **Neue Residenz,** now houses a world-famous collection of fossils dug from brown coal deposits in the Geiseltal Valley near Halle. On the other side of the Saale River (cross the Schiefer bridge to get there) is another interesting museum, the **Halloren- und Salinemuseum,** which traces the history of the salt trade on which early Halle built its prosperity. It includes a full-scale replica of a salt mine, a chilling reminder of the price paid by the working man in centuries past for extracting one of life's necessities from the earth. *Mansfelderstr. 52. Admission: DM 2 adults, DM 1 children. Open Apr.–Sept., Tues.–Sun. 10–5; Oct.–Mar., Tues.–Sun. 10–4.*

③ From just outside Halle, take the autobahn 20 kilometers (12½ miles) to **Leipzig.** With a population of about 560,000, this is the second largest city in eastern Germany (Berlin is the largest) and has long been a center of printing and bookselling. Astride major trade routes, it was an important market town in the Middle Ages, and it continues to be a trading center to this day, thanks to the trade fairs that twice a year (March and September) bring together buyers from the former East and West.

Those familiar with music and German literature will associate Leipzig with the great composer Johann Sebastian Bach (1685–1750), who was organist and choir director at the Thomaskirche (St. Thomas church); with the 19th-century composer Richard Wagner, who was born here in 1813; and with German Romantic poets Goethe and Schiller, both of whom lived and worked in the area.

In 1813 the Battle of the Nations was fought on the city's outskirts, in which Prussian, Austrian, Russian, and Swedish forces stood ground against Napoléon's troops. This battle (the *Völkerschlacht*) was instrumental in leading to the French general's defeat two years later at Waterloo, and thus helped to decide the national boundaries on the map of Europe for the remainder of the century.

Following the devastation of World War II, little is left of old Leipzig. Considerable restoration has been undertaken in the old city, however, and the impression is certainly that of a city with touches of Renaissance character, although some of the newer buildings (notably the university skyscraper tower) distort the perspective and proportions of the old city. Guided bus tours of Leipzig are conducted daily at 10 and 1:30 (from March to mid-October, there's also a tour at 4); tours leave from the information center downtown at Sachsenplatz 1 (tel. 0341/ 79590).

Numbers in the margin correspond to points of interest on the Leipzig map.

❹ Railroad buffs may want to start their tour of Leipzig at the **Hauptbahnhof,** the main train station. With its 26 platforms, it is the largest in Europe. In 1991 it was expanded to accommodate the anticipated increase in traffic after reunification. But its fin-de-siècle grandness remains, particularly in the staircase that leads majestically up to the platforms. As you climb it, take a look at the great arched ceiling high above you; it's unique among German railway stations.

From the station, cross the broad expanse of the Platz der Republik, crowded with nascent capitalists selling everything from shaving soap to Czech Pilsner beer. Better shopping is to be found in the narrow streets opposite you. Behind them is a characterless square, Sachsenplatz, where you'll find Leipzig's main tourist office, Leipzig Information (open Mon.–Fri. 9–7, Sat. 9:30–2). Continue south one block, along Katharinenstrasse, passing the "Fregehaus," number 11, with its fine oriel and steep roof. In two minutes you'll enter Leipzig's showpiece plaza, the city's old market square, the huge **Markt.** One side is occupied completely by the recently restored Renais-
❺ sance city hall, the **Altes Rathaus,** which now houses the municipal museum, where Leipzig's past is well documented. *Markt 1. Admission: DM 3 adults, DM 1.50 children. Open Tues.–Sun. 9–5.*

Starting from all sides of the Markt you'll find small streets that attest to Leipzig's rich trading past, and tucked in among them glass-roofed arcades of surprising beauty and elegance. Invent a headache and step into the Apotheke at Hainstrasse 9, into surroundings that haven't changed for 100 years or more, redolent of powders and perfumes, home cures, and foreign spices. It's spectacularly Jugendstil, with finely etched and stained glass and rich mahogany. Or make for the antiquarian bookshops of the nearby Neumarkt Passage. Around the corner, on Grimmaischestrasse, is Leipzig's finest arcade, the
❻ **Mädlerpassage,** where the ghost of Goethe's Faust lurks in every marbled corner. Here you'll find the famous Auerbachs Keller restaurant, at number 2, where Goethe set a scene in *Faust* (*see* Dining, below). A bronze group of characters from the play, sculpted in 1913, beckons you down the stone staircase to the cellar restaurant. A few yards away down the arcade is a delightful Jugendstil cafe called Mephisto, decorated in devilish reds and blacks.

Behind Grimmaischestrasse, on Nikolaistrasse, is a church that stands as a symbol of German reunification. It was here,

Leipzig

Altes Rathaus, **5**

Bosehaus, **12**

Botanischer
Garten, **15**

Exhibition Pavilion, **16**

Gohliser
Schlösschen, **18**

Grassimuseum, **14**

Hauptbahnhof, **4**

Leipzig University
tower, **8**

Mädlerpassage, **6**

Museum der Bildenden
Künste, **13**

Neues Gewandhaus, **9**

Nikolaikirche, **7**

Opera House, **10**

Schiller's House, **19**

Schloss Dölitz, **20**

Thomaskirche, **11**

Völkerschlacht-
denkmal, **17**

7 before the undistinguished facade of the **Nikolaikirche,** that thousands of East Germans demanding reform gathered every Monday in the months before the communist regime finally collapsed under the weight of popular pressure. "Wir sind das Volk" ("We are the people") was their chant as they defied official attempts to silence their demands for freedom. In the white and pastel-colored interior of the church, much more impressive than the exterior would lead you to believe, is a soaring Gothic choir and a 16th-century nave, both cloaked in late-18th-century surface decoration. A diamond-patterned ceiling is supported by classical pillars that end in green palm-tree-like flourishes, a curious combination of styles that successfully meld. Luther is said to have preached from the ornate 16th-century pulpit.

8 Towering over the Nikolaikirche and every other building in the center of the city is the 470-foot-high **Leipzig University tower,** dubbed the "Jagged Tooth" by some of the young wags who study there. They were largely responsible for changing the official name of the university, replacing the postwar title of Karl Marx University with its original one. In the shadow of the skyscraper, which houses administrative offices and lecture rooms, is the glass and concrete **Neues Gewandhaus,** the **9** modernistic home of the Gewandhaus Orchestra, one of Germany's greatest. (Its popular director, Kurt Masur, recently added to his duties the directorship of the New York Philharmonic Orchestra.) In the foyer you can see one of Europe's largest ceiling paintings, a staggering allegorical work devoted to the muse of music by Sighard Gilles, who employed 716 square meters to monumental effect. The statue of Beethoven that stands in the foyer won first prize for sculptor Max Klinger at the World Art Exhibition in Vienna in 1912. The acoustics of the Gewandhaus, by the way, are world renowned, enhancing the resonance of every tone by a full two seconds.

10 Opposite the Gewandhaus, on the north side of the Augustus-Platz, is the modern, boxy **Opera House,** the first postwar theater to be built in communist East Germany.

Time Out   You'll find several cafés lining Grimmaischestrasse, leading out of the square, but why not buy an ice cream from one of the ubiquitous stands there. The eastern Germans are in love with *Eis* and consume it all year round. The Italian-style ice cream is quite authentic.

11 Continue west on Grimmaischestrasse to Thomasgasse and the **Thomaskirche,** the Gothic church where Bach was choirmaster for 27 years and where Martin Luther preached on Whit Sunday, 1539, signaling the arrival of Protestantism in Leipzig. Originally the center of a 13th-century monastery that was rebuilt in the 15th century, the tall church now stands by itself, but the names of adjacent streets recall the cloisters that once surrounded it. While in Leipzig Bach wrote five masses, two Passions, and the Magnificat, and composed most of his cantatas for the church's famous boys choir, the Thomasknabenchor, which was founded in the 13th century; the church continues as the choir's home as well as a center of Bach tradition. In the Middle Ages, the choir was assembled to sing at every public function—from the installation of bishops to the execution of criminals. Its ranks thinned rapidly when the boys were engaged to sing while plague victims were carted to graves outside the city walls.

Bach's 12 children and the infant Richard Wagner were baptized in the church's early-17th-century font; Karl Marx and Friedrich Engels also stood before this same font, godfathers to Karl Liebknecht, who grew up to be a revolutionary too!

The great music Bach wrote in his Leipzig years commanded little attention in his lifetime, and when he died he was given a simple grave, without a headstone, in the city's Johannisfriedhof cemetery. It wasn't until 1894 that an effort was made to find where the great composer lay buried, and after a thorough, macabre search his coffin was removed to the cemetery church, the Johanniskirche. The church was destroyed by Allied bombs in December 1943, and Bach found his final resting place in the church he would have selected: the Thomaskirche. It's now a place of pilgrimage for music-lovers from all over the world, and his gravestone below the high altar is never without a floral tribute. Fresh flowers also constantly decorate the statue of Bach that stands before the church. *Thomaskirchhof. Admission free. Open daily 9–6.*

⑫ The Bach family home, the **Bosehaus,** still stands, opposite the church, and is now a museum devoted to the life and work of the composer. (The exhibits are in German only; a guide to the museum in English can be purchased in the shop.) Of particular interest is the display of musical instruments dating from Bach's time. *Thomaskirchhof 16. Admission: DM 2 adults, DM 1 children. Open Tues. Thurs.–Sun. 9–5, Wed. 1 PM–9 PM.*

Time Out   Tea-time? On the corner of Thomaskirchhof, opposite the church, is the charming **Teehaus** café, offering more varieties of tea than you'd think it was possible to find in eastern Germany. Etched and beveled Jugendstil glass, brass, and dark wood paneling are the perfect complement to the delicate teas, which are served by an enthusiastic staff. *Open daily 10–6.*

From the Thomaskirche, follow Burgstrasse southward, past the 19th-century neo-Gothic monstrosity that now serves as Leipzig's city hall, and you'll come to the city's most outstanding museum, the **Museum der Bildenden Künste,** an art gallery ⑬ of international standard that is especially strong in early German and Dutch painting. The art collection occupies the ground floor of the former Reichsgericht, the court where the Nazis held a show trial against the Bulgarian communist Georgi Dimitroff on a trumped-up charge of masterminding a plot to burn down the Reichstag in 1933. *Georgi-Dimitroff-Platz 1. Admission: DM 3 adults, DM 1.50 children. Open Tues. and Thurs.–Sun. 9–5, Wed. 1 PM–9:30 PM.*

Head up Rossplatz and turn right onto the short Grimmaisch Steinweg to reach the **Grassimuseum** complex (Johannespl. 5– ⑭ 11. Admission: DM 3.05 adults, DM 1.55 children). It includes the **Museum of Arts and Crafts** (open Tues.–Fri. 9:30–6, Sat. 10–4, Sun. 9–1), the **Geographical Museum** (open Tues.–Fri. 10–3, Sun. 9–1), and the **Musical Instruments Museum** (enter from Täubchenweg 2; open Tues.–Thurs. 3–6, Fri. and Sun. 10–1, Sat. 10–3).

⑮ The **Botanischer Garten** (Botanical Gardens) is a set of splendid open-air gardens and greenhouses. *Linnestr. 1. Admission:*

American Express offers Travelers Cheques built for two.

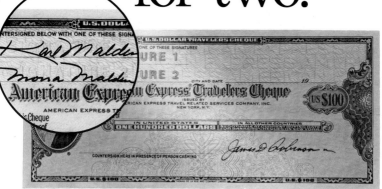

American Express® Travelers Cheques *for Two*. The first Travelers Cheques that allow either of you to use them because both of you have signed them. And only one of you needs to be present to purchase them.

Cheques *for Two* are accepted anywhere regular American Express Travelers Cheques are, which is just about everywhere. So stop by before your next trip and ask for Cheques *for Two*.

 Travelers Cheques®

2½ Hours
VHS-C

2½ Hours
8mm

SONY

PACK WISELY.

Given a choice, the seasoned traveler always carries less.
Case in point: Sony Handycam® camcorders, America's most
popular. They record up to 2½ hours on a single tape.
VHS-C tapes record only 30 minutes.* And why carry five tapes
when you can record everything on one? Which brings us
to the first rule of traveling: pack a Sony Handycam camcorder.

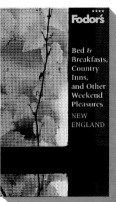

DM 2. Open weekdays 9–4, Sun. 10–4; greenhouses Sun. 10–12:30 and 2–4.

Still farther out, via streetcars No. 15, 20, 21, or 25, is the
⑯ Exhibition Pavillion at Leninstrasse 210. Its main feature is a
vast diorama portraying the Battle of the Nations of 1813 (open
Tues.–Sun. 9–4). Slightly farther on Leninstrasse is the mas-
⑰ sive **Völkerschlachtdenkmal,** a memorial in the formal park; it,
too, commemorates the battle (open daily 9–4). Rising out of
suburban Leipzig like some great Egyptian tomb, the somber,
grey pile of granite and concrete is more than 300 feet high. Despite its ugliness, it's well worth a visit if only to wonder at the
lengths—and heights—to which the Prussians went to celebrate their military victories, and to take in the view from a
windy platform near the top (provided you can also climb the
500 steps to get there). The Prussians did make one concession
to Napoléon in designing the monument: A stone marks the
spot where he stood during the battle.

Outside of the center of Leipzig but reachable by public transportation (streetcars No. 20 and 24, then walk left up
Poetenweg, or streetcar No. 6 to Menckestr.) is the delightfully
⑱ Rococo **Gohliser Schlösschen** (Gohliser House), the site of frequent concerts. *Menckestr. 23.*

⑲ Beyond that is **Schiller's House,** for a time the home of the
German poet and dramatist Friedrich Schiller. *Menckestr. 21.
Admission: DM 2 adults, DM 1 children. Open Tues., Wed.,
Fri., and Sat. 11–5.*

⑳ **Schloss Dölitz** (streetcars No. 22 or 24, walk up Helenstrasse)
contains an exhibition of *Zinnfiguren*, historical tin soldiers.
*Torhaus, Schloss Dölitz, Helenstr. 24. Admission: DM 3. Open
Sun. 9–1.*

Meissen and Dresden

*Numbers in the margin correspond to points of interest on the
Eastern Germany map.*

㉑ Route 6 out of Leipzig will take you to **Meissen,** about 80 kilometers (50 miles) away. This romantic city on the Elbe River is
known the world over for its porcelain, bearing the trademark
crossed blue swords. The first European porcelain was made in
this area in 1708, and in 1710 the royal porcelain manufacturer
was established in Meissen, close to the local raw materials.

The story of how porcelain came to be produced in Meissen
reads like a German fairy tale: Free-spending Prince August
the Strong (ruled 1697–1704, 1710–33) urged alchemists at his
court to search for the secret of making gold, which he badly
needed to refill a Saxon state treasury depleted by his expensive building projects and extravagant lifestyle. The
alchemists failed to produce gold, but one of them, Johann
Friedrich Böttger, discovered a method for making something
almost as precious: fine hard-paste porcelain. Prince August
consigned Böttger and a team of craftsmen to a hill-top castle
outside Dresden—Albrechtsburg in Meissen—and set them to
work. August hoped to keep their recipe a state secret, but
within a few years fine porcelain was being produced by
Böttger's method in many parts of Europe.

The porcelain works outgrew their castle workshop in the mid-19th century, and you'll find them today in the town at the foot of the castle mount at Leninstrasse 9. There you can see demonstrations of pieces being prepared. In the same building, a museum displays Meissen porcelain, a collection that rivals that of the Porzellansammlung in Dresden. The 18th-century commemoration pieces and figurines are especially fine. Upstairs are the lesser known, 20th-century designs. Not surprisingly, there's a small gift shop on the premises. *Tel. 03521/541. Open April–Oct., Tues.–Sun. 8:30–4:30.*

Meissen porcelain is to be found in one form or another all over town. A set of porcelain bells at the late-Gothic **Frauenkirche**, on the beautifully restored central market square, the Marktplatz, was the first of its kind anywhere when installed in 1929; they are rung six times a day. Opposite is the 500-year-old town hall, with three unusual dormers. The largest set of porcelain figures ever crafted can be found in another Meissen church, the **Nikolaikirche**, which also houses remains of early Gothic frescoes. Also of interest in the town center is the 1569 **Old Brewery**, graced by a Renaissance gable; **St. Francis**, now housing a city museum; and **St. Martins**, with its late-Gothic altar.

Time Out   Snuggling up to the Frauenkirche is one of Meissen's oldest wine taverns, the **Weinschenke Vinzenz Richter** (Marktplatz 3). Meissen has some of Europe's northernmost and smallest vineyards, producing an excellent white wine. This is the place to try it. *Closed Mon. and Tues.*

It's a bit of a climb up Burgstrasse and Amtsstrasse to the **Albrechtsburg** castle, where the story of Meissen porcelain really began, but the effort is worthwhile. The 15th-century Albrechtsburg is Germany's first truly "residential" castle, a complete break with the earlier style of fortified bastion. It fell into disuse and neglect as nearby Dresden rose to local prominence, but it's still an imposing collection of late-Gothic and Renaissance buildings. In the central courtyard, a typical Gothic *Schutzhof* protected on three sides by high rough-stone walls, is an exterior spiral staircase, **the Wendelstein**, hewn from one massive stone block in 1525, a masterpiece of early masonry. Ceilings of the halls of the castle are richly decorated, although many date only to a restoration in 1870. Adjacent to the castle is a towered early Gothic cathedral, whose west entrance hall contains the graves of Saxon kings with covers designed by Cranach and Dürer that resemble giant etching plates. The sculptures of Otto I and his wife, Adelheid, are considered to be supreme examples of German medieval sculpture.

22   Another 20 kilometers (12 miles) southeast on Route 6 will take you to **Dresden.** Splendidly situated on a bend in the Elbe River, Dresden is a compact city easy to explore. In its Rococo yellows and greens, it is enormously appealing, and the effect is even more overwhelming when you compare what you see today—or what Canaletto paintings reflect of a Dresden centuries earlier—with the photographs of Dresden in 1945, after a British bombing raid almost destroyed it overnight. It was one of the architectural and cultural treasures of the civilized world, and the fact that, despite lack of funds and an often uncooperative communist bureacracy, the people of Dresden succeeded in rebuilding it is an enormous tribute to their skills and dedication.

Their efforts restored at least the riverside panorama to the appearance Canaletto would have recognized, but some of the other parts of the city center look halfway between construction and demolition. In the coming years the city will look more like a building site than ever as 20 new hotels are added to provide the accommodations the city so desperately needs. Don't think of visiting Dresden without reserving a hotel room well in advance.

Dresden was the capital of Saxony as early as the 15th century, although most of its architectural masterpieces date from the 18th century, when the enlightened Saxon ruler August the Strong and his son, Frederick Augustus II, brought leading Italian and Bavarian architects and designers up from the south. The predominantly Italianate influence is evident today in gloriously overblown Rococo architecture. Streetcar tours leave from Postplatz Tuesday–Sunday at 9, 11, and 1:30; bus tours, leaving from Dr.-Külz-Ring, run on Tuesday, Wednesday, and Thursday, at 11 (call 0351/495–5025 for details).

Numbers in the margin correspond to points of interest on the Dresden map.

The best introduction to Dresden is to arrive by ship (*see* Essential Information, above), but for motorists or train passengers, the starting point of a Dresden tour will be the main railway station (which has adequate parking). To reach the old part of the city and its treasures you'll first have to cross a featureless expanse surrounded by postwar high rises, leading into the pedestrians-only Pragerstrasse (the tourist information office is at number 8). Cross busy Dr.-Külz-Ring and you'll

㉓ enter a far different scene, the broad **Altmarkt,** whose colonnaded beauty has managed to survive the disfiguring efforts of city planners to turn it into a huge outdoor parking lot. The church on your right, the Kreuzkirche, is an interesting combination of Baroque and Jugendstil architecture and decoration. A church stood here in the 13th century, but the present structure dates from the late 18th century. (Its Renaissance tower, which can be seen in Canaletto's paintings of Dresden, collapsed in 1765.) The church is home to the famous Kreuzchor (choir of Kreuzkirche). The rebuilt Rathaus is on your left, as is the 18th-century yellow-stucco Landhaus, which contains the Museum für Geschichte der Stadt Dresden (City Historical Museum). The Rococo staircase in the entrance hall is particularly graceful. *Wilsdrufferstr. 2. Admission: DM 2 adults, DM 1 children. Open Mon.–Thurs. and Sat. 10–6.*

At the northern end of the Altmarkt cross Wilsdrufferstrasse (or pause for a window-shopping break on this broad boulevard) into the **Neumarkt** (New Market), which is, despite its name, the historic heart of old Dresden. The ruins on your right are all that remain of Germany's greatest Protestant church after the bombing raid of February 1945. These jagged, precariously tilting walls were once the mighty Baroque

㉔ **Frauenkirche,** so sturdily built that it withstood a three-day bombardment during the Seven Years' War only to fall victim to the flames that followed the World War Two raid. Like the Gedächtniskirche in Berlin, the Frauenkirche has been kept in its ruined state as a war memorial, although plans were announced in 1991 to rebuild it as a European cultural center.

Dresden

KEY

AE American Express Office

Albertinum, **25**
Altmarkt, **23**
Augustusbrücke, **31**
Brühlsche
Terrasse, **26**
Frauenkirche, **24**
Johanneum, **27**

Katholische
Hofkirche, **29**
Residenzschloss, **28**
Semperoper, **30**
Zwinger, **32**

25 The large, imperial-style building looming behind the Frauenkirche is the famous **Albertinum,** Dresden's leading art museum. It is named after Saxony's King Albert, who between 1884
and 1887 converted a royal arsenal into a suitable setting for
the treasures he and his forebears had collected. The upper story of the Albertinum, accessible from the Brühlsche Terrasse,
houses the Gemäldegalerie Alte und Neue Meister (Gallery of
Old and Modern Masters), temporarily displaying the highlights of the Sempergalerie while it is being restored (*see* below). Permanent exhibits include outstanding work by German
masters of the 19th and 20th century (Caspar David Friedrich's
haunting *Das Kreuz im Gebirge* is here) and French Impressionists and Post-Impressionists.

Equally impressive is the Grünes Gewölbe (Green Vault).
Named after a green room in the palace of August the Strong,
this part of the Albertinum (entered from Georg-Treu-Platz)
contains an exquisite collection of unique objects d'art fash-
ioned from gold, silver, ivory, amber, and other precious and
semi-precious materials. Among the crown jewels is the world's
largest "green" diamond, 41 carats in weight, and a dazzling
group of tiny gem-studded figures entitled *Hofstaat zu Delhi
am Geburtstag des Grossmoguls Aureng-Zeb.* The name gives
a false idea of the size of the work, dating from 1708, which rep-
resents a birthday gathering at the court of an Indian mogul;
some parts of the tableau are so small that they can only be admired through a magnifying glass. Somewhat larger and less
delicate is the drinking bowl of Ivan the Terrible, perhaps the
most sensational of the treasures to be found in this extraordinary museum. Next door is the Skulpturensammlung (Sculpture Collection) that includes ancient Egyptian and classical
works and examples by Giovanni da Bologna and Adriaen de
Vries. *Am Neumarkt. Gemäldegalerie Alte und Neue Meister
admission: DM 5 adults, DM 2.50 children. Open Tues. and
Thurs.–Sun. 9–5, Wed. 9–6. Grünes Gewölbe and Skulpturensammlung admission: DM 5 adults, DM 2.50 children. Open
Fri.–Tues. 9–5, Wed. 9–6.*

26 If you leave the Albertinum by the **Brühlsche Terrasse** exit
you'll find yourself on what was once known as the "Balcony of
Europe," a terrace high above the Elbe, carved from a 16th-
century stretch of the city fortifications; from the terrace a
breathtaking vista of the Elbe and the Dresden skyline opens
up. The southern exit of the Albertinum brings you back to the
Neumarkt and to another former royal building that now serves
27 as a museum, the 16th-century **Johanneum,** once the regal stables. Instead of horses, the Johanneum now houses the
Vekehrsmuseum, a collection of historical vehicles, including
vintage automobiles and engines. *Neumarkt. Admission: DM
4 adults, DM 2 children. Open Wed.–Sun. 9–5, Tues. 9–6.*

Walk behind the Johanneum and into the former stable exercise
yard, enclosed by elegant Renaissance arcades and used in the
16th century as an open-air festival ground. To spare the royal-
ty on horseback the trouble of dismounting before ascending to
the upper-story to watch the jousting and jollities in the yard
below, a ramp was built to accommodate both two- and four-
legged guests. (From the top of the ramp you can look down on
the ruined royal palace being reconstructed.) You'll find the
scene today much as it was centuries ago, complete with jousting markings in the ground. More popular than even than joust-

ing in those days was *Ringelstechen*, a risky pursuit in which riders at full gallop had to catch small rings on their lances. Horses and riders often came to grief in the narrow confines of the stableyard.

On the outside wall of the Johanneum is a remarkable example of Meissen porcelain art: a painting on Meissen tiles of a royal procession, 102 meters (336 feet) long. More than one hundred members of the royal Saxon house of Wettin, half of them on horseback, are represented on the giant jigsaw made up of 25,000 porcelain tiles, painted in 1904–07 after a design by Wilhelm Walther. Follow this unusual procession to the end and (28) you will come to the former royal palace, the **Residenzschloss**, where restoration work is under way behind the fine Renaissance facade. Although the work is expected to last well into the 1990s, some of the finished rooms are hosting historical exhibitions normally housed at the Zwinger (*see* below). The main gate of the palace, the Georgentor, has acquired its original appearance, complete with an enormous statue of the fully armed Saxon Count George, guarding the portal that carries his name. The palace housed August the Strong's Grünes Gewölbe before it was moved in its entirety to the Albertinum. *Sophienstr. Admission: DM 5 adults, DM 2.50 children. Open Mon., Tues., Thurs.–Sun. 9–5.*

Next to the Residenzschloss is the largest church in Saxony, (29) the **Katholische Hofkirche,** also known as the Cathedral of St. Trinitas. The son of August the Strong, Frederick Augustus II, (ruled 1733–63) brought architects and builders from Italy to construct a Catholic church in a city that had been the first large center of Lutheran Protestantism. They worked away by stealth, so the story goes, and Dresden's Protestant burgers were presented with a fait accompli when the church was finally consecrated in 1754. Seventy-eight historical and biblical figures decorate the Italian High Baroque facade; the chaste white interior's treasures include a beautiful stone pulpit by the royal sculptor Balthasar Permoser and a 250-year-old church organ said to be one of the finest ever to come from the mountain workshops of the famous Silbermann family. Peek behind the main altar into the two Rococo chapels, with charming illusionistic ceiling paintings and applied gold scroll decoration. In the cathedral's crypt are the tombs of 49 Saxon rulers and a precious vessel containing the heart of August the Strong.

Opposite the cathedral on the Theaterplatz is the restored (30) **Semperoper** (Semper Opera House), justifiably one of Germany's best-known and most popular theaters. Richard Wagner's *Rienzi, Der Fliegende Holländer,* and *Tannhäuser,* and Richard Strauss's *Salome, Elektra,* and *Der Rosenkavalier* all premiered here. The masterful Dresden architect Gottfried Semper built the opera house in 1838–41, in Italian Renaissance style, and then saw his work razed in a fire caused by a careless candle-lighter. Semper had to flee Dresden because of his participation in a democratic uprising, so his son Manfred rebuilt the theater according to his father's new designs, in the neo-Renaissance style you see today. Even Manfred Semper's version had to be rebuilt, after the devastating bombing raid of February 1945. On the 40th anniversary of that raid—February 13, 1985—the rebuilt Semperoper reopened with a performance of *Der Freischütz* by Carl Maria von

Weber, another composer who did so much to make Dresden a leading center of German music and culture. The demand to experience the Semper Opera again in all its glory is enormous, and tickets are difficult to obtain in advance (*see* The Arts and Nightlife, below). If you're lucky enough to get in, however, an overwhelming experience awaits you. Even if you're no opera buff, the Semper's lavish interior, predominantly crimson, white, and gold, can't fail to impress. Marble, velvet, and brocade create an atmosphere of intimate luxury (it seats 1,323), and the uninterrupted views and flawless acoustics are renowned.

Time Out On the riverbank side of the Theaterplatz you'll see the pavilionlike **Italienisches Dörfchen**, constructed in 1911–13 on the site of housing for the Italian workers who erected the nearby Hofkirche. The café is a perfect spot for taking a break over a glass of local beer or a pot of coffee.

31 The impressive bridge behind the cathedral, the **Augustus-brücke**, is a rebuilt version of an historic 17th-century bridge blown up by the SS shortly before the end of World War II. Renamed for the Bulgarian Communist accused by the Nazis of instigating the Reichstag fire, Georgi Dimitroff, the restored bridge, after the fall of communism, has gotten its original name back honoring August the Strong. You'll find this process of curing the unpleasant hiccups of communist rule still underway throughout eastern Germany.

Back on the Theaterplatz, in the center of the square directly in front of the opera house, you'll see a proud equestrian statue of King Johann, who ruled Saxony when Gottfried Semper was at work. Don't be misled by Johann's confident pose in the saddle—he was terrified of horses and never learned to ride.

The southwestern side of the square is taken up by another Gottfried Semper creation, the Sempergalerie, part of the **32** largely 18th-century **Zwinger** palace complex. Built by the great architect to house parts of the art collections of the Saxon royal house, it contains the world-renowned Gemäldegalerie Alte Meister (Gallery of Old Masters). The Zwinger was scheduled to reopen after restoration in October 1992. Until then, the Sempergalerie paintings were temporarily on display at the Albertinum (*see* above). The Porzellansammlung (Porcelain Collection), zoological museum, and Mathematisch-Physikalischer Salon (displaying old scientific instruments) remain open at the palace (*see* below). Call the Zwinger (tel. 0351/ 48420) for the latest information on when the collections will be reunited at the palace complex.

Among the priceless paintings in the Sempergalerie collection are examples by Dürer, Holbein, Jan van Eyck, Rembrandt, Rubens, van Dyck, Hals, Vermeer, Raphael (*The Sistine Madonna*), Titian, Giorgione, Veronese, Velázquez, Murillo, Canaletto, and Watteau. On the wall of the entrance archway you'll see an inscription in Russian, one of the few amusing reminders of World War II in Dresden. It reads, in rhyme: "Museum checked. No mines. Chanutin did the checking." Chanutin, presumably, was the Russian soldier responsible for checking one of Germany's greatest art galleries for anything more explosive than a Rubens nude.

The Sempergalerie forms one side of the fabulous Zwinger, the pride of Dresden and perhaps one of the greatest examples of Baroque architecture. There are two entrances to the Zwinger; the Kronentor (Crown Gate), off of Ostra-Allee, is the one through which August the Strong and his royal retinue once paraded. August hired a small army of artists and artisans to create a "pleasure ground" worthy of the Saxon court, building it on a section of the original city fortifications (the "Zwinger"). They were placed under the general direction of the architect Matthäus Daniel Pöppelmann, who was called reluctantly out of retirement to design what came to be his greatest work, started in 1707 and completed in 1728. Completely enclosing a central courtyard, filled with lawns and pools, the complex comprises six linked pavilions, one of which boasts a carillon of Meissen, hence its name: Glockenspielpavillon. It's an extraordinary scene, a riot of garlands, nymphs, and other Baroque ornamentation and sculpture on the edge of an urban landscape etched in somber gray. The contrast would have been much greater if Semper had not closed in one side of the Zwinger, which was originally open to the riverbank. Stand in the center of this quiet oasis, where the city's roar is kept at bay by the palatial wings that form the outer framework of the Zwinger, and imagine the scene on summer evenings when August the Strong invited his favored guests to celebrate with him—the wedding, for instance, of his son, Prince Friedrich August, to Maria Joseph, Archduchess of Austria. The ornate carriage-style lamps shone, the fountains splashed in the shallow pools, and wide staircases beckoned to galleried walks and the romantic Nymphenbad, a coyly hidden courtyard where nude female statues are protected in alcoves from a fountain that spits unexpectedly at unwary visitors.

The Porzellansammlung, stretching from the curved gallery adjoining the Glockenspielpavillon to the long gallery on the east side, is considered to be one of the best porcelain collections in the world. The focus, naturally, is on Dresden and Meissen china, but there are also outstanding examples of Japanese, Chinese, and Korean porcelain. *Porzellansammlung admission: DM 5 adults, DM 2 children. Open Sat.–Thurs. 9–4:30. Zoological Museum, Mathematisch-Physikalischer Salon admission: DM 3 adults, DM 1.50 children. Open Fri.–Wed. 9–4.*

Other less central curiosities in Dresden include the **Armeemuseum** (Military Museum), which covers military history predating the German Democratic Republic (Dr.-Karl-Fischer-Pl., admission DM 3, open Tues.–Sun. 9–5); the **Buch-Museum** (Book Museum), which traces the history of books from the Middle Ages to the present (Marienallee 12, admission free, open Mon.–Sat. 9–5); and the **Deutsches Hygiene-Museum** (German Museum of Health), with historical displays of medical equipment and a unique glass anatomical figure (Lingnerpl. 1, admission DM 3 adults, DM 1.50 children. Open Sat.–Thurs. 9–5).

Numbers in the margin correspond to points of interest on the Eastern Germany map.

From Dresden, you can either take the autobahn E40 or, if you have the time, the more scenic road via Freital to **Freiberg**. Once a prosperous silver-mining community, Freiberg is highlighted by two picturesque Gothic town squares, the Upper and

Lower Markets. The late Gothic cathedral, with its Golden Gate of 1230, has a richly decorated interior and a Silbermann organ dating from 1711.

㉞ Route 173 continues on via Oederan and Flöha to **Chemnitz** (on older maps, Karl-Marx-Stadt), about 65 kilometers (41 miles) down the E40 from Dresden. In recognition of the labor movement, East German officials renamed the city in 1953 to honor Karl Marx; in 1990 the population, now free to express a choice, overwhelmingly voted to revert to the original name. Badly damaged during World War II, Chemnitz has revived as a center of heavy industry, but it never had the architectural attractions of others in the area. Stop to see the rebuilt 12th-century **Red Tower** in the center of the city; the **Altes Rathaus** (Old City Hall), dating to 1496–98, now incorporating a variety of styles following many reconstructions; and the 250-million-year-old petrified tree trunks, unique in Europe, alongside the city museum. Look, too—assuming it's still there—at the massive stylized head of a meditative Karl Marx, sculpted by the Soviet artist Lew Kerbel, in front of the district council building in the new city center. Behind it is the motto, "Working Men of All Countries, Unite!"—in German, Russian, French, and English.

㉟ Take E40 out of Chemnitz to **Gera,** about 65 kilometers (41 miles) away. Once a princely residence and center of a thriving textile industry, the city has been largely rebuilt after the heavy damage sustained in World War II. Gera has often been compared to old Vienna, although today you have to search long and hard—and even then exercise some imagination—to discover any striking similarities between the German provincial town and the Habsburg capital. After the combined destruction of a world war and more than four decades of communist mismanagement, some ornate albeit crumbling house facades, however, do betray Gera's rich past, although the palace in which prince-electors once held court was destroyed in the final weeks of the war and never rebuilt. The palace's 16th-century **Orangerie,** though, does still stand, in the former Küchengarten in the suburb of Untermhaus. An imposing semicircular Baroque pavilion, it now houses an art gallery and a separate collection of works by Gera's most famous son, the satirical Expressionist painter Otto Dix (1891–1969). The Dix gallery was renovated in 1991 for the centenary of the painter's birth, and by 1993 it is hoped that some of Dix's works that vanished in the Nazi purge in the 1930s of "decadent" art will have been added to the collection. *Dimitroffallee 4. Admission: DM 2 adults, DM 1 children. Open Mon.–Thurs. 10–5, Sat.–Sun. 10–6.*

Don't leave Gera without lingering in the central town square, the Marktplatz, its Renaissance buildings restored with rare (for eastern Germany) care. The 16th-century city hall, the Rathaus, has a vividly decorated entrance. Note the weird angles of the lower-floor windows; they follow the incline of the staircase that winds up the interior of the building's picturesque 57-meter-high (185-foot-high) tower.

Time Out At the city hall's vaulted cellar restaurant, the **Ratskeller,** Gera's medieval past crowds in on you from all sides, with painted scenes on glass partitions and on the gnarled walls themselves. The restaurant is open daily from mid-morning until midnight, so it's an ideal place for coffee, lunch, or dinner.

Close by is the Baroque **Regierungsgebäude** (government building), incorporating pieces from an earlier 16th-century building.

Take the E40 another 53 kilometers (33 miles) to **Weimar.** Sitting prettily on the Ilm River between the Ettersberg and Vogtland hills, Weimar has a place in German political and cultural history out of all proportion to its size (population: 63,000). It's not even a particularly old city by German standards, with a civic history starting as late as 1410. But by the early 19th century it had become one of Europe's most important cultural centers, where poets Goethe and Schiller were neighbors, Johann Sebastian Bach played the organ for his royal Saxon patrons, Carl Maria von Weber wrote some of his best music, and Liszt was director of music, presenting the first performance of *Lohengrin*. Walter Gropius founded his Staatliches Bauhaus here in 1919, and behind the classical pillars of the National Theater the German National Assembly in 1919–20 drew up the constitution of the Weimar Republic. After the collapse of the ill-fated Weimar government, Hitler chose the unsuspecting little city as the site for the first national congress of his new Nazi Party. On the outskirts of Weimar, the Nazis built—or forced prisoners to build it for them—the infamous Buchenwald concentration camp.

Weimar owes much of its greatness to a woman, the widowed Countess Anna Amalia, whose son Carl August ruled the duchy of Saxony-Weimar, and who went talent-hunting in the late-18th century for cultural figures to decorate the glittering court that her Saxon forebears had set up in the town. Goethe was among them, and he served the countess as a counselor, advising on financial matters and town design. Schiller followed, and the two became valued visitors to the Countess's home. Their statues stand today before the **National Theater,** on Theaterplatz, two blocks west of the Markt, the central market square. The famous pair—Goethe with a patronizing hand on the shoulder of the younger Schiller—should be gleaming, having just been restored. The theater, sadly, isn't the one where Goethe and Schiller produced some of their leading works; the Baroque building became too small to admit the increasing numbers of visitors to Weimar, and it was demolished in 1907, replaced by a larger one with better technical facilities. That theater was bombed in World War II and rebuilt in its present form in 1948. It reopened with a performance of Goethe's *Faust*, which was written in Weimar.

Adjacent to the National Theater is the surprisingly modest home of the Countess Anna Amalia, the **Wittumspalais.** Within this exquisite Baroque house you can see the drawing-room where her soirées were held, complete with the original cherry-wood table at which the company sat. The east wing of the house contains a small museum that is a fascinating memorial to those cultural gatherings. *Admission free. Open Wed.–Sun. 9–noon and 1–5*.

Goethe spent 57 years in Weimar, 47 years in the house that has since become a shrine for millions of visitors. The **Goethehaus** is at the entrance of the street called Frauenplan, two blocks south of Theaterplatz. It's now a museum containing a collection of writings that illustrate not only the great man's literary might but his interest in the sciences, particularly medicine, and his administrative skills (and frustrations) as Weimar's exchequer. You'll see the desk at which Goethe stood to write (he liked to work standing up), his classical sculpture collection that fills the rooms, his own paintings (he was an accomplished watercolorist), and the modest bed in which he died. The rooms are dark and often cramped, but an almost palpable intellectual intensity seems to illuminate them. *Frauenplan 1. Admission: DM 5 adults, DM 3 children. Open Tues.–Sun. 9–5.*

Around the corner from Goethe's house, on a tree-shaded square, is Schiller's sturdy, green-shuttered home, in which he and his family spent a happy, all-too-brief three years (Schiller died there in 1805). Schiller's study was tucked up underneath the mansard roof, a cozy room dominated by his desk, where he probably completed *William Tell.* Much of the remaining furniture and the collection of books were added later, although they all date from around Schiller's time. *Neugasse. Admission: DM 5 adults, DM 3 children. Wed.–Sun. 9–5.*

On the nearby central town square, **Marktplatz,** you'll find another historic Weimar house, the home of the painter Lucas Cranach the Elder, who lived there during his last years, 1552–53. Its wide, imposing facade is richly decorated and bears the coat of arms of the Cranach family. It now houses a modern art gallery.

Around the corner to the left is Weimar's 16th-century **Residenzschloss** (Grand Ducal Palace), with its restored classical staircase, festival hall, and falcon gallery. The tower on the southwest projection dates to the Middle Ages, but got its Baroque overlay circa 1730. The castle houses eastern Germany's third largest art collection, including several fine works by Cranach and many early 20th-century pieces by such artists as Böcklin, Liebermann, and Beckmann. *Admission: DM 4 adults, DM 2 children. Open Tues.–Sun. 10–6.*

As in so many East German towns, Weimar's old town center has been reconstructed. Stop by the late Gothic **Herderkirche,** named after 18th-century theologian and philosopher Johann Gottfried Herder, who was the church's chief pastor. Its large winged altar was started by Lucas Cranach the Elder and finished by his son in 1555. Herder died in 1803 and is buried in the church. Nearby in Jakobstrasse you'll spot the Baroque facade of the **Kirms-Krackow** house, currently closed for restoration. The second floor houses a museum dedicated to Herder. Take time to visit the small garden with the teahouse. *Jakobstr. 10. Admission: DM 1. Open 9–noon, 1–5. Closed Mon.*

A short walk south, past Goethehaus and across Wieland Platz, brings you to the cemetery where Goethe and Schiller are buried, the **Historischer Friedhof** (Historic Cemetery). Their tombs are in the vault of a classical-style chapel in the leafy cemetery, where virtually every gravestone commemorates a famous citizen of Weimar. The Goethe-Schiller vault can be visited daily (except Tues.) 9–1 and 2–5.

On the other side of the Ilm, amidst meadowlike parkland, you'll find Goethe's beloved **Gartenhaus** (Garden House), where he met with his mistresses and where he wrote much poetry and began his masterpiece *Iphigenie auf Tauris* (admission: DM 3 adults, DM 2 children; open daily 9–noon and 1–5).

Goethe is said to have felt very close to nature here, and you can soak up the same rural atmosphere today on footpaths along the peaceful little river, where time seems to have stood still. Just across the river from the Gartenhaus is a generous German tribute to another literary giant, William Shakespeare, a 1904 statue showing him jauntily at ease on a marble plinth and looking remarkably at home in his foreign surroundings.

Just south of the city, the lovely 18th-century yellow **Belvedere Palace** once served as a hunting and pleasure castle; today you'll find a Baroque museum inside. The formal gardens were in part laid out according to Goethe's concepts. At press time, the palace was closed for restoration.

In the Ettersberg hills just north of Weimar is a blighted patch of land that contrasts cruelly with the verdant countryside that so inspired Goethe: **Buchenwald.** This was one of the most infamous Nazi concentration camps, where 65,000 men, women and children from 35 countries met their deaths through forced labor, starvation, disease, and gruesome medical experiments. Each is commemorated today by a small stone placed on the outlines of the barracks, which have long since disappeared from the site, and by a massive memorial tower built in a style that some critics find reminiscent of the Nazi megalomania it seeks to condemn. The tower stands on the highest point of Buchenwald, approached by a broad, long flight of steps and sheltering at its base a sculpted group representing the victims of Buchenwald. *Campsite admission: free. Open Tues.–Sun. 9:45–4:30. Bus tours to the site are organized by Weimar's tourist office, Weimar-Information, Markstr. 4 (tel. 03643/2173).*

Twenty-five kilometers (15 miles) west of Weimar (take the B-7 route, running parallel to the autobahn) lies one of the most picturesque and best-preserved cities of Thuringia: the "flowers **37** and towers" city of **Erfurt.** Erfurt emerged relatively unscathed from World War II, most of its innumerable towers intact (although restored in the early 1970s). Flowers? Erfurt is the center of the eastern German horticultural trade and Europe's largest producer of flower and vegetable seeds, a tradition begun by a local botanist, Christian Reichart, who pioneered seed research. The city outskirts are smothered in greenhouses and plantations, and one of Germany's biggest horticultural shows, the Internationale Gartenbauaustellung, takes place here every year from the end of March through September.

With its highly decorative and colorful facades, this is a fascinating city to discover on foot, and a photographer's delight. Erfurt is dominated by its magnificent cathedral, the 14th-century Gothic **Dom,** reached by a broad staircase from the expansive cathedral square. The Romanesque origins of the cathedral (Romanesque foundations can still be seen in the crypt) are best preserved in the choir, where you'll find glorious stained-glass windows and some of the most beautifully carved choir stalls in all Germany. They have a worldly theme, tracing the vintner's trade back through the centuries. Nearby, look for a remarkable group of free-standing figures: a man flanked by two women. The man is the 13th-century Count von Gleichen. But the two women? There are two stories: one, the respectable version, has it that the women are the count's wives, one of whom he married after the death of the other.

The other, possibly older story claims that one of the women is the count's wife, the other his mistress, a Saracen beauty who saved his life under mysterious circumstances during a crusade. The cathedral's biggest bell, the Gloriosa, is the largest free-swinging bell in the world. Cast in 1497, it took three years to install, in the tallest of the three sharply pointed towers, painstakingly lifted inch by inch with wooden wedges. No chances are taken with such a heavy treasure; the bell is rung only on special occasions. *Dom open May–Oct., Mon.–Fri. 9–11:30, 12:30–5, Sat. 9–11:30, 12:30–4:30, Sun. 2–4; Nov.–April, Mon.–Sat. 10–11:30, 12:30–4, Sun. 2–4.*

Next to the cathedral and linked to it by a 70-step open staircase is the Gothic church of **St. Severus.** Step inside, if only to admire the extraordinary font, a masterpiece of intricately carved sandstone that reaches practically to the roof of the church.

The cathedral square is bordered by attractive old houses dating back to the 16th century. Behind the predominantly neo-Gothic city hall, the **Rathaus,** you'll find Erfurt's outstanding attraction, the **Krämerbrücke** (Shopkeepers' Bridge), spanning the Gera River. You'd have to travel to Florence in Italy to find anything else like this, a Renaissance bridge incorporating shops and homes. Built in 1325 and restored in 1967–73, the bridge served for centuries, as an important trading center, where goldsmiths, artisans, and merchants plied their wares. Today, antique shops are in the majority among the timber-framed houses that are incorporated into the bridge, some dating to the 16th century. The area around the bridge is crisscrossed with ancient streets lined with picturesque and often crumbling homes. The area is known as **Klein Venedig** (Little Venice), not because of any real resemblance to the lagoon city but for the recurrent flooding caused by the nearby river.

On the way back to the center of town from the Krämerbrücke, follow Gotthardstrasse and you'll pass the **St. Augustine cloisters,** where the young Martin Luther spent formative years. Today it's a seminary. In nearby Leninstrasse you'll find Erfurt's interesting local-history museum, housed in a late-Renaissance house, **Zum Stockfisch.** *Leninstr. 169. Admission DM 1 adults, 50 pf children. Open Sun.–Thurs. 10–6.*

Leninstrasse brings you to the pedestrian-zoned **Anger,** an old street lined with restored Renaissance houses. The **Bartholo-mäusturm,** base of a 12th-century tower, holds a 60-bell carillon.

Just outside of the center is the **International Garden Exhibition** (open daily 10–7). Slightly farther afield is **Schloss Molsdorf,** one of the most stunning Rococo castles in Thuringia, set in a lovely park in the village of Molsdorf. The complex dates to 1736–45, but has been considerably renovated since. *Grounds open daily, castle open Wed.–Sun. 2–5. Tours are given hourly.*

38 **Eisenach,** 58 kilometers (36 miles) west on either the main B–7 highway or the autobahn E–63 (or an hour's journey by rail), is a historic old city that has managed to retain its medieval atmosphere better than most others in eastern Germany. Standing in its ancient market square, ringed by half-timbered houses, it's difficult to imagine that this town was an important center of the eastern German automobile industry, home of the now-shunned Wartburg. The solid, noisy staple of the East Germany auto trade was named after the famous castle that broods over Eisenach, high atop one of the foothills of the Thuringian Forest.

Begun in 1067 (and added to throughout the centuries), **Wartburg castle** hosted the German minstrels Walter von der Vogelweide and Wolfram von Eschenbach, Martin Luther, Richard Wagner, and Goethe. Johann Sebastian Bach was born in Eisenach in 1685 and must have often climbed the hill to the castle. Legend has it that von der Vogelweide, Germany's most famous minstrel, won a celebrated song contest here, the "contest of the Minnesingers" immortalized by the Romantic writer Novalis and Wagner's *Tannhäuser*. Luther sought shelter within its stout walls from papal proscription, and from May 1521 until March 1522 translated the New Testament from Greek to German, an act that paved the way for the Protestant Reformation. The study in which Luther worked can be visited; it's basically the same room that he used, although the walls have been scarred by souvenir-hunters who, over the centuries, scratched away the plaster and much of the wood paneling. Luther's original desk was vandalized, and the massive table before you is a later addition, although a former possession of the Luther family.

There's much else of interest in this fascinating castle, including a portrait of Luther and his wife by Cranach the Elder, and a very moving sculpture, the *Kneeling Angel*, by the great 15th-century artist Tilman Riemenschneider. The 13th-century great hall is breathtaking; it's here that the minstrels are said to have sung for courtly favors. Don't leave without climbing the belvedere for a panoramic view of the distant hills of the Harzgebirge (Harz mountains) and Thüringer Wald (Thuringian Forest) and soak in the medieval atmosphere of the half-timbered, cottage-style interior courtyards of the castle. *Admission: DM 3 adults, DM 1.50 children. Open Nov.–Feb., daily 9–5, Mar.–Oct., daily 8:30–5:30.*

The castle, accessible only from the north bridge, is an easy stroll from the center of town, along Friedrich-Engels-Strasse and Reuterweg. On the way, you'll pass the **Reuter-Wagner Museum,** at Reuterweg 2, which has a comprehensive exhibition on Wagner's life and work (DM 1.05 adults, 55 pf children; open Mon.–Fri. 9–12:30 and 2–5, Sun. 9–4). The town also has two museums devoted to Luther and Bach: the **Lutherhaus,** Lutherplatz 8 (open Mon.–Sat. 9–1 and 2–5, Sun. 2–5) and the **Bachhaus,** Frauenplan 21, which is devoted to the whole Bach family, and includes a collection of historical musical instruments (open Mon., Tues., Thurs., and Fri. 9–5; weekends 9–12:30 and 1–5). At Johannesplatz 9, look for what is allegedly the narrowest house in East Germany, built in 1890; the width is just over 2 meters (6 feet, 8 inches), the height 7½ meters (24½ feet), and the depth 10½ meters (34 feet).

Our tour of the southern part of eastern Germany ends here. You can continue west on E40 into western Germany, which leads into Route 5 to Frankfurt-am-Main. To return to Berlin, the fastest route is east on E40 and north on E51. For a change of scenery, turn off E40 onto Route 4 north to Nordhausen, where you pick up Route 81 to Magdeburg (*see* Excursions from Berlin, Chapter 4, above), and from there the E30 autobahn back into Berlin.

What to See and Do with Children

In **Dresden,** the penguin house at the zoo is particularly appealing; the zoo houses about 2,000 animals of some 500 species. *Open summer 8–5:30, winter 8–4:30.*

Automobiles have been manufactured since 1896 at **Eisenach,** the third-oldest production center in Germany. The automobile works operates an exhibition hall, showing cars from earlier years. Even the most recent car manufactured here, the Wartburg, looks none too modern by Western standards. *Open daily 9–7.*

Also in Eisenach, at the Wartburg castle, kids can ride donkeys from the *Eselstation* at the start of the pathway to the castle.

Off the Beaten Track

Hellerau, 10 kilometers west of Dresden, on the Elbe River is the site of one of Europe's first experiments in William Morris-style "garden towns." It was founded in 1910 by Walt Dohrn, but the experiment (a furniture factory employing "happy, fullfilled workers" housed in idyllic rural cottages) foundered with his death in a Swiss skiing accident in 1914. Hellerau took off again between the two world wars, but since the end of World War II, the premises that made it famous—an avant-garde theater and an international boarding school—have been a Red Army barracks. The Soviets have been moving out and there are plans to turn Hellerau into a European cultural center.

The **Feengrotte** (Fairy Grotto) at **Saalfeld,** near Gera, is a unique underground lake, transformed into a spectacular fairyland of colored stalactites as you travel through by boat.

Shopping

Souvenirs to buy in Saxony and Thuringia include wooden carvings, old books and prints, and glass Christmas ornaments. You can look for porcelain, but much of the good Meissen is exported. The gift shop at the Meissen factory occasionally has very good seconds that are (relative) bargains. There's also a large Meissen shop in the Bellevue Hotel in Dresden. Neither shop is equipped to ship, so be prepared to carry your purchases home very gingerly. What the shops offer is mainly Dresden, which at its finest rivals Meissen, or Thuringian china, only for lovers of Rococo design. None of it—if it's good—is inexpensive.

In **Leipzig,** shop on Grimmaischestrasse and the arcades along Sachsenplatz and the Markt. You'll find an excellent bookstore run by the Evangelical church opposite the entrance to Leipzig's St. Thomas church. **Dresden's** shopping districts include Ernst-Thälmann-Strasse, the nearby Neumarkt, and Strasse der Befreiung.

Sports and Fitness

Biking Cycling is not as yet a well-developed recreation in eastern Germany, but trails will unquestionably spring up quickly with the political changes. Bicycle rentals will most certainly be among the early private undertakings to open in the eastern districts. If you're taking your own bicycle, be sure to bring essential spare parts with you. There's good cycling in Dresden along both sides of the Elbe River. Only the really fit should consider the upland Sächsische Schweiz, which is recommended for hikers and climbers.

Fishing The Elbe river tributaries south of Magdeburg offer excellent fishing; also try the rivers and streams around Erfurt and Eisenach. Conditions should improve as the polluted waters are cleaned up.

Hiking From Eisenach, hike into the nearby nature preserve area to the southeast.

Skiing The region south of Erfurt, centering around Oberhof, is a popular winter sports area, with comfortable hotels and full sports facilities.

Water Sports The Gera and Saale rivers provide opportunities for canoeing; contact the tourist offices at Gera and Halle for rental information.

Winter Sports The upland, heavily forested Thüringer Wald is eastern Germany's second favorite holiday destination, in summer and winter. Its center is Suhl, administrative center of an area where every 10th town and village is a spa or mountain resort. Suhl's tourist office, Suhl Information, is at Steinweg 1, tel. 066/20052.

Dining and Lodging

Dining

Many of the best restaurants are in the larger hotels. Regional specialties include *Thüringer Sauerbraten mit Klössen* (roast corned beef with dumplings), *Bärenschinken* (cured ham), and *Harzer Köhlerteller mit Rostkartoffeln* (charcoal-grilled meat with roast potatoes). Seafood is plentiful in the lake areas.

Highly recommended restaurants in each price category are indicated with a star ★.

Category	Cost*
Very Expensive	over DM 40
Expensive	DM 25–DM 40
Moderate	DM 15–DM 25
Inexpensive	under DM 15

*per person for a three-course meal and a beer or glass of wine

Lodging

The choice of hotels in Saxony and Thuringia remains limited, and although private householders may now rent rooms, these are also hard to come by, as the demand is far greater than the supply. Contact the local tourist information offices for names of bed and breakfasts.

Note that during the Leipzig fair—early March and early September—all Leipzig hotels increase their prices.

Highly recommended hotels are indicated by a star ★.

Category	Cost*
Very Expensive	over DM 230
Expensive	DM 190–DM 230
Moderate	DM 130–DM 190
Inexpensive	under DM 130

Prices are for two people in a double room.

Chemnitz
Lodging

Chemnitzer Hof. Look carefully at this older hotel (built in 1930, now on the national register) and you'll spot its origins in the early Bauhaus style, in which ornamentation was discarded in favor of abstract design. Inside, rooms are attractive and the service friendly. You'll be in the heart of the city; you might enjoy the sense of living in another era. *Theaterplatz 4, tel. 0371/6840. 106 rooms with bath. Facilities: 2 restaurants, Bierstube, bar, nightclub, sauna, garage. AE, DC, MC, V. Very Expensive.*

Kongress. This modern 26-story skyscraper close to the town center stands in dramatic contrast to the rest of the city, but you'll find comfortable rooms in friendly surroundings here. Preferred rooms are on the upper floors, overlooking the city. The restaurants, at least under the old regime, leaned heavily toward Russian cuisine. *Karl-Marx-Allee, tel. 0371/6830. 369 rooms with bath. Facilities: 4 restaurants, café, bar, nightclub, sauna, solarium, fitness room, garage. AE, DC, MC, V. Very Expensive.*

Moskau. Accommodations in this modern but plain blocklike structure near the town center are not particularly fancy, but you'll find everything you need. The outdoor cafés in summer are particularly relaxing. *Strasse der Nationen, tel. 0371/6810. 111 rooms with bath. Facilities: restaurant, cafés, nightclub, sauna, garage. AE, DC, MC, V. Moderate.*

Dresden
Dining

Kügelnhaus. The complex here includes a grill, coffee bar, restaurant, and historic beer cellar, all justifiably popular, so go early or book ahead. *Hauptstr., tel. 0351/52791. Reservations advised. Dress: informal. No credit cards. Moderate.*

Sekundogenitur. This famous complex consisting of a restaurant, now connected to the Dresdner Hof hotel complex (*see* Lodging, *below*), is on the banks of the Elbe. There is outside dining when the weather permits. The Wiener schnitzel is excellent. *Brühlsche Terrasse, tel. 0351/495–1772 or 0351/48410. Reservations advised. Dress: informal. No credit cards. Closed Mon. Moderate.*

Lodging

Bellevue. Across the river from the Zwinger Palace, opera, and main museums, this fairly new hotel cleverly incorporates an old restored town house. The hotel views of the historic center are terrific, the rooms luxurious, and the service good. The Café Pöppelmann is especially recommended for its atmosphere and hearty dishes. *Meissnerstr., Grosse Meissner Str., 8060 Dresden, tel. 0351/56620. 328 rooms with bath. Facilities: 4 restaurants, bar, café, indoor pool, sauna, solarium, fitness room, bowling, jogging course, boutiques. AE, DC, MC, V. Very Expensive.*

Dresdner Hof. The city's newest hotel fits snugly into a corner of the old town and is only a short distance from the Zwinger palace, Albertinum, and other major sights. Housing a wine cellar, several bars, a bistro, and smart restaurants, it offers every possible comfort. The lobby is a stunning black-and-white evocation of Jugendstil. *An der Frauenkirche 5, tel. 0351/48410. 340 rooms with bath. Facilities: 7 restaurants, 2 bars, café, Bierclub, nightclub, indoor pool, sauna, solarium, fitness room, spa, garage. AE, DC, MC, V. Very Expensive.*

Newa. This modern monolith offers less charm than the Dresdner Hof or the Bellevue but is a good choice for comfort and is close to the main train station. The Newa is on the package-tour route and is often booked well in advance. In keeping with the name, the restaurants emphasize Russian cuisine; the main specialty restaurant enjoys a fairly good reputation. *St.-Petersburger-Str. 34, tel. 0351/496–7112. 314 rooms with bath. Facilities: 2 restaurants, bar, café, sauna, garage. AE, DC, MC, V. Expensive.*

Astoria. A half mile from the city center but close to the Dresden Zoo (take bus 72 from the main train station), the Astoria is a modern five-story hotel with a garden terrace. The staff is pleasant, but the decor hardly fancy—"minimalist" describes it best. *Strehlener Platz 2, tel. 0351/471–5171. 82 rooms, most without bath. Facilities: restaurant, bar, shop. AE, DC, MC, V. Moderate.*

Interhotel Prager Strasse. This modern complex of two hotels in tandem, the **Königstein** and **Lilienstein,** is named for the two promontories overlooking the Elbe river south of the city. The hotels are side by side on a pedestrian street between the train station and the city center. Rooms are modern if unexciting; the favored rooms (for the view) overlook the Prager Strasse, although the back rooms are slightly quieter. *Prager Str., tel. 0351/48560. 300 rooms each. Facilities: 3 restaurants, sauna, garage. AE, DC, MC, V. Moderate.*

Parkhotel Weisser Hirsch. You'll be a considerable distance from city center here (if driving, take Bautzenerstrasse from Platz der Einheit) in pleasant country surroundings. Facilities are simple, but the parklike setting makes up for the lack of luxury. *Bautzner Landstr. 7, tel. 0351/36851. 54 rooms, none with full bath. Facilities: restaurant, café (dancing in evenings). No credit cards. Inexpensive.*

Eisenach
Dining

Gastmahl des Meeres. You're always well served at this popular fish restaurant chain in eastern Germany, and Eisenach's version is among the best. It's a large, friendly place, smothered in flowers as fresh as the fish that's caught from the restaurant's tanks. *Auf der Esplanade, tel. 030/3885. No reservations. Dress: informal. MC. Closed weekends. Moderate.*

Waldschanke. This charming old restaurant is difficult to find, hidden away in a wood on the outskirts of town, but the hunt is well worth it (follow the Wartburgallee for about a mile and then watch for the signs to Prinzenteich). You'll eat lakeside in a former hunting lodge, and if you're lucky, fresh-caught fish or in-season venison will be on the menu. *Johannistal 57, tel. 030/ 4465. Reservations advised. Dress: informal. No credit cards. Closed Thurs. and Fri. Moderate.*

Lodging **Auf der Wartburg.** In this historic castle, where Martin Luther, Johann Sebastian Bach, and Richard Wagner were also guests, you'll get a splendid view over the town and surrounding countryside. The standard of comfort is above average, and antiques and oriental rugs mix with modern, moderately stylish furnishings. The hotel runs a shuttle bus service to the rail station. *Wartburg, tel. 03643/5111. 30 rooms, most with bath. Facilities: restaurant. No credit cards. Moderate.*

Hospiz "Glockenhof-Sophienhof." At the base of the Wartburg castle, this hostel, run by the Evangelical church, occupies a half-timbered brick-roofed house that radiates personality fitting to the town. Facilities are modest but rooms are pleasant. *Grimmelgasse 4, tel. 03643/3562. 23 rooms, most with bath. Facilities: restaurant. No credit cards. Inexpensive.*

Erfurt **Hohe Lilie.** Sweden's King Gustav Adolph established his court
Dining in the Renaissance building housing this first-class restaurant. The atmosphere is aptly regal—and so are the prices. But the menu offers good value for money, and some of the dishes—the steak "Erfurtas" for instance—are, by eastern German standards, quite exceptional. *Domplatz 31, tel. 0361/22578. Reservations necessary. Jacket and tie required. AE, DC, MC, V. Expensive.*

Vital. If the Hohe Lilie is too expensive, or booked up, try the nearby Vital. Good portions of typical Thuringian fare (lots of local sausage) are served in simple but pleasant surroundings. Even after German unification it was possible to eat well here for less than DM 20, but prices are bound to rise. *Domplatz 3, tel. 0361/24317. Reservations advised. Dress: informal. No credit cards. Inexpensive.*

Dining and Lodging **Erfurter Hof.** This inviting house in a traditional elegant style is under historic preservation, but the interior has been fully renovated to bring it up to modern standards. You're right at the train station and an easy stroll from the town center. The restaurant features cuisine of the Thuringen region, with an emphasis on fish and grilled meats. *Am Bahnhofsvorplatz 1–2, tel. 0361/24016. 197 rooms, all with bath. Facilities: 2 restaurants, café, wine cellar, bar, nightclub, sauna, garage. AE, DC, MC, V. Very Expensive.*

Kosmos. This recent multistory intruder from outer space is out of place in this town, but you'll be halfway between the train station and the town center. At least the views are splendid; ask for a room on an upper floor overlooking the old city. The prices at Orbis restaurant and Galaxie café are not as far out as the names would imply. *Juri-Gagarin-Ring 126–127, tel. 0361/551–294. 320 rooms, all with bath. Facilities: restaurant, café, bar, sauna, garage. AE, DC, MC, V. Moderate–Expensive.*

Gera **Gera.** The rooms inside this centrally located modern monolith
Lodging are fortunately far more inviting than the nondescript facade suggests. The specialty restaurants—Ganymed (French), Lotos (East Asian), Elsertal (German), and Bierhöler (local Thüringen cuisine)—have good reputations. Guest rooms are standard but comfortable. Book ahead around Leipzig fair time. *Strasse der Republik, tel. 0970/22991. 330 rooms with*

bath. *Facilities: 3 restaurants, Bierstube, café, sauna, solarium, garage. AE, DC, MC, V. Very Expensive.*

Halle **Stadt Halle.** Inside, this central hotel is considerably more ap-
Lodging pealing than the rather cold facade would lead you to believe.
Rooms offer the standard comforts, but several of the public
rooms such as the Ufa restaurant (Russian specialties, and
from the central Russian republic of Bashkir at that) and the
Messe Club bar are quite attractive. Halle also takes overflow
from Leipzig at fair time, so plan and book accordingly. *Ernst-
Thälmann-Pl., tel. 0345/38041. 345 rooms with bath. Facili-
ties: 2 restaurants, café, bar, nightclub, garage. AE, DC, MC,
V. Very Expensive.*

Leipzig **Auerbachs Keller.** This historic restaurant (built 1530) in the
Dining city center is immortalized in Goethe's *Faust.* The menu fea-
★ tures regional dishes from Saxony, often with Faustian names.
There is a good wine list. Both a visit and a reservation are
musts. *Grimmaische Str. 2–4, tel. 0341/209–131. Jacket and tie
required. AE, DC, MC, V. Moderate.*

Paulaner. Intimate, attractive, and quiet, this small place offers a limited selection of good local food. *Klostergasse 3, tel.
0341/281–985. Reservations advised. Dress: informal. No
credit cards. Expensive.*

Sakura. Located in the Hotel Merkur (*see* Lodging, *below*), the
Sakura offers good Japanese cuisine, perhaps out of respect for
the Japanese firm that designed and built the hotel. *Gerberstr.
15 (in Hotel Merkur), tel. 0341/799. Reservations required.
Jacket advised. AE, DC, MC, V. Expensive.*

Altes Kloster. Game is featured in this fascinating restaurant,
once part of a cloister. The Old World ambience enhances the
excellent food. *Klostergasse 5, tel. 0341/282–252. Reservations
advised. Jacket and tie required. No credit cards. Moderate.*

Burgkeller. Romanian specialties are served here in the Doina
Restaurant; the keller, at least, is authentic German.
*Naschmarkt 1–3, tel. 0341/295639. Reservations not neces-
sary. No credit cards. Moderate.*

Kaffeebaum. Reputedly the country's oldest café (established
1694), Kaffeebaum has a limited menu, but the atmosphere of
this Burgerhaus plus its regulars make a visit worthwhile. At
press time (summer 1992) the restaurant was closed for renovation, and the opening date was not available. It is advisable to
call ahead. *Fleischergasse 4, tel. 0341/200452. Reservations advised. No credit cards. Moderate.*

Paulaner. This intimate restaurant is recommended for its
quiet atmosphere and good regional cooking. *Klostergasse 3,
tel. 0341/281985. Reservations advised. Dress: informal. No
credit cards. Moderate.*

Ratskeller. This large restaurant, which also has a *Jagdzimmer*
(Hunting Room), prides itself on its good *bürgerliche* (plain-
and-hearty) cooking. Specialties include the popular *Ratskeller Topf,* a savory stew with vegetables; homemade pasta;
and *Schweineschnitzel* (pork cutlet). *Lotterstr. 1, tel. 0341/791–
6201. Reservations advised. No credit cards. Closed Sun. dinner. Moderate.*

Lodging **Astoria.** Many prefer this older hotel for its solid comfort and
atmosphere in the grand style, as well as for its central location
by the main train station. There's considerable traffic in the
area, so you'll do best with a quieter room on the side rather
than the front. The Galerie restaurant literally puts you into an

art museum of Social Realist murals for lunch or dinner. *Platz der Republik 2, tel. 0341/72220. 309 rooms with bath. Facilities: 2 restaurants, bar, dance café, nightclub, sauna, garage. AE, DC, MC, V. Very Expensive.*

Merkur. The city's newest and by far most luxurious hotel is imposing for its high-rise profile as well as its Japanese restaurant and garden. Rooms in this Japanese-built hotel offer every luxury, including full air-conditioning, and you're close to the main train station. *Gerberstr. 15, tel. 0341/7990. 440 rooms with bath. Facilities: 4 restaurants, 2 bars, coffee bar, nightclub, indoor pool, sauna, solarium, spa, bowling, shops, parking. AE, DC, MC, V. Very Expensive.*

Hotel am Ring. This hotel is the logical choice for those who want to be close to the opera house and concert hall. The hotel is modern and efficiently run. Rooms at the rear are quieter. *Palais Platz 5–6, tel. 0341/79520. 275 rooms with bath. Facilities: 2 restaurants, bar, nightclub, sauna, shops, parking. AE, DC, MC, V. Expensive.*

Stadt Leipzig. Considering its central location close to the main train station, this postwar modern monolith from the '60s is surprisingly quiet. Public rooms are attractive: dark wood paneling in the Vignette restaurant sets the tone for a quiet meal. *Richard-Wagner-Str. 1–6, tel. 0341/288–814. 340 rooms with bath. Facilities: 3 restaurants, café, bar, nightclub, sauna, garage. AE, DC, MC, V. Expensive.*

International. This traditional hotel offers appropriate charm and friendly personnel. You're within steps of the heart of the city, and not far from the train station either. The spacious rooms offer old-fashioned comfort but with modern facilities. The sidewalk café is popular. *Tröndlinring 8, tel. 0341/71880. 108 rooms with bath. Facilities: restaurant, Bierstube, bar, café, garage. AE, DC, MC, V. Moderate.*

Zum Löwen. This is another of the postwar modern hotels built to handle Leipzig fair traffic, but in this case, the house is personable and cheerful, if not opulent. Around the corner from the Astoria, you'll be near the train station and within an easy stroll of city center. *Rudolf-Breitscheid-Str., tel. 0341/72220. 108 rooms with bath. Facilities: restaurant. AE, DC, MC, V. Moderate.*

Parkhotel. The location directly across from the train station could hardly be better, but the accommodations are simple if not downright spartan—virtually none of the rooms have baths. *Richard-Wagner-Str. 7, tel. 0341/7821. 174 rooms, none with bath. Facilities: restaurant, parking. No credit cards. Inexpensive.*

Meissen
Dining and Lodging

Bahnhofshotel. This small hotel is at the train station and convenient to the center of town. Rooms have a dated modern decor but are attractive, with satisfactory baths. The restaurants remind one a bit of the train station, which is only appropriate. *Grossenhainer Str. 2, tel. 03521/3320. 18 rooms with bath. Facilities: restaurant, parking. AE, DC, MC, V. Moderate.*

Weimar
Dining

Weisser Schwan. This historic restaurant in the center of town, right by Goethehaus (*see* Exploring, above), dates to 1500. Its various rooms, including the library, offer international and Thuringian specialties, particularly fish and grilled meats. *Frauenstorstr. 23, tel. 03643/61715. Reservations essential. Jacket and tie advised. AE, DC, MC, V. Closed last Mon. of month. Expensive.*

Elephantenkeller. In the ancient vaulted cellar restaurant of the Elephant Hotel (*see* Lodging, below), you'll eat well on traditional Thuringian cuisine in surroundings that haven't changed much since Goethe's day. Only the functional 1950s style of some of the furnishings disturb the overall atmosphere reinforced by the well-worn flagstones of the floor and the squat sandstone pillars behind which many lunchtime deals are being sealed in post-reunification Germany. Try the *Weimarer Zwiebelmarkt* soup, an onion soup made with pork knuckle stock. *Markt 19, tel. 03643/61471. Reservations advised. Dress: informal. No credit cards. Moderate.*

Ratskeller. This historic restaurant is located in the cellar of the Stadthaus (City Hall), a Renaissance building dating to the 17th century. The wholesome regional fare includes grilled sausages with sauerkraut and onions, and Thuringian onion soup. *Markt 10, tel. 03643/64142. Reservations not necessary. AE, DC, MC, V. Moderate.*

Felsenkeller. In this warm, rustic, country-style restaurant and drinking establishment in the Gasthaus Brauere, a variety of warm dishes is offered at prices between DM 5 and DM 30. The beer is brewed on the premises. *Humboldtstr. 37, tel. 03643/61941. Reservations not necessary. No credit cards. Inexpensive.*

Gastmahl des Meeres. Centrally located, this restaurant offers a wide range of fish dishes, as well as meat. It has fast service and friendly waiters but tends to get crowded between 1 PM and 2 PM, so its best to arrive early for lunch. *Herder Platz 16, tel. 03643/4521. No reservations. No credit cards. Inexpensive.*

Lodging **Belvedere.** Opened in 1990, this luxurious hotel is about 1½ kilometers (1 mile) outside of the town center, across from a gorgeous wooded park—Goethe helped plan the layout—which is worth a stroll even if you're not staying at the Belevedere. Rooms are, if anything, overly complete; you'll lack nothing, except proximity to Weimar's center. *Belvedere Allee, tel. 03643/621–3477. 300 rooms with bath. Facilities: 2 restaurants, café, beer pub, three bars, indoor pool, sauna, solarium, fitness room, spa, bowling, garage. AE, DC, MC, V. Very Expensive.*

Elephant. This hotel, dating to 1696, is one of the Germany's most famous; you'll follow the choice of Goethe, Schiller, Herder, Liszt—and Hitler—all of whom have been guests here. Behind the sparkling white facade are comfortable modern rooms, thanks to recent renovations, but a feeling for the historic past is ever present. Book well ahead. *Am Markt 19, tel. 03643/61471. 116 rooms with bath. Facilities: 4 restaurants, bar, nightclub, sauna, garage. AE, DC, MC, V. Expensive.*

Hospiz. This hostel run by the Evangelical church is only steps away from Goethe's house. Rooms are modest, but so is the price; the public rooms are attractively furnished with antiques. In 1991, bathrooms were being added to the rooms and old furniture replaced. *Amalienstr. 2, tel. 03643/2711. 21 rooms, 12 with bath. Facilities: restaurant, parking. No credit cards. Moderate.*

Russischer Hof. This charming hotel built in 1805 was modernized and expanded in 1989. The rooms are attractively furnished, each equipped with bath, shower, TV, and radio. *Goethe Platz 2, tel. 03643/62331. 85 rooms with bath. Facilities: 2 restaurants, bar, beer cellar, garage. AE, DC, MC, V. Moderate.*

The Arts and Nightlife

The Arts

Opera   The opera in **Dresden** has regained its international reputation
since the house, which was almost totally destroyed in World
War II, was reopened in 1985 following an eight-year reconstruction. Just to see the magnificent house alone is worth the
trip; a performance is that much better. Tickets are reasonably
priced but also hard to get; they're often included in package
tours. Try your luck at the evening box office (the *Abendkasse*,
left of the main entrance) about a half hour before the performance; there are usually a few dozen tickets available.

Several smaller cities, notably **Chemnitz**, also have opera
houses that turn out interesting performances, occasionally of
relatively little known or contemporary works.

Music   The Neues Gewandhaus in **Leipzig**, a controversial piece of architecture, is home to a splendid orchestra. Tickets to concerts
are very difficult to obtain unless you reserve well in advance
and in writing only (Gewandhaus zu Leipzig, Augustus-Platz,
Leipzig 7010). Sometimes spare tickets are available at the box
office a half hour before the evening performance. Of the music
festivals in the area, the best known are the Handel festival in
Halle (June) and the Music Days in **Leipzig** (June), as well as the
International Bach Festival held every four years during September and October. **Dresden** organizes an international
Dixieland festival each May.

Nightlife

Leipzig comes to life particularly during fair time, although in
the past, this was as much to extract hard currency from the
visitors as it was to entertain them. In most cities the leading
hotels run nightclubs year-round (*see* Lodging, above), and
many of these are not bad at all. In **Leipzig**, try the Merkur,
Kongress, Chemnitzer Hof, and Moskau; in **Dresden**, the
Dresdner Hof; in **Gera**, the Gera; in **Erfurt**, the Erfurter Hof;
and in **Weimar**, the Belvedere and Elephant hotels.

Index

Fodor's Travel Guides

U.S. Guides

Alaska

Arizona

Boston

California

Cape Cod, Martha's Vineyard, Nantucket

The Carolinas & the Georgia Coast

Chicago

Disney World & the Orlando Area

Florida

Hawaii

Las Vegas, Reno, Tahoe

Los Angeles

Maine, Vermont, New Hampshire

Maui

Miami & the Keys

New England

New Orleans

New York City

Pacific North Coast

Philadelphia & the Pennsylvania Dutch Country

San Diego

San Francisco

Santa Fe, Taos, Albuquerque

Seattle & Vancouver

The South

The U.S. & British Virgin Islands

The Upper Great Lakes Region

USA

Vacations in New York State

Vacations on the Jersey Shore

Virginia & Maryland

Waikiki

Washington, D.C.

Foreign Guides

Acapulco, Ixtapa, Zihuatanejo

Australia & New Zealand

Austria

The Bahamas

Baja & Mexico's Pacific Coast Resorts

Barbados

Berlin

Bermuda

Brazil

Budapest

Budget Europe

Canada

Cancun, Cozumel, Yucatan Penisula

Caribbean

Central America

China

Costa Rica, Belize, Guatemala

Czechoslovakia

Eastern Europe

Egypt

Euro Disney

Europe

Europe's Great Cities

France

Germany

Great Britain

Greece

The Himalayan Countries

Hong Kong

India

Ireland

Israel

Italy

Italy's Great Cities

Japan

Kenya & Tanzania

Korea

London

Madrid & Barcelona

Mexico

Montreal & Quebec City

Morocco

The Netherlands Belgium & Luxembourg

New Zealand

Norway

Nova Scotia, Prince Edward Island & New Brunswick

Paris

Portugal

Rome

Russia & the Baltic Countries

Scandinavia

Scotland

Singapore

South America

Southeast Asia

South Pacific

Spain

Sweden

Switzerland

Thailand

Tokyo

Toronto

Turkey

Vienna & the Danube Valley

Yugoslavia

Special Series

Fodor's Affordables

Affordable Europe

Affordable France

Affordable Germany

Affordable Great
Britain

Affordable Italy

**Fodor's Bed &
Breakfast and
Country Inns Guides**

California

Mid-Atlantic Region

New England

The Pacific Northwest

The South

The West Coast

The Upper Great
Lakes Region

Canada's Great
Country Inns

Cottages, B&Bs and
Country Inns of
England and Wales

The Berkeley Guides

On the Loose in
California

On the Loose in
Eastern Europe

On the Loose in
Mexico

On the Loose in the
Pacific Northwest &
Alaska

**Fodor's Exploring
Guides**

Exploring California

Exploring Florida

Exploring France

Exploring Germany

Exploring Paris

Exploring Rome

Exploring Spain

Exploring Thailand

Fodor's Flashmaps

New York

Washington, D.C.

Fodor's Pocket Guides

Pocket Bahamas

Pocket Jamaica

Pocket London

Pocket New York
City

Pocket Paris

Pocket Puerto Rico

Pocket San Francisco

Pocket Washington,
D.C.

Fodor's Sports

Cycling

Hiking

Running

Sailing

The Insider's Guide
to the Best Canadian
Skiing

**Fodor's Three-In-Ones
(guidebook, language
cassette, and phrase
book)**

France

Germany

Italy

Mexico

Spain

**Fodor's
Special-Interest
Guides**

Cruises and Ports
of Call

Disney World & the
Orlando Area

Euro Disney

Healthy Escapes

London Companion

Skiing in the USA
& Canada

Sunday in New York

**Fodor's Touring
Guides**

Touring Europe

Touring USA:
Eastern Edition

Touring USA:
Western Edition

**Fodor's Vacation
Planners**

Great American
Vacations

National Parks of the
West

**The Wall Street
Journal Guides to
Business Travel**

Europe

International Cities

Pacific Rim

USA & Canada

WHEREVER
YOU TRAVEL,
*H*ELP IS NEVER
FAR AWAY.

From planning your trip to replacing
lost Cards, American Express® Travel Service
Offices* are always there to help.

BERLIN
Kurfuerstendamm 11
30-882-7575

Friedrichstrasse 172
30-238-4102-5

DRESDEN
Grosse Meissner Strasse 15
(At Hotel Bellevue)
51-566-2865